A Long, Long Way

A Long, Long Way

Hollywood's Unfinished Journey from
Racism to Reconciliation

GREG GARRETT

OXFORD
UNIVERSITY PRESS

OXFORD

UNIVERSITY PRESS

Oxford University Press is a department of the University of Oxford. It furthers
the University's objective of excellence in research, scholarship, and education
by publishing worldwide. Oxford is a registered trade mark of Oxford University
Press in the UK and certain other countries.

Published in the United States of America by Oxford University Press
198 Madison Avenue, New York, NY 10016, United States of America.

© Greg Garrett 2020

Library of Congress Cataloging-in-Publication Data
Names: Garrett, Greg, author.
Title: A long, long way : Hollywood's unfinished journey from racism
to reconciliation / Greg Garrett.
Identifiers: LCCN 2019035566 (print) | LCCN 2019035567 (ebook) |
ISBN 9780190906252 (hardback) | ISBN 9780190906276 (epub) |
ISBN 9780190906269 (updf) | ISBN 9780197502549 (online)
Subjects: LCSH: African Americans in motion pictures. |
Race in motion pictures. | Race relations in motion pictures. |
African Americans in the motion picture industry—United States—History. |
Motion pictures—United States—History.
Classification: LCC PN1995.9.N4 G37 2020 (print) |
LCC PN1995.9.N4 (ebook) | DDC 791.43/652900973—dc23
LC record available at https://lccn.loc.gov/2019035566
LC ebook record available at https://lccn.loc.gov/2019035567

1 3 5 7 9 8 6 4 2

Printed by LSC Communications, United States of America

*For the Very Rev. Lucinda Laird and
the people of the American Cathedral in Paris*

The camera sees what you point it at: the camera sees what you want it to see.

James Baldwin, *The Devil Finds Work*

All the stolen voices
Will one day be returned.

U2, "The Miracle (of Joey Ramone)"

Contents

1

Introduction

A Long, Long Way

Wake Up: Race and American Film

We all need a myth to guide our lives, and if we don't claim
a myth, one will claim us.

Phyllis Trible

Movies are not about Blacks, but what Whites think about
Blacks.

Ralph Ellison

On August 10, 2018, Spike Lee's movie *BlacKkKlansman* premiered in
the United States, one year after white supremacists had marched in
Charlottesville, Virginia. In the climactic moments of the film, echoing
the editing of D. W. Griffith, who pioneered the art of cross-cutting
between story elements to build suspense, Lee moves back and forth
between two scenes in which Griffith's 1915 film *The Birth of a Nation*
plays a pivotal role. In one, a Ku Klux Klan initiation ceremony led
by Grand Wizard David Duke (Topher Grace) is capped by an approving and enthusiastic screening of the film, which helped to create
the modern Klan. In the other scene, Jerome Turner (Harry Belafonte)
describes to a roomful of African American students the 1916
lynching of his friend Jesse Washington, who was burned, castrated,
and tortured in front of a crowd of 16,000 people in Waco, Texas, the
place where I have taught for three decades. Jerome cites *The Birth of a
Nation* as a cause for that horrific public violence, as indeed it was.

These two scenes show how powerful a film can be in shaping or reinforcing attitudes about race, violence, and identity. "The language of the camera," as James Baldwin tells us, "is the language of our dreams."[1] And, of course, our nightmares.

But in Lee's film we also see how movies can push back against stereotypes, can speak truth to power, and can move audiences not to hate but toward understanding. Although it is set in the 1970s, in its final scenes *BlacKkKlansman* connects the violence and racism of the distant past and of the movie's present with our own present (as critic Oliver Jones wrote, "Yes, this is a period movie; it's just that the period is now, then, before and always"), and Lee reminds us that while film can carry horrible messages, it can also offer the possibility of hope.[2] With our clear-eyed awareness that movies and other media have been a force for bigotry and hatred, we can identify and reject myths that are soul-killing and seek out myths that are soul-filling.[3] We can watch a film; recognize elements that are racist, stereotyped, or simplistic; and hold it to account, even as we seek out stories that embrace diversity and the full humanity of every character.

In our history, as in *BlacKkKlansman*, race and the media are inextricably linked. Over the past century racists have used the medium of film to perpetuate harmful stereotypes and offer warped narratives, or they have portrayed white reality as though it were the only reality that mattered. A second phase followed, as white filmmakers of conscience recognized that propensity for racism and sought to make incremental changes in the stories they told. Other white storytellers launched a third phase, attempting to portray the lives of people of color in a more significant and representative way. Later, in a fourth phase, people of color began to tell their own stories and portray their own lives, and, in a fifth phase, Hollywood films began to display a casual multiculturalism in which racial difference is taken for granted. Finally we arrive at the sixth phase, where, as in *BlacKkKlansman*, movies made for mainstream audiences by people of color are overturning the harmful myths of the past, denying the dangerous stories of American culture, and even turning the techniques and genres of Hollywood storytelling back upon themselves so that they become tools for awareness and reconciliation.

The task of this book is to interrogate these six phases of Hollywood treatment of race, moving from our undoubtedly racist past to our still-troubled but perhaps slightly more hopeful present. As a middle-aged white man, I can hardly make credible use of the word "woke," yet it is a crucial idea to understand in connection with our current moment and the interrogation we are about to undertake. Spike Lee knows this. Before Erykah Badu, Trayvon Martin, and Black Lives Matter, his films were calling us to wake up. This call is the final line in *School Daze* (1988) and the opening line of *Do the Right Thing* (1989). It echoes throughout *BlacKkKlansman*. All Americans—not just African Americans—are called to be awake, to pay attention, to look through new lenses, to see what really is as opposed to what we would like to or have been encouraged to see. Another middle-aged white man, David Brooks, defined it this way: "To be woke is to be radically aware and justifiably paranoid. It is to be cognizant of the rot pervading the power structures."[4] Thankfully, what we will find when we investigate the hatred and bigotry, the stories and the images of one hundred years of Hollywood filmmaking, is more than just rot: It's also a way forward.

The Atlantic writer Vann Newkirk and I were part of an onstage conversation about race, film, and healing that followed a screening of *Get Out* in Washington National Cathedral in February 2018. In his introduction to the film, Vann talked about Dr. Martin Luther King, Jr.'s final Sunday sermon, delivered from the cathedral's Canterbury Pulpit just behind us:

> It was in one way a standard theological examination. He begins with scripture from the book of Revelation. But then he goes to talking about the story of Rip Van Winkle, a fellow who fell asleep for twenty years and woke up—he fell asleep during the time the United States was controlled by the crown, and woke up in a post-revolutionary era. King used that example sort of as a parable to warn people about how to remain awake during a great revolution. What he talked about was how to stay woke, as lots of people say. But also how to, if you were in the process of waking up, how to have your racial awakening, and how to get to the point where you could critically engage with life, with race, with becoming an anti-racist.[5]

That is the ultimate goal of our project, to critically engage with life and race. By exploring racism in American film from 1915 to the present, by exposing and rejecting the pernicious myths and embracing the good, by understanding how these films might lead (and have led) to useful conversations about race and prejudice, and by trying to become, in the process, anti-racist, we will offer correctives to *Birth of a Nation* in our past and to the neo-Nazis of Charlottesville in our present. Dr. King's goal—an America, a world, where people would be judged less on the color of their skin than on the content of their character—remains elusive. Yet it is a goal supremely worth seeking, and strangely enough, our often-racist literature and culture might be a part of our progress toward it.

I began my formal research toward this work at a research library in the United Kingdom during July 2016. Just before I arrived, a national referendum in Great Britain, fueled to a large degree by nativist concerns about immigrants and refugees, had pushed that nation in the direction of cutting ties with Europe and trying to control the flow of people into their country. "Brexit" was all anyone there could talk about—until, within hours of each other, two African American men were killed by police officers on camera, very publicly joining a sad roll call for that year to date of five hundred deaths in America at the hands of police (with blacks 2.5 times more likely to be killed than whites).[6] Shortly afterward, an African American veteran, home from the Middle East, opened fire on police officers at a Black Lives Matter rally in Dallas, Texas, with a military-grade assault weapon. His sole motivation, he said before himself being blown up by military ordnance, was that he wanted to kill white policemen.

Protests, shootings, and shouting matches followed. President Barack Obama cut short a state visit to Europe to return to the United States to deal with the crisis. Many Americans gave voice to anger, despair, or near hopelessness in regard to the questions of race and violence that were shaking our country. On the front page of its July 9th edition, the centrist London newspaper featured a banner headline that seemed aptly to characterize our new normal: "America's Race Hate Nightmare."

Many people—including me, I must confess—tried to read the election of Barack Obama as marking a new chapter in American racial life. But by this summer of 2016 it was painfully clear that this early optimism was misplaced, that the idea that we were living in a postracial society was purest delusion. A comprehensive study by the Pew Research Center found that blacks and whites continued to view events and issues in wildly different ways, that racial optimism stemming from the election of an African American president had subsided for whites and blacks both; while whites thought there was too much focus on race, blacks thought there was not nearly enough. Although whites were evenly divided on the state of race relations, "by a nearly two-to-one margin, blacks are more likely to say race relations are bad (61%) rather than good (34%)."[7] In his 2016 study of President Obama, Michael Eric Dyson identified what seems to be an inescapable truth about our continuing struggle: "What many Americans of all colors believe is that race fundamentally defines America and is a dividing line drawn in blood through the nation's moral map."[8] But white and black people on either side of that dividing line view race and prejudice in fundamentally different ways.

At about the same time that I began working on this book— although entertainment news seemed, at first glance, hardly so weighty as the front-page headlines—the Academy of Motion Picture Arts and Sciences announced that it was inviting new members to join, 46 percent of the nominees women, 41 percent of them people of color. This was widely perceived as a response to the #oscarssowhite controversy and an attempt to combat the perception that the Academy (and the entertainment industry as a whole) was racist or, at the very least, complicit in barring people outside the white mainstream from wider recognition and opportunity.[9]

Ignited by the second straight year in which the Academy failed to nominate a single African American for a major award, the #oscarssowhite social media campaign swept the nation and the world in early 2016. Reactions were predictably varied. Some—many—were appalled that the year's group photo of Oscar nominees looked like a vast bowl of vanilla ice cream with a jot of caramel in it. (Mexican director Alejandro González Iñárritu, who won his second straight Best Director trophy for *The Revenant*, was the sole person of color nominated in a major category.) Others suggested that perhaps no African American performances were worthy of nomination; still others claimed not to understand what the fuss was about. All of these responses, however, entered into the larger American dialogue about race, prejudice, opportunity, justice, racial violence, difference, and representation. As perhaps our greatest mythmaker, what Hollywood thinks about race does matter.

Actual racial violence and the representation of race in American culture are connected because Hollywood, pop music, television, and other cultural media have long excluded people of color, have depicted them as subhuman or unimportant or as stereotypes, have refused to allow them to tell their own stories, and have given greater exposure to whites at the expense of perhaps equally talented people of color. Any objective media history of African Americans, Asians, Hispanics, Jews, Native Americans, Italian Americans, members of the LGBTQ community, and other minority groups reveals a century or more of prejudice, insult, injury, and neglect, a century of works that have shaped their audiences and members of those groups in ways benign and malignant. Our primary focus in this work will be on African American representation and oppression, but a similar work, full of sadness and full of hope, could be written about any of these groups.

As a culture, we have regressed since the summer of 2016. America is now more obviously divided on racially charged issues like law enforcement and immigration than at any moment in my lifetime. At the end of 2017, 60 percent of those polled by the Pew Research Center said that the election of Donald J. Trump had worsened racial tensions. A majority of black respondents said that racial tensions overall have increased. (Republicans—and white Americans in general—were both less likely to believe this and more likely to opine that racial tensions are largely unchanged and not a serious problem.)[10]

Yet the worsening racial climate notwithstanding, the past hundred years offer us a history of tiny strides, moments of grace and understanding, universally appreciated performances and transformative narratives, and some movement toward true equality. Perhaps America is now the land of Muslim bans and diatribes against immigrant rapists and murderers, but it also the land of *Moonlight* (2016), *Get Out* (2017), *Black Panther* (2018), and *BlacKkKlansman*.

We are not in the Promised Land yet, but there are signs of hope.

Race and Representation: We've Come
a Long, Long Way

In 1966, Dr. King spoke at Southern Methodist University in Dallas, then as now a bastion of white privilege. He said this:

> I guess probably more than any other question, the one that I get over and over again as I journey around our nation is the question whether we are making any real progress in race relations. . . . I guess the only answer that I can give to that question is what I consider a realistic one. It avoids the extremes of both a deadening pessimism and a superficial optimism. I would say that we have come a long, long way in our struggle to make justice a reality for all men, but we have a long, long way to go before the problem is solved.[11]

Perhaps all those that Dr. King would call "people of goodwill" would agree that the racism and prejudice in our culture continue to offend our Creator, who sees us all as beloved children. But as a film historian and cultural theologian, I can make this initial statement about race and film in America: We have come a long, long way, even if we still have a long, long way to go.

In the early years of American film, audiences received a vision of African Americans, Asian Americans, Arabs, Native Americans, and other cultures outside the white middle-class mainstream that was almost always filtered through the sensibility of white male writers and directors—and, often, through the performances of white actors as well.[12] From the corked-up villains of *The Birth of a Nation*, to Russian-born Jewish Al Jolson singing in blackface, from Swedish actor Warner Oland as the Chinese detective Charlie Chan and Hungarian Peter Lorre as the Japanese detective Mr. Moto, to white actors and stunt people in dark makeup as Native Americans, minority groups were often denied even the solace of seeing themselves depicted by actors from their culture. It's no wonder that in the early 1960s James Baldwin would write that the world is white, and black people (and others outside the white mainstream) were forced to define themselves in opposition to this whiteness—and often to despise themselves because they did not share it.[13]

Ta-Nehisi Coates said something similar in his National Book Award–winning *Between the World and Me*: "That beauty that Malcolm [X] pledged us to protect, black beauty, was never celebrated in movies, in television, or in the textbooks I'd seen as a child. Everyone of any import, from Jesus to George Washington, was white . . . We were black, beyond the visible spectrum, beyond civilization."[14] Whether misrepresented or left out of the media, people of color did not see themselves portrayed in the culture; they could not have their lives confirmed in the way white audiences did without even a thought about it. As a white person, I saw myself and lives like mine depicted on TV and in the movies from my earliest days. I now understand as I did not before beginning this book that this was an important force in creating my identity and validating my presence on the planet.

Film, media, and other cultural depictions—or vacuums—matter because they are powerful ways that people create meaning. When a population is constantly depicted in a certain way, those depictions take on a mythic life of their own. People who are consistently excluded from depiction begin to define themselves in terms of that very exclusion, an awareness that they are not "normal" or mainstream, that in some important sense they and their stories are outside of history, somehow not worth telling. When the Second Avenue Subway in New York City opened in early 2017, the new stations were adorned with large and colorful mosaics. The art elicited powerful responses and actually brought some onlookers to tears:

On Sunday, New Yorkers were mesmerized by the artwork adorning the walls. At the 72nd Street stop, Sumana Harihareswara stopped to gaze at a mosaic of a woman of South Asian descent dressed in a burgundy sari, looking at her cellphone. Ms. Harihareswara was overcome with emotion.

"I don't think I've ever come across subway art before that makes me feel so seen," she said through tears. "This woman could be my aunt; she could be my cousin."

She and a stranger exchanged a knowing glance. "Representation matters," they agreed. Ms. Harihareswara, a longtime transit enthusiast from Astoria, Queens, said she was struck by the diversity portrayed in the mosaics, including a mural of a gay couple holding hands.[15]

Hurr Murtaza, one of my Muslim students at Baylor University, wrote in his reading journal in the fall of 2017 that to enjoy a story, he had to find himself in it somehow. He expanded his thinking in a later email by saying, "One pillar to *Black Panther*'s success was quenching a need for representation on the big screen. There are plenty of stories that I feel I am not represented in whether that be in simple terms such as life experiences or personality, or in terms of race. There are times where the lack of representation can be offputting or disheartening. However, what's worse is representation in a negative aspect. For me, an example would be a broad stroke, painting Muslims to be terrorists."[16]

The director of the acclaimed 2016 film *Moonlight*, Barry Jenkins, echoes Hurr's thought: "Representation does matter . . . if you do not see your face, it is if you do not exist."[17] If you cannot find yourself in the stories and culture you consume, where are you? Who are you? And in terms of the culture itself, what are you? Setting aside the question of enjoyment, when a buffet of white people is all that's on offer, these myths shape all of the audiences who consume them, including white mainstream audiences; when you define yourselves in terms of characters who are consistently depicted as superior to all others, it is hard to avoid the sense, conscious or unconscious, that you are, truly, above others.

Not to see yourself can be damaging. To see yourself and the life you live up there on the screen, larger than life, in the same place where John Wayne and Humphrey Bogart and Marilyn Monroe and Julia Roberts have lived and died, loved and fought, elevates your existence. You are seen and affirmed. You are real. I had seen myself onscreen from my childhood and did not for many years think about the fact that others did not have that luxury. The African American theologian Kelly Brown Douglas had a different experience. Evoking a transformative (for me) conversation she and I had previously had, she told an audience at a screening of *Guess Who's Coming to Dinner* (1967) at the Washington National Cathedral about her first viewing of the movie and why it mattered so much to her:

I could not wait to see the black man in the movie that all the adults were talking about. From the minute that Sidney Poitier came onto the screen, I was transfixed, and I will admit that I've been transfixed by him ever since. But most importantly, at that time for me, it was monumental, for this was the first time that I saw a black man, in fact any black person, in a major movie role. As an eleven-year-old growing up in a time when the most black representation that I saw on the screen was that of Buckwheat and Stymie from *Little Rascals*, and *Amos and Andy*, seeing a proud black man was, for me, consequential. It made me proud . . . to see him was to see the black men that I knew: proud black men. And so, the point of the matter is that even though I was not really the targeted demographic of the film, in that it was really, I think, not written for those who looked like me, it mattered to me. It wasn't about the interracial couple, though my friends and I had plenty of conversations about that, but it was about seeing the black people, especially seeing a black doctor on the screen.[18]

Conversations about film with the Very Rev. Dr. Douglas, who is a canon of the cathedral and dean of Episcopal Divinity School, have shaped my perceptions as a critic and theologian as well, because they have taught me that when white filmgoers see lives that do not look precisely like theirs, faces from other cultures and other races depicted on the screen, it likewise normalizes them. In *Guess Who's Coming to Dinner*, Sidney Poitier appears alongside screen icons Spencer Tracy and Katherine Hepburn (and on the movie poster, he is given equal stature). If we can imagine seeing a black face here, couldn't we also imagine seeing a black face elsewhere? Asked why today he loves science fiction, Sen. Cory Booker answered with a story about his father, "who made me watch *Star Trek* with him, to see an African American woman and an Asian man as a view of the future. For a man who in the '60s, when the show came out, was dealing with unconscionable discrimination, *Star Trek* (1966–69) was a hopeful beacon. My dad brought me up to understand that art—even in the most unconscionable, painful, degrading present—can help us pull ourselves and our society to a higher level."[19]

At its best, that is what art can do, and why film representation matters. But Ralph Ellison's pungent comment that films are about what white people think about black people speaks to those times when minorities have been badly or untruthfully depicted in our culture by white storytellers. Sadly, in the first fifty years of Hollywood, what whites thought about blacks—or about any minority group— was often (and here's that word again) appalling. As we learn from Donald Bogle's classic study *Toms, Coons, Mulattoes, Mammies, and Bucks* (1973) and Marlon Riggs's Emmy-winning documentary *Ethnic Notions* (1987), for hundreds of years American material and popular culture regularly placed black characters into narrow and demeaning stereotypes and tended to depict them as less than fully human, often as mere products of their biological impulses. At that February 2018 event at the Washington National Cathedral, the Very Rev. Dr. Douglas wondered why for so long these characters were depicted in such a way: "What was it about white America, and what were they trying to say to white America about black people?" Our conclusion was that the consistency of these tropes could only be explained by the fact that white audiences liked or even needed to see black characters depicted in these ways.[20] And it can only be explained if, as Bogle says, these stereotypes were included in film and culture to entertain and confirm white audiences "by stressing Negro inferiority."[21]

These stereotypes had plenty of company; material and popular culture tended to denigrate and degrade all ethnic and cultural groups outside the white Anglo-Saxon mainstream. The 1934 Warner Brothers musical *Wonder Bar* presented Al Jolson and a seeming cast of thousands in blackface performing the musical number "Going to Heaven on a Mule." Jolson sings of a place where pork chops grow on trees and watermelons abound. The sequence contains so many offensive stereotypes that it's hard to imagine it could be surpassed if the makers of *Family Guy* or *South Park* today had set out to be deliberately provocative. Equally offensive to us now, although perhaps at least understandable as wartime propaganda, is the representation of Japanese people as jabbering buck-toothed simians in films and cartoons (including Disney cartoons) released during World War II. These are only two of many occasions when films and other forms of popular culture presented a way to keep nonwhites in their place—a place distinctly below or in opposition to white Americans.

When minority actors were permitted to depict themselves, they were often placed in bit roles. D. W. Griffith employed white actors in blackface for all the meaty villain roles in *The Birth of a Nation*, while black actors and actresses were seen only in the background. The astonishingly talented singer and actress Lena Horne often found herself featured in extraneous musical numbers that were not integrated into the plot of the film. In Southern states where black performers could not be shown in theaters, her footage was thus easily and unnoticeably cut before the film was screened.

But despite all this, Hollywood, like the nation, wanted to do better and was wrestling with thinking about race in new ways. Some strong characters of color emerged. In 1940, Harriet McDaniel, though literally cast as "Mammy," became the first black American to win an Academy Award. In *Gone with the Wind* (1939), her character stood up to her mistress, Scarlett O'Hara (Vivien Leigh), and shook her head over Rhett Butler (Clark Gable). As Ms. McDaniel pointed out, her grandmother had actually worked on a plantation; now, she was receiving an Oscar for portraying that reality onscreen. In 1942's *Casablanca*, Dooley Wilson played Sam, the friend and confidant of Humphrey Bogart's Rick. Sam, like Mammy, is given the strength of character to stand up to the movie's leads, and the film makes a clear statement about dignity and equality when Rick responds to a request that he sell Sam: "I don't buy or sell human beings."

In the years leading up to the civil rights era, we saw additional progress alongside continuing racism. A number of so-called problem films from the 1950s explored prejudice against blacks, Jews, and other groups. Nat King Cole became the first African American entertainer to star in a variety show on television. In the 1950s and 1960s, the great Western film director John Ford began to represent Native Americans as something more than stock villains, and in *The Searchers* (1956) and *Cheyenne Autumn* (1964) he not only depicted them with more sympathy but explored the destructive power of prejudice in the American West through John Wayne's iconic character Ethan Edwards in *The Searchers*.

The Sixties offered a number of major steps in representation of people of color as they began to emerge from the shadows into the spotlight. Bill Cosby, whatever we might think of him today, became the first lead black character on a scripted network television series, *I Spy* (1965). The Black Panther, the first black superhero in mainstream comics, debuted in 1966 and became a member of Marvel's superteam The Avengers in 1968. In 1967, Sidney Poitier demonstrated his strength, intelligence, and dignity in three films dealing with race and racism and became the top box-office draw of that year. It's true that these characters were still written and directed by white storytellers, but the problems of prejudice and representation were at least out in the open. Sympathetic minority characters began to challenge the earlier offensive and reductive stereotypes. American film and media slowly—very slowly—began to look more like the larger America as figures like Dr. King and Malcolm X began to offer religious and political challenges to bigotry and prejudice.

From there, we were only one very big step away from the obvious and necessary step: allowing people of color, women, and other underrepresented groups to tell their own stories instead of having them told for them, even by sympathetic observers. In this respect, *The Godfather* represented a watershed moment. In 1972, Italian Americans, like other ethnic groups, were used to being written about and represented by writers and actors from the Anglo mainstream. In films, they often appeared as shifty, shiftless, criminal, unintelligent, and sometimes seemed scarcely human. In *The Godfather* Italian American writers, filmmakers, and actors created multifaceted characters. Although the movie portrayed the Italian mob, its characters behaved with recognizably human motivations. They made difficult ethical choices. They loved their families, they tried to protect and provide for them, and even though they were far from perfect, they were offered the gift of human dignity. In the process, of course, they created a story that moved from particular to universal; as Al Pacino later described it, "The movie had a lot to do with family and people related to it. You didn't have to be Italian-American to appreciate it."[22] For once, white audiences were asked to identify with people from another ethnic group, and they discovered that their entertainment and appreciation did not depend on their own experience being represented onscreen.

This trend began to change the way movies are made and the way they were consumed. Blaxploitation films of the 1970s may not have been high art, but they offered black filmmakers and actors a chance to tell black stories. Martial arts films, both imported and American-made, offered audiences a chance to see Asian characters in action and to encounter Asian culture. Television shows like *Sanford and Son* (1972–77), *Good Times* (1974–79), and *The Jeffersons* (1975–85) achieved mainstream popularity despite their ethnic casts and their often racially specific storylines. Pamela S. Deane notes that *Good Times* based storylines around "evictions, gang warfare, financial problems, muggings, rent parties and discrimination"; viewers watched the Evans family deal with unemployment and with bigotry in a tenement apartment in an urban slum.[23] These were storylines that may not have represented the experience of white middle-class viewers in the Seventies, but they certainly resonated with some minority viewers, while the universal themes of family, fairness, and economic adversity allowed everyone to connect with the characters.

In the 1980s, *The Cosby Show* (1984–92) presented a black family simply as a part of the American mainstream. While their color was occasionally an issue, the Huxtable family was headed by two professionals, and the series more often explored the familial trials and celebrations common to every family married with children. Then, in the persons of Spike Lee and John Singleton, minority filmgoers got to celebrate great filmmakers who received critical acclaim for their work about black people. Singleton became both the youngest and the first African American ever nominated for best director (for *Boyz in the Hood*, 1991), while Lee's *Do the Right Thing* (1989) remains one of the most celebrated and discussed works of American cinema thirty years after its release. The films of these talented cinematic storytellers became part of the larger landscape. Stories about and by those outside the white mainstream were no longer radical exceptions; they begin to represent a new normal, and the voices of people of color began to color the larger discourse of the culture.

In recent years, actors who are outside of the white heterosexual mainstream have appeared in many popular films, while some of our best literary and cultural artists have continued to explore race directly or indirectly. Quentin Tarantino, a provocative writer and director considered by some to be the greatest American filmmaker of his generation, has taken race as one of his great themes in films including *Pulp Fiction* (1994), *Jackie Brown* (1997), and *Django Unchained* (2012). Bill Clinton was once said by Toni Morrison to be our first African American president (by which I believe she meant that President Clinton understood the dynamics of powerlessness and poverty, the loss of control over one's body and one's narrative). Tarantino might be described as a white filmmaker exploring those dynamics in his films, even though admittedly (like President Clinton) he does so from a position of relative white privilege.[24] In the meaty roles he has written for actors like Samuel L. Jackson, Pam Grier, and Jamie Foxx; in *Inglourious Basterds* (2009), which rewrites history to give Jews the power to take revenge on villainous Nazis; and in *Django*, a revenge fantasy that offers an escaped slave the chance to exercise retributive violence against slavers and plantation owners, Tarantino has offered us all the opportunity to discuss how we talk about race, how people without power seek equilibrium, and even whether he, as a white man, should have the right to speak for his black characters.

In the past decade an African American man has been elected president of the United States (twice!) and a Hispanic woman has been appointed to the U.S. Supreme Court. Despite such gains, we know, of course, that prejudice continues to rears its ugly head. The Black Lives Matter movement and the rhetoric of exclusion and fear deployed in the 2016 presidential campaign bear witness to the fact that however far we have come, we have miles to go. Nia-Malika Henderson noted that in the presidential campaign, "racial issues aren't just sparking the occasional flashpoint this campaign cycle—they are a constant and troubling feature of the contest."[25] Race continues to be a political football as I complete this book in 2019. President Donald Trump has continued to talk about Mexican rapists and denigrate the intelligence and patriotism of African American athletes, to equate neo-Nazis in Charlottesville, Virginia, with "very fine people."[26] Nonetheless, we do see signs of progress; despite what happens in the age of Trump, we have entered an age of casual multiculturalism. Perhaps future generations will see the struggle for human dignity differently because of it.

In 2006, *Crash*, produced by Don Cheadle and starring Cheadle, Michael Peña, Thandie Newton, Terrence Howard, and Ludacris (among others), won Best Picture at the Academy Awards. In 2008, *Slumdog Millionaire*, a film with a rainbow cast, took Best Picture at the Academy Awards as well as at the BAFTAs (the British Academy Awards). In 2012, black British actress Naomie Harris was cast in the archetypal role of Moneypenny in the Bond franchise; she reprised it in 2015's *Spectre*. In 2013, *12 Years a Slave*, based on a slave narrative, made Steve McQueen the first black director/producer ever to win an Oscar. (In addition to the Academy Award for Best Film, *12 Years a Slave* also won best picture at the Golden Globes and the BAFTAS.) In 2015, Lin-Manuel Miranda cast his Broadway phenomenon *Hamilton* with numerous people of color portraying white historical figures, and it became and remains the hardest ticket to get in the world. (It has been seen by everyone from Barack Obama and Hillary Clinton to Mitt Romney and Dick Cheney, from Beyoncé and Jay-Z to Amy Schumer and George R. R. Martin, and President Donald Trump launched a Twitter war with the cast over a perceived insult to Vice President Mike Pence.)[27] For Miranda, this casting decision, which would have seemed impossible even decades ago, was intuitive: " 'Our cast looks like America looks now, and that's certainly intentional,' said Mr. Miranda, who originated the title character, Alexander Hamilton. 'It's a way of pulling you into the story and allowing you to leave whatever cultural baggage you have about the founding fathers at the door.' "[28] Race becomes, instead of a way of excluding people, a way of more strongly drawing them into the story.

It's probably worth noting that for all the understandable furor about the exclusion of people of color from the Academy Awards in 2016, people of color have been well represented at the awards since. *Moonlight* was the surprise winner of Best Film in 2017. No 2018 Oscar film had more buzz than Jordan Peele's *Get Out*, and the 2019 Oscars broke new ground for people of color both onscreen and behind it. The world's top-grossing films now often prominently feature people of color, opening doors for new writers, directors, actors, and other professionals. The opening two films of the third Star Wars trilogy (*Star Wars: The Force Awakens*, 2015, and *Star Wars: The Last Jedi*, 2017), among the most successful movies of all time (grossing over $4 billion worldwide), featured a wildly multicultural cast (although some conservative fanboys complained about those multiracial casting decisions). In February 2018, an Afrocentric superhero film with black writers, a black director, and an almost entirely black cast began breaking box-office records around the world, becoming a cultural event celebrated by black audiences but enjoyed by audiences of every color. *Black Panther* grossed over $1.35 billion, by far the most ever earned by a film made by a black director, and was the highest-grossing film of 2018, with *Avengers: Infinity War* (which features characters from *The Black Panther* and a multiracial cast) second, while 2019's *Avengers: Endgame*, another multiracial film, has earned $825 million domestically and almost $3 billion worldwide. No longer are audiences clamoring for simple stereotypes and monochromatic casts. *Black Panther* and other recent films prove that there is a demand for well-told stories, whoever writes, directs, and acts in them, and remind us again that in a diverse culture, all people want, need, and deserve to have their stories told.

We've come a long, long way. We still have a long, long way to go. Those realities can live together in tension, in the culture, just as they do in life. But we need to talk about them, because the success of a movie about a black superhero doesn't automatically change the lives of people of color in America.

Film, Conversation, and Reconciliation

How do we do that hard work of talking? The thesis of this book—and of much of my writing and teaching—is that narrative can help us to have hard conversations, to grow as human beings, and to develop compassion for others. And to illustrate that, I'll tell a story. About a story.

In fall 2016, I taught a repugnant movie. On purpose. In my film class at Baylor University, I assigned D. W. Griffith's *The Birth of a Nation*. This early American feature film, adapted from Thomas Dixon's polemical novel *The Clansman*, follows the intertwined stories of two families—one Northern, one Southern—through the Civil War and Reconstruction. In its stirring finale the newly created white vigilante group the Ku Klux Klan rides to the rescue of white womanhood and civilization. Although African American characters are among its prime villains, they are played by white actors and actresses in obvious blackface, perhaps the most appalling of the film's many appalling elements.

The Birth of a Nation captured the imagination and inflamed the passions of the nation when it first appeared. It was responsible in a very real way for the birth of the Hollywood film industry as we now know it, and also for the early stirrings of film censorship. It doubled the membership of the NAACP and also relaunched the modern Ku Klux Klan. It was, for many years, the top-grossing film in American history and, adjusted for inflation, is still one of the most popular films of all time.

Today, *The Birth of a Nation* is rarely taught and rarely seen in its entirety, despite its cinematic and cultural importance. James Baldwin argued that the film was clearly a work of artistic genius. It was also, he said, "an elaborate justification of mass murder."[29] As I told my students, a work of art can, sadly, be both.

The Birth of a Nation occupies a strange shadow status in our culture: It is one of the most important American movies ever made, yet one that is rarely watched and even more rarely discussed. It is a work that deals with some of our most fundamental American conflicts, but it has been pushed outside of public discourse. The American Movie Classics channel occasionally airs it with elaborate presentations of its historical and critical context, which do not forestall heated protests whenever it is shown. College professors may fear that students won't be able to talk critically about a work so blatantly ideological in its portrayal of the superiority of whites, so they don't teach it, or show only snippets. And when in 1992 the film was named to the National Film Registry, the Library of Congress's index of major American films, the action was roundly condemned.[30]

Some people are offended by the movie's racism. Some are offended by having to talk about the movie's racism. But this failure to talk about the past and its implications for the present seems to be a problem we find throughout American society. We are finding it harder and harder to talk about race these days, and often when we do, we enter those conversations with our minds already made up. As suggested by the Pew Research Center report on racial attitudes in America, our thinking about racism has become calcified.[31] If we are white, it may be that we are sick of talking about racism and our possible complicity in it, and may even believe it is no longer an issue. (As Hadley Freeman wrote in *The Guardian*, the 2016 election suggested that many straight white males are offended by continued talk of identity politics, and certainly that has been borne out in conversations I have moderated over the past three years.)[32] If we are people of color, we may be sick of talking about it because nothing seems to change, even though we believe it is most certainly still an issue. For people of color, race cannot be ignored, and even moments of hope can be tarnished by apprehension. In the acclaimed 2016 episode "Hope" from the series *Black-ish*, Dre (Anthony Anderson) talks with his family that even the election of Barack Obama didn't change the way things felt to him and to many African Americans: "We saw him get out of that limo and walk alongside of it, and wave to that crowd. Tell me, you weren't terrified when you saw that. Tell me you weren't worried that someone was gonna snatch that hope away from us like they always do."[33]

In refusing to have a conversation about *The Birth of a Nation* (or about the essays of Toni Morrison and James Baldwin, or about *Black-ish*, or about any of the other works that deal directly or indirectly with the question of race, prejudice, and how our culture thinks about them), we are missing out on a prime opportunity to have a conversation not about our own entrenched positions but about the positions of the characters in a story. Over the years, I have taught *The Adventures of Huckleberry Finn* many times at Baylor, and while that work too depicts a racist society, it also offers us the chance to talk about what makes us all human. We begin with suspicion; we end, if all goes well, with some understanding.

During Lent 2016, the Rev. David Andrews, an Episcopal priest in Wilmington, Delaware, and now a dear friend, invited me to lead a retreat on race and film for his inner-city mixed-race parish, which had been formed when a failing white congregation and a black congregation were combined. Although they worshiped together on Sunday and worked together on peace and justice issues all week long, his congregation had never, David said, had the hard conversations about race and identity. They had not truly talked to each other about who they were, how they saw themselves, and how they saw others. He was ready to finally initiate that conversation.

Over the course of a weekend together, we watched *Guess Who's Coming to Dinner, Do the Right Thing,* and *Crash.* We talked about how those films had been understood by their original audiences, what they seemed to be about, and how we received them now. We were offended and inspired. We agreed and disagreed with the decisions made by characters. We told our own stories and listened to those of others. And in the process, we had a powerful conversation about race and, perhaps more important, about the powerful human connections that unite rather than divide us.

In the three years since then, I have repeated that experience for other churches and institutions and in the classroom and have observed the very same result: Speaking about race and prejudice becomes more possible when we start not with ourselves and our experience but with characters in a narrative. I have read widely and learned many things formally, but these screenings and public and private conversations were the essential research for this book; I could not have written it without the things other viewers, critics, and theologians taught me about race and film. The conversations were that important.

So while I would never show a film or teach a book simply to shock someone, and as a child of the American South race and prejudice remain my most sensitive issues, sometimes—as with *The Birth of a Nation*—a text that offends all or many can also open a window into a new way of seeing the world if we talk about it, which is all any teacher hopes to do. I'll continue to be appalled by *The Birth of a Nation,* and I'll continue to show it, teach it, write about it, and discuss it.

A note on methodology before we close: In this book I have chosen not to write a history of race in America, or even a history of race in American cinema. Both of those have been done, and done well, by other writers, some of whom I cite here. As ever, what I am interested in is the interplay of culture and narrative: how we have been shaped by the stories we have watched, and how responding consciously to the myths and meanings of these films might reshape us.

Films have power. Their stories, the way they tell them, and the ways we understand them can bring us together or tear us apart. It isn't ridiculous to explore film as a vehicle for meaning. In an essay titled "The Power of Movies to Change Our Hearts," civil rights leader Vernon Jordan wrote that "[d]ivision has always been a product of assumption—assuming that our story is the only story, or that our lives are harder than someone else's, or that people who don't look like us don't have the right to live and work for the American dream. But no matter how divisive life in this country may become, the movie theater has always been a place where we can rediscover what unites us."[34]

I take this as an article of faith. In over thirty years of teaching film and narrative, in three years of showing films and leading conversations on films on race, I have seen, over and over again, the power of stories to change minds and hearts. Film critic A. O. Scott extends Jordan's thesis. While we go to the movies for entertainment, he says, we also go looking for the truth: "In a time of confusion, the best films can offer clarity, comfort and a salutary reminder of complexities that lie beyond the bluster and expedience of political discourse and conventional journalism."[35] Film and narrative can make us more aware by taking us into lives outside our own, characters making choices different from ours. But we have to ask good questions, watch with open hearts, and understand the worlds of the text.

To do this, in each succeeding chapter, we'll focus on an American film illustrating one of the major movements in Hollywood's treatment of race, and employing a common structure. I'll begin each chapter with **relevance**, discussing the context of the film and how it both responded to and reshaped notions of race in American culture at the time, including some conversation about how the film functions cinematically as that is relevant. I'll consider next **representation**, how characters outside the white mainstream are depicted (if in fact they are depicted at all) and what sorts of myths and stereotypes the film creates or perpetuates. Lastly, I'll consider how these works and our discussion about them might be part of the necessary work of **reconciliation**. Vernon Jordan argues that "[w]hen we see injustice from another perspective on the screen, it makes us more aware of real-life injustices around us."[36] How can we make that true? Do these films offer positive lessons we might carry forward into our lives and society at large? How do the myths expressed in these films broaden us as human beings? How might they be harmful to us? How do other formative myths or teachings about race and our treatment of each other offer a hope for reconciliation? Our conclusion will offer next steps about how our consideration of these film narratives might help us wrestle with the existential questions of race in America.

In exploring the ways in which our works of culture have offered up myths about race and prejudice and thinking about the task of reconciliation, I will necessarily bring them into conversation with our wisdom traditions. The Abrahamic faiths (I identify as a Christian theologian, so this is my own starting point) contain many teachings about compassion and hospitality, many commandments to love and honor those who differ from us, and, at the same time, some disturbing exclusionary teachings intended at the time of their writing to elevate the followers of a particular faith or people of a particular tribe. Other traditions, at the heart of belief for millions, also contain essential insights into race, prejudice, and reconciliation. Just as works of literature and culture do, religion presents myths about existence (in the highest meaning of the word *myth*; that is, as a story or belief that shapes us and helps us comprehend our lives, our society, our world, and the cosmos). In the interplay of the stories from our culture and the stories from our faith traditions, we may find agreement as well as discord, and in this book we'll be asking what we can learn from each way of hearing the truth—and where each might lead us astray.

In February 2019 at St. Paul's Chapel in New York City, mere blocks from where hatred and prejudice brought down the Twin Towers, Dr. Catherine Meeks, who heads racial healing efforts for the Episcopal Church, asked a challenging but essential question, quoting Jesus in the Gospels: "Do we want to be healed?" That is: Do we want to do better? Do we want to live in a society where all of us are regarded as worthy? Do we want to live in a culture where no one will suffer because of the color of their skin? It was a stirring moment, and although the question was delivered to a roomful of what Dr. King would have called people of good conscience, it was still a challenge: Are we willing to do the hard work of ending racism, to commit ourselves to the long and arduous process it will require?[37]

Ultimately, cultural works dealing with race, along with wisdom teachings dealing with identity and purpose, help us understand who we are and how we fit into the universe, where exactly we belong. Sometimes our religious understandings of ourselves are based on ancient normative beliefs about humanity that require gentle revision. Sometimes we have forgotten to apply the whole of our wisdom traditions to our relations with other human beings. Sometimes our cultural understandings of ourselves are damaged and damaging, and we need to call those to account and seek higher wisdom. But together they offer us the chance to consider who we think we are, who we think others might be, and why we find ourselves locked into intractable conflicts about equality. Those paradoxes and moments of insight, those places of intersection and diversion, will be the focus of our journey together.

In the spring of 2018, at another of the conversations I convened during my research for this book, I showed *Guess Who's Coming to Dinner*, *Do the Right Thing*, and *Get Out* to a diverse audience in downtown Houston. One of the audience members was an elderly white woman who told me before *Get Out* that she had never watched a horror film, and she was visibly nervous about doing it now. During the discussion with local pastor Sean Palmer that followed the screening, when we suggested that it was a film that audiences needed to see more than once to fully understand what it is trying to accomplish, the woman made a horrified face, made shooing motions with her hands as though she wanted to push the idea away from her, and mouthed the word "no" to me up on stage.

But afterward she came up to me, and with her jaw jutting, resolute, she told me that as hard as it had been for her to watch *Get Out* the first time, she was going to commit to watch it again, "because I live in a racist culture and I want to understand how we can change that."

One of the event coordinators pulled me aside after and asked, "Do you know who that woman is?"

I shook my head. It turned out that she was a longtime member of the Houston Episcopal Cathedral's peace and justice community. And then the coordinator told me it was pretty amazing that she was even there to watch those movies, since she was a hundred years old.

"Wow," I said.

I looked back at that woman. What changes she had seen in the world—from *Birth of a Nation* to *Get Out*. From public lynchings to a black president. And what courage, to take on a cinematic story that was hard for her for multiple reasons, but to do so understanding how important the work of racial healing was, and how this story might help her participate in conversations toward that goal.

For some of us who are white, we have had to go on a journey of discovery, recognition, and transformation. We may still need to set out on that journey. Former New Orleans mayor Mitch Landrieu talks about how hard it can be for that to happen and why we might believe it doesn't have to:

> The way that most white people have a discussion about race is, "Well, we had the Revolution, then we had the Civil War, and then we had the civil rights movement. Okay, that's good. We're done with that because we elected a black president." . . . On race, what I've learned over time, since the time that I was born until today, is that you can't go around it; you can't go over it; you can't go under it. You actually have to go through it and talk through it so there can be some reconciliation. And we really haven't had that.[38]

Talk—both public and private—is at the heart of the possibility of reconciliation.

It remains difficult to talk about race, but it is a conversation that still—perhaps always—needs to take place. You have to go through it and talk through it, and in the past three years of reading, screening, speaking, asking questions, and, perhaps most important, listening, I've marveled at how movies can be of real use in helping us do just that. I'd like for you to know about this as well.

Do we want to be healed?

Turn the page and join me as we see how far we've come, and how far we still need to go.

2

The Birth of a Nation

Seeing the Other as Subhuman

Marching by Torchlight: Racism in America

On August 11, 2017, torch-carrying white supremacists marched through the University of Virginia campus in Charlottesville, Virginia, chanting "White Lives Matter!" "You will not replace us!" and "Jews will not replace us!" They confronted a group of counterprotestors who encircled the statue of Thomas Jefferson, the founder of the university and himself a slaveholder, and taunted black counterprotesters by making monkey noises.

The following day, the full-blown "Unite the Right" rally took place. As the *Washington Post*'s Joe Heim reported, "At 9:30 a.m., about 30 clergy members clasped arms and began singing 'This Little Light of Mine.' Twenty feet away, the white nationalists roared back, 'Our blood, our soil!'"[1]

For many of us the idea that in the Year of Our Lord 2017 neo-Nazis could demonstrate in America not just in the dark of night but in broad daylight was astonishing. For others, the idea that anyone could still give credence to these old myths of blood and soil—the tragic noble defeat of the Confederacy, the danger of whites being replaced by people of color, the superiority of all whites, the need to rule over Americans of African descent, who at best were children and at worst animals—was mortifying. Yet these myths have been part of American history and policy for hundreds of years and were forever enshrined in perhaps the most influential motion picture of all time, D. W. Griffith's *The Birth of a Nation.*

Some films are cinematic events, notable for their brilliantly told stories or their technological advances. Some are cultural events, capturing the zeitgeist of a moment and perhaps influencing their viewers in the process. And some very few not only do these things, but they change history. *The Birth of a Nation* was an incredible advance in cinematic technique and storytelling. It established the feature film as the primary American filmgoing experience and incorporated the advances and cinematic experience Griffith had gained in making over four hundred short films, solidifying a grammar and rhetoric of film, camera angles and placements, editing devices, special effects, and use of color that continue to shape our moviegoing experience today. James Baldwin, who could not help but be appalled by the messages of the film, still described it as "one of the great classics of the American cinema."[2] As a cultural event, the film drew huge crowds of middle- and upper-class filmgoers to beautiful theaters, changing filmgoing from the province of the lower classes consuming short films at nickelodeons to a truly American pastime, and allowing film exhibitors to charge higher prices for the experience.

But *The Birth of a Nation* was one of those rare films that not only excited audiences and moved cinema forward but also both reflected and altered the country. During the Civil War, President Abraham Lincoln is said to have said to Harriet Beecher Stowe, the author of *Uncle Tom's Cabin*, "So you're the little lady that started this big war." At the request of his old acquaintance Thomas Dixon (author of the movie's source novel, *The Clansman*), President Woodrow Wilson screened *The Birth of a Nation* in the White House. Although Dixon had told the president "I would show him the birth of a new art—the launching of the mightiest engine for moulding public opinion in the history of the world," he had an ulterior motive. The molding Dixon hoped for was the transfer of racism from the South to the North through the medium of Griffith's film.[3]

On February 18, 1915, the president, his family, the cabinet, and their wives watched the movie in the East Room of the White House. Wilson was still in mourning for his wife, Ellen, or he might have attended an official Washington showing set up at the Press Club on the following night, and the implied approbation of a White House screening might have been avoided.[4] Although the remark is probably apocryphal, history has recorded that Wilson said that *The Birth of a Nation* was "like history writ with lightning" and "so terribly true."

Whether President Wilson actually said these words, Dixon and director Griffith insinuated that he had approved of the film by screening it, and Wilson refused to denounce it. He seems, in fact, to have liked the film. He wrote Griffith in March 1915 to congratulate him on "a splendid production," and in his later statements on the film, Wilson seems to have "deplored stirring up emotions and showing bad manners" on the part of protesters more than the racist messages of Dixon's novel and Griffith's movie.[5]

The president's tenuous affirmation set to one side, the film had larger political and social effects. *The Birth of a Nation* was, as Paul McEwan has pointed out in his book-length study for the British Film Institute, "a racist work of art made in a racist culture."[6] In response to its message of white superiority and black inferiority, the movie led to the twentieth-century resurgence of the long-dormant Ku Klux Klan. It also mobilized the National Association for the Advancement of Colored People—the NAACP—as a force against the racism of the culture, making the film a marker in the ongoing battle for civil rights in America. The messages and myths of the movie, so much more mainstream in 1915, continued to resonate throughout America, and we could see the recent marchers in Charlottesville as standing in a direct line of descent from the audiences who drank in *The Birth of a Nation* in 1915.

Dixon's set purpose for his tale—the exploration of white supremacy over blacks—was not Griffith's reason for choosing *The Clansman* as a story to adapt. What he found irresistible was the sweep of its historical subject and the possibilities for epic set-pieces as well as smaller sentimental scenes. But in adapting the novel he did not discard Dixon's ideology. Indeed, in some ways, he made Dixon's racism more emotionally available and more normative by attaching it to sympathetic (or repulsive) characters, by offering his film as an authoritative history even though it departs almost completely from the facts, and by cementing the audience's reaction to the story with expert use of camera angles, lighting, editing, music, production design, acting, and other cinematic elements. As recently as 2013, critic Xan Brooks enthused in *The Guardian*, "Griffith's language is so fluent, so confident."[7] My students are typically as impressed by Griffith's artistry as they are repelled by the film's message, but the truth is that the method and the meaning are intertwined, as they always are in great art. Were *The Birth of a Nation* not such a narrative and cinematic achievement, its repulsive moral could never have had such an impact.

A title card at the film's opening states its central thesis: "The bringing of the African to America planted the first seed of disunion." Slavery is important in the film not because it is morally wrong, but because it becomes a dividing line between white men, "Aryans" who should recognize their solidarity and rule together, North and South, without discord. What sort of nation is being born in this film? It is not the birth of a new nation through the shedding of blood in the Civil War. In the Gettysburg Address, Abraham Lincoln, who appears as a sort of historical character in Griffith's film, hopes "that this nation, under God, shall have a new birth of freedom—and that government of the people, by the people, for the people, shall not perish from the earth."[8] What Dixon and Griffith argue is that African men and women brought to America have stood in the way of that Aryan nationhood. Until the issue of the African's status is agreed upon by all white people and resolved, until they occupy their rightful places, that new birth of freedom is impossible.

Dixon and Griffith loft a rallying cry: Let America be America. But the America they envision is in startling contrast to what others have meant by that cry. The prejudice and bigotry of *The Birth of a Nation* stand at odds with the historical Lincoln's call to the higher angels of our nature in his first inaugural address and offer a bleakly ironic contrast to the repeated refrain of Langston Hughes's masterful poem about American prejudice and injustice, "Let America Be America Again":

> O, let America be America again—
> The land that never has been yet—
> And yet must be—the land where *every* man is free.[9]

In the face of that most inspiring vision of brotherhood and amity, what does *The Birth of a Nation* have to offer? Its own sort of inspiration: the depiction of the true connection of all white people, regardless of their seeming separation by region, philosophy, or even warfare. The film's opening minutes set up the two families who are the center of the epic: the slaveholding Camerons in Piedmont, South Carolina, and the abolitionist Stonemans in the North. Congressman Austin Stoneman (Ralph Lewis) is in some ways the film's nominal villain early on, but the family is normalized by his daughter Elsie (Lillian Gish, the film's biggest star) and her brothers Phil (Elmer Clifton) and Tod (Robert Harron), who are shown at their home in Pennsylvania relaxing and playing affectionately with each other.

The Camerons, likewise, are presented at home, and their idyllic existence (a way of life "that is to be no more," a title card announces) too is marked by family love, civility, and playfulness. We are introduced first to Ben Cameron (Henry Walthall), the picture of style and manners; he will go on to become the primary protagonist of the film. His father, Dr. Cameron (Spottiswoode Aitken), is described as "the kindly master of Cameron Hall"; when first we meet him, the camera at first frames him reading the paper with a kitten in his arms, then tilts down slowly to show two puppies playing at his feet. Around him on the porch, the family plays, reads, and spends a lazy Southern day. It is impossible not to like the Camerons upon first meeting them.

Phil Stoneman and Ben Cameron are friends from boarding school, and Phil and younger brother Tod come for a visit in 1860, prior to the war. During that trip, Phil falls in love with the elder Cameron daughter, Margaret (Miriam Cooper), Ben develops an infatuation for Phil's sister Elsie after seeing (and then stealing) her photo, and the two younger sons become fast friends, as demonstrated by their slapstick play together. Both young men are depicted much more like silent-film comedians such as Buster Keaton than as characters in a drama or historical epic, which makes them immediately likeable and enlists our support in their friendship. While the audience experiences the dramatic irony of knowing that these two lovely families will soon be on opposite sides of a bloody war, we can see their similarities and easy compatibility. Despite their differences, it is easy to imagine them as one extended family.

Black characters are also presented as being in sympathy with the ideology of the film, embodying the idea that slaves prefer to be slaves than free. Early in the film, slavery is presented as humane and perhaps even idyllic. After showing slaves picking cotton with energy and seeming enjoyment, a title card tells of the two hours slaves are allotted for dinner, and the Cameron slaves are invited to dance for the visiting Stoneman brothers, which they do gladly and with great gusto. When the Southern soldiers set out from Piedmont in a marvelous parade, slaves cheer them and celebrate the spectacle as the Camerons and their allies ride and march away. Griffith himself often held up as exemplary characters the two Faithful Retainers who had been slaves of the Camerons, who remain with them after they are freed, and who eventually even engineer the rescue of Dr. Cameron when he is put on trial for being in the Klan. Mammy (Jennie Lee, playing in blackface) and the unnamed male slave (perhaps Harry Braham, also in blackface) rescue their old master, demonstrating that they may not have the capacity to understand how completely they are acting against their own best interests, but they are completely devoted to their master, the family they serve, and the only way of life they know. Mammy goes so far as to dress down a liberated black from the North, railing against blacks who set themselves up above their station. In this way, Griffith presents black characters allied with the white vision for the future, a vision from the past in which kindly and paternal whites rule over their black servants.

The depiction of white characters with much in common and of black characters in sympathy with the project of white America stands in contrast to the depiction of those black and "mulatto" characters, who—as we will see—embody common negative stereotypes and stand in the way of the creation of this best of all possible nations, white America. Their animal cruelty, their selfishness, their lust, their scheming for power, and their indolence (yes, the black characters have a laundry list of contradictory stereotypes to live up to!) prove that it is foolish to imagine blacks can ever master themselves, let alone be placed as rulers over others. These nonwhite characters of *The Birth of a Nation* who cannot accept their place, not the battling soldiers of the Civil War, represent the greatest threat to the health and vitality of the nation.

The dramatic impact of the portrayal of the characters who represent the film's ideology is reinforced by the film's supposed historicity. Advertisements lauded the realistic depictions of major events in the Civil War and Reconstruction and, despite its many factual and interpretive liberties, audiences actually understood *The Birth of a*

Nation to be history onscreen. An unnamed reviewer of the film for the *Dallas Morning News* spoke of "the picture's obvious fidelity" and "the astonishing realism," and called the film "history in motion."[10] The matter-of-fact assertion that the slaves were given a two-hour dinner period is one of many titles in the film that build a casual authority. In its reenactments of familiar and important scenes from the historical record—Lincoln calling up troops, the assassination at Ford's Theatre, the meeting of Grant and Lee at Appomattox—the film represents itself as truly and correctly showing what happened, although it is also clearly supplying its own emotional nuances and commentary. Note, for example, how Lincoln wipes tears from his eyes after signing the order calling for Northern troops to go to war against the South. Perhaps Lincoln did feel an overwhelming sense of sadness at having to perform this act. But clearly Griffith is enlisting the beloved character of Lincoln as an ally in evoking appropriate emotion from his viewers, and reminding us that conflict between members of the white race is tragic and counterproductive. We who have so much in common should not be enemies.

The film cites authorities for its representation of historical scenes, ranging from famous paintings of events to Woodrow Wilson's own *History of America*. A series of title cards quoting Wilson announce that "Adventurers swarmed out of the North, as much the enemies of the one race as of the other, to cozen, beguile, and use the negroes" and suggest that the white South was put under the heel of the black South, which led naturally and organically to the rise of the Ku Klux Klan, which was purely an agent of white self-defense. Depicting the black South Carolina legislature during Reconstruction, Griffith deploys a title card claiming to show "An historical facsimile of the State House of Representatives of South Carolina as it was in 1870. After Photograph by the 'The Columbia State.'" The card refers to a photo of the chamber, empty, but Griffith then dissolves from the empty chamber to one in which black legislators eat, put their feet up on desks, ogle white women in the gallery, and push through legislation legalizing mixed-race marriage. As Mimi White points out, this dissolve, very rare in *The Birth of a Nation*, allows Griffith to take his historically accurate photo and transfer the authenticity to his imagined scene of a state house debauched.[11]

This is Griffith's method throughout the film. He uses the claim of historical accuracy in support of the film's racism and advocacy of white superiority. What brings all these elements together is how powerfully they are contained in and expressed by the film's cinematic elements. It is important to note, first, that silent films were not necessarily silent; they were often accompanied by organists or even by an orchestra. *The Birth of a Nation* was the first film to have its own original soundtrack. The music from the original score for the film, composed by Joseph Carl Breil, offers auditory reinforcement to the idea that the dancing slaves are happy and free in their servitude and the Camerons, who own them, are also living an idyllic life. The "Negro Theme," a motif Breil uses first for the introduction of the Negro to America, becomes more and more important in the second half of the film as black characters scheme for power and influence over whites, and Breil's instrumentation, gloomy woodwinds with the primitive sound of tom-toms, emphasizes that these characters do not belong in white civilization. In a Wagnerian turn now typical of movie soundtracks, Breil offers a sinister musical theme to accompany Austin Stoneman's misguided benevolence toward people of color and his misdirected ambition, which almost wrecks the nation. The theme contributes as powerfully as the writing and acting to the characterization of Stoneman and is also used on several occasions to introduce his protégé Silas Lynch (George Siegmann, in blackface), a mulatto politician who eventually replaces Stoneman as the film's primary villain.

Performances are styled to convey racial attitudes as well. The film's major villains are African American but are played, without exception, by whites in blackface. All at times act with more than the usual exaggerated motions of the silent film actor; in his final scenes of the film with Elsie, for example, Silas Lynch becomes more simian, carrying the unconscious Elsie as though he is an ape, with little regard for whether or not he hurts her. According to Donald Bogle, Lillian Gish spoke in the 1930s of how "the colored man picks up the Northern girl gorilla-fashion."[12] Gus (Walter Long) plays his role with great physicality, appearing less than human in his movements, often waving his arms, leaping, and scrambling on all fours. Silas too sometimes drops the semblance of human form and resembles nothing so much as a great ape. Bogle sums up these depictions and their purpose: "Griffith played hard on the bestiality of his black villainous bucks and used it to arouse hatred."[13] By contrast, even in times of great agitation and action, white characters such as Ben are depicted as thoughtful, graceful, and ever conscious in their movements.

Careful use of shot, camera angle, or camera movement is deployed throughout the film to fortify the film's themes, sometimes used to illustrate Griffith and Dixon's concern for white womanhood and the menacing sexuality of black men. Near the movie's climax, Elsie Stoneman has fallen into the clutches of Silas and he wrenches her to his side. It was, as Bogle notes, a startling use of contrast: "the powerful black man and the frail blonde girl—was a master stroke and brilliant use of contrast, one that drew its audiences into the film emotionally."[14] This image displays an amazingly insightful use of star power. As Griffith made her one of America's most popular movie stars, Gish had established the persona of a modest, virginal, delicate, retiring young woman. Her *New York Times* obituary notes that "Miss Gish evoked an aura of fragility, and hers was a vulnerable waiflike beauty."[15] In this shot toward the end of *The Birth of a Nation*, that ethereal blonde beauty contrasts with the bestial black figure of Silas; white audiences could be counted on to respond to this image with fear and panic. In a single image, their worst racial nightmare was brought to life.

Late in the film, Margaret Cameron is hiding in a cabin with members of her family surrounded by a black army force. Griffith irises in on a close-up of her face. She looks pensively off camera, and a lone tear traces down her face. Any viewer would be stricken with sympathy for the plight of this lovely and innocent girl. This is shortly followed by shots in which Dr. Cameron stands poised above Margaret holding a pistol, ready to strike her dead with the butt if the black enemy should break through. As seen earlier in regard to the death of another young woman, better a white woman dead than defiled. The framing of these shots and the tension in the poses of the actors elicits our sympathy and builds suspense, reinforcing our identification with the film's prevailing ethos. What sort of monsters would place a father in a situation where murder is his best choice for his child?

A short close-up of Gus looking longingly at the younger Cameron sister, Flora (Mae Marsh; Flora is also called "The Pet Sister" in the cast list), also illustrates the monstrous sexuality of the black male. Flora has been established throughout the film as a playful and innocent girl who dotes on Ben. This close-up, so tight that Gus's face occupies half the screen, directs our attention to his eyes, staring at Flora, obviously desiring her. It is the sort of shot that might be used before a murder; the sense of menace is palpable, and the shot is made even more frightening by the fact that Gus is in shadow. What follows does not surprise us. Gus intends to harm this sweet little girl, and this visual prompt prepares us for that attack.

In affirmation of the title card mourning the end of the Southern way of life, Griffith stylishly films the 1861 Piedmont farewell ball in such a way as to show that this is a truly beautiful society, and that its demise is to be mourned. He films the ball in a slow shot drawing back, with the camera dollying regretfully away from the swirling flower-like women in their beautiful dresses, and the men, straight and tall, all of them dancing in a world that is about to end.

Another example of effective camera work comes when Ben Cameron meets with friends in his home in Piedmont following the political victories enjoyed by Stoneman and Lynch; black people are now in power and white people under their thumbs. The camera holds on Ben and his friends, seated with a stairway in the background. The shot holds a surprising amount of unused space as Ben recounts the various "outrages" of this new regime: white people put on trial before a black judge and jury, white citizens brutalized by black soldiers. At last he cannot contain himself; he rises, filling the frame, his fist raised, before the camera irises in on him. Griffith uses artistic composition and our unconscious knowledge of it to frame Ben Cameron as a heroic figure worthy of our support and admiration through the rest of the film. Our unresolved (and perhaps unrealized) tension about the unfilled cinematic space has been satisfied, and we associate Ben's action with our own feelings that things are now finally as they should be.

Griffith in Black and White

Griffith is justly lionized for his mastery of film editing, which he learned in the four hundred short films he directed and brought to this feature film in scenes that could not help but excite and involve audiences emotionally. One of the most important incidents in the film is the attempted rape and suicide of Flora Cameron, which Griffith films in an exciting eight-minute sequence. Gus (described in the cast listing as a renegade Negro) seems to be a freed slave now in army uniform; he can be observed in the center of the frame in the early scenes of slaves dancing for the Camerons and their guests. The editing of this sequence varies in different versions of the film, but they all intercut three important elements: Flora goes into the woods to fetch water and becomes distracted by a squirrel in a tree; Gus sees Flora alone and desires her, first shadowing her, then directly menacing her; and Ben goes in search of Flora, becomes convinced that something is wrong, and moves closer and closer to where she is.

We can follow Ben's progress through the landscape by familiar settings in which we have earlier seen Flora and Gus. As in much of Griffith's work, the tension is built by the suspenseful juxtaposition of individual shots: Here is Flora, running from Gus; here is Gus, pursuing her and drawing ever closer; here is Ben, calling Flora's name and looking for her. Will Flora elude Gus? Will Ben arrive in time? The answer to both questions is "No."

Gus's pursuit, and the perceived threat of sexual assault, induces Flora to leap from a rocky cliff to her death. An earlier title card has Gus saying that he will not hurt Flora, but his eyes, his carriage, and his continued pursuit say otherwise. The editing builds in pace as she jumps, as Gus flees, as Ben arrives, too late, atop the rocks. He looks down and sees his sister, broken at the base of the crag. At last, Griffith closes the sequence with a long-held shot of Ben wiping blood from Flora's face, holding her while she dies, and then clearly plotting revenge for this outrage. The long pause is necessary for the scene to have its full emotional effect, an outpouring of sadness and rage that is made perhaps even more powerful by the sentimental title that leaves no doubt how we are intended to think about the action we have observed: "For her who had learned the stern lesson of honor we should not grieve that she found sweeter the opal gates of death." But of course we do; that is *why* we grieve.

Her death is the result of her desire to remain pure in the face of a monstrous and inhuman attacker, and Griffith has used his skills as director to build our own sadness and rage against Gus, the renegade

Negro, the unfaithful slave—and against all who might resemble him. After Gus is caught and lynched by the KKK, his body is thrown onto a porch to be found by Silas; audiences of the day—and perhaps even in our day—remembered how Griffith made them feel during Flora's chase and death and resonated with the title card about Gus's lynching, chilling in its simplicity: "The answer to the blacks and carpetbaggers." Vigilante justice is often satisfying in American films, and this is one of its earliest and most powerful manifestations.

The most famous sequence in the film—and one of the most notable in film history—is the gathering and ride of the KKK at the film's climax. This sequence too is marked by brilliant editing and juxtaposition intended to engage our emotions and our outrage. It actually begins when Elsie Stoneman is at the mercy of Silas Lynch, who has proposed to marry her and clearly has designs upon her person. Two riders gallop through the countryside. Even before the KKK has been apprised of Elsie's predicament, we in the audience have witnessed it, and as the number of horsemen grows, Griffith adds additional elements to build the tension. Austin Stoneman arrives, discovers that Lynch intends to marry his daughter, and as he struggles to rescue Elsie, realizes his folly in elevating any person not wholly white to a position of power. The streets fill with the "crazed negroes" brought in by Lynch and Stoneman to intimidate the white townspeople. Dr. Cameron, Margaret, and others have joined two Union veterans in a cabin besieged by black Union soldiers.

Griffith cuts back and forth between the scenes, the emotional pitch and sense of menace rising. The Klan has raised an army of riders, but will they arrive in time? The threats against white womanhood— Lynch's announced desire for Elsie, the implied threat to Margaret inside the cabin—are imminent and very real. Not only do we have two heroines in danger, but Griffith ups the ante, intercutting scenes of blacks rioting in the street and doing violence to Klan sympathizers while "helpless whites" look on from their living rooms as they read the Bible and pray that they are not the next to be attacked.

It is no wonder that audiences leapt to their feet as the Klan arrived to save the day and right these cosmic wrongs; Griffith has pushed every emotional button, mustered every sympathy, and employed every form of identification that a well-told cinematic narrative has to offer. By intercutting the stories and the use of rhythmic editing, he has built an almost-unbearable suspense that only now can be relieved. I love an old, probably apocryphal, story about Soviet filmmakers who came to Hollywood and were told they were going to be shown *The Birth of a Nation* as the highest expression of the American cinematic art. These Soviet directors scoffed at the idea. "We have heard of this film," they said, "of the hateful ideas it expresses, of the many divisions it has caused. Such a film could not interest us." But they sat down, and they watched, and, so the story goes, when the KKK rode to the rescue in the final reel, they too stood to their feet and cheered.

Whether or not Soviet filmmakers ever cheered on the rise of the KKK, this is what biblical scholar Marcus Borg called a parabolic story; whether or not the story is objectively true, it is mythically true—that is, it expresses something real and authentic. This film has the power to make even those who resist its deep-seated ideology stand up and cheer for its protagonists. The challenge for us is clear: We must, on the one hand, hold the film up as a marvel of cinematic accomplishment and, on the other, repent of its hateful ideology and virulent racism.

How can we do these things? How can we be appreciative of how the film communicates but also be wary of *what* the film communicates? A focus on the stereotypical representation of black and nonwhite characters may offer us the best way to hold *The Birth of a Nation* responsible for its sins. While the film certainly did not create these stereotypes—most had been present in American culture for a century at least—it offered potent versions of these myths that infiltrated our thinking and influenced the way we view each other down to the present day. In these stereotypes, we see how profoundly dangerous *The Birth of a Nation* was, has been, and still could be, if the Charlottesville rally is any example.

The list of African and African American character stereotypes in *The Birth of a Nation* is a veritable roll call of offensive terms. I use them here noting that Donald Bogle's landmark study of blacks in American film employed them long ago. They are descriptive categories that identify long-lasting myths about black people and their humanity or perceived lack of it. They matter because they have often become a primary way that white audiences see black people. Racial theorist bell hooks argues that challenging the harmful ways that white people see black people is an important move toward liberation and equality.[16] But these stereotypes are also sadly influential in how black people see themselves. To accept reductive views of other people is tragic, to accept them as views of yourself perhaps even more so. In his letter to his nephew, James Baldwin said that his brother, his nephew's father, had lived a hard and terrible life, "defeated long before he died, because, at the bottom of his heart, he really believed what white people said about him."[17] To identify these stereotypes, to call them out as reductive and harmful, and to seek better, more complex characterizations is an important part of our task in this book.

Mammy, played in *The Birth of a Nation* by white actress Jennie Lee in blackface, is, of course, an example of the Mammy, one of the most pervasive of the racial caricatures associated with black women. Mammy is obese, dark-skinned, and asexual; wears a bandanna; and is completely devoted to the white family she serves, to the exclusion even of her own family or people. This familiar archetype has been around since the days of slavery and has appeared in advertising, in popular culture, and in material culture such as figurines, salt and pepper shakers, and cookie jars. The Mammy archetype has appeared in products for American consumers. Many readers will recall how Aunt Jemima, before the recent redesign of the model as a modern (and slender) African American mother, used the image of the Mammy to sell pancakes, syrup, and other breakfast foods. The first spokesperson for Aunt Jemima was Nancy Green, born a slave in Kentucky. From the 1890s to her death in 1923 she actually portrayed the character of Aunt Jemima, helping to build the brand into a national success.[18] Pinnacle Foods, the holding company that now owns the Aunt Jemima brand, does not address the racial legacy of Aunt Jemima. It simply describes it as "one of the oldest and most-recognized trademarks in America" and says that "Aunt Jemima has been an indispensable part of American breakfasts for over 120 years."[19] The Mammy stereotype is a perfect match for something like breakfast food; a previous brand owner, Quaker Oats, described Aunt Jemima in this way: "The image symbolizes a sense of caring, warmth, hospitality and comfort."[20]

Although she too had these positive traits, Mammy in *The Birth of a Nation* also carried all the harmful racial myths attributed to the Mammy stereotype. She is depicted as humorously illiterate. Her girth is used to depict her as something other than a desirable sexual being and is played for laughs when she flattens a soldier to allow Dr. Cameron to escape. Mammy's dark skin (with the black makeup, Jennie Lee looks, in fact, grotesque), unflattering dress, and big soft body are supposed to suggest that black women are not attractive to whites, which of course is patently untrue. Throughout the antebellum period, black women were raped, gave birth to mixed-race children, and were routinely treated as sexual objects. Female slaves "were sexually exploited by rich whites, middle class whites, and poor whites . . . All black women and girls, regardless of their physical appearances, were vulnerable to being sexually assaulted by white men. The mammy caricature tells many lies; in this case, the lie is that white men did not find black women sexually desirable."[21] The Mammy figure could, however, be used to sweep that horrible reality under the rug and engender a myth that allowed white men to have their black mistresses and deny their desirability at the same time.

Mammy in the film and as a stereotype is an idealized caregiver, so good at taking care of others that it is her only role in life—a role she was born to and in which she delights. She would rather stand up for the family she serves than for herself, and while she is sometimes paired with an unnamed male servant, her fellow Faithful Retainer, her care and her focus are devoted to the white family she serves as house slave, not to her own family, whoever and wherever they might be. When we first see Mammy in the film, it is on the porch of the Camerons' house in Piedmont, where she affectionately embraces Flora Cameron. Throughout the course of the film, she remains a house servant, but her focus continues to be how best she can protect and serve the Camerons, which leads in the climactic action of the film to her role in the besieged cabin, where she bashes one black invader after another over the head with a stick. The film thus advances a myth of happy and willing servitude that absolves whites of the responsibility for slavery—and also suggests that servitude is the most felicitous state for black people.

Although the Mammy stereotype is simply that, a stereotype that does not conform to the experience of many black lives, its representation in *The Birth of a Nation* and other cultural works continues to shape the way we think about black women—and the way black women think about themselves. In the course of her research for her book *Sister Citizens*, Melissa Harris-Perry conducted focus groups with African American women in Oakland, Chicago, and New York City. While many of the women in her groups defined themselves as having characteristics we associate with the Mammy figure (such as kindness, generosity, compassion, dependability), they went out of their way to explain that those traits were not directed toward white employers, but to their own families and communities.[22] In fact, Harris-Perry suggested that the desire not to be seen as a Mammy in the service of whites may stand in the way of useful alliances with white women. "The legacy of Mammy and the resulting suspicions of white women and their motivations can limit the range of political possibilities open to black women."[23]

Another familiar stereotype that appears in *The Birth of a Nation* is that of the Jezebel, an oversexed black woman who uses her sexuality to gain what she wants, including power over white men. Lydia (Mary Alden in blackface), Austin Stoneman's maid, is portrayed as a temptress who captivates Stoneman and generates many of the film's complications. The character of Lydia is drawn from the real-life Lydia Hamilton Smith, the biracial housekeeper of Thaddeus Stevens, the Radical Republican congressman upon whom Stoneman is based. In Dixon's *The Clansman*, Stoneman is intimate with his housekeeper, as indeed many have supposed the real Stevens was with Mrs. Smith; historian Joshua Zeitz calls this relationship "the worst-kept secret in Washington."[24] In the closing scene of Steven Spielberg's *Lincoln* (2012), Thaddeus Stevens (Tommy Lee Jones) is shown in bed with Mrs. Smith, although Spielberg presents the relationship very differently from Griffith, not as a weakness but a strength, a sign of Stevens's empathy with American blacks and his commitment to their cause.

Unlike the Mammy, in *The Birth of a Nation* Lydia is not depicted as a diligent worker, and her service to her master does not seem to consist in house labor. Her life is not bound up in faithful service to her master and white family, as Mammy's is; she is described as a person with ambition. After a conference between Stoneman and Sen. Charles Sumner, a title tells us that "the mulatto [is] aroused from ambitious dreamings by Sumner's curt orders." Furious at being treated like a slave, she drops to the floor and tears wildly at her clothing. We see an idea come to her: She will say that Sumner assaulted her. A title card precedes Stoneman's entry into the room. It effectively summarizes the action we are about to see: "The great leader's weakness that is to blight a nation." Finding Lydia in disarray, Stoneman reaches for her bare shoulder as if mesmerized, then pulls her into an embrace. As in the clinch and fade out convention of classic Hollywood, we infer that something sexual happens, although it cannot be depicted onscreen.

James Baldwin noted that the film's two primary villains, Lydia and Silas, are mulattos "driven by a hideous lust for whites."[25] The hideous lust of the Jezebel frees white men from responsibility for their desire for women of color and of responsibility for their acts of rape or coercion. As Ibram X. Kendi observes in his National Book Award–winning study *Stamped from the Beginning*, this stereotype of the hypersexual black woman began in Europe and spread to America, where in colonial times, "white men continued to depict African women as sexually aggressive, shifting the responsibility of their own sexual desires to the women."[26] This story continues to be told down to the present. In her willingness to use her body to advance her ambitions, Lydia does fit a stereotype of sexualized, often lighter-skinned, black women. Donald Bogle identifies Lydia as the Tragic Mulatto. While he does mark her as the lone passionate female in the film, he also describes her as the only black character with some sort of interior life, saying that Lydia projects "genuine mental anguish . . . over her predicament as a black woman in a hostile white world."[27] Certainly she is one of the black characters in the film who acts rather than being acted upon. In Dixon's novel *The Clansman*, the Lydia character is called "The First Lady of the Land." Despite her clear narrative role as a villain, Lydia might even be viewed as a sympathetic character, perhaps owing to Mary Alden's performance. In a world dominated by white men, how does one get what one wants? What weapons does a person of color have available to deploy when white men hold money, power, and position? Lydia uses her sex and her brains to make her way in the world.[28] The Mammy and the Jezebel are potent stereotypes, and as Melissa Harris-Perry's research indicates, they are still pervasive today. Harris-Perry's focus groups reported that it is still all too easy for a black woman to feel that people see her as either a sexless servant or a sexy gold digger.

Another offensive racial stereotype represented in *The Birth of a Nation* is the Uncle Tom, the good Negro who is submissive, generous, kind, and longsuffering. The unnamed male counterpart to Mammy in the film is a Tom, although his role is smaller than Mammy's and his actions and loyalty are less dramatic. The film also contains numerous examples of what Bogle calls the Coon stereotype, Negro characters presented as buffoons who are objects of amusement. The Coon is, Bogle says, "the most degrading of all black stereotypes," depicting as it does lazy, shiftless, subhuman blacks whose lives are marked by "eating watermelons, stealing chickens, shooting crap, or butchering the English language."[29] The slaves singing and dancing for their master and his guests are Coons, as are the barefoot black Congressmen who take over the South Carolina legislature. The slave children who fall off the back of a wagon are a subset of Coons, pickaninnies, shiftless and racially exaggerated black children who are often depicted in danger or menaced in some way for the enjoyment of a white audience.

But by far the most important stereotype Dixon and Griffith employ in *The Birth of a Nation* is that of the Buck, a stereotype that is emotionally and thematically at the heart of their story. Lydia is presented as a vamp and Mammy as a sexless lump, but white audiences were far less concerned about the sexuality of black women than the sexuality of black men. The myth of the hypersexuality of black people—particularly black men—goes back at least as far as the first European writing about Africa. The fifteenth-century papal theologian Joannes Annius wrote a commentary on the story of Ham in Genesis (the supposed genesis of the black race) describing black skin as a sign of sin and sexuality. In the sixteenth century, Leo the African wrote in his *Dell descrittione dell'Africa* that black people were more drawn to sexual indulgence than any other beings.[30] Both works were widely translated and highly influential. We have seen that Americans consumed these same myths. In America, because of slavery, those myths about black sexuality took on added power. The children born of female slaves were born enslaved to the master, but what about a child fathered by a black man and born to a white mother? This was a religious, social, and economic conundrum best answered by the belief that no white woman would willingly give herself to a black man. The explanation was that black men were insatiable, powerful, and compelled to desire white women. White women must be protected from this hideous lust, which meant vigilance, separation, and the readiness to punish any black men who transgressed.

In *The Birth of a Nation*, Gus and Silas are two hypersexual black men who cannot control their desire for young white women. Dixon and Griffith frame these cases as typical (remember that in the film the black South Carolina legislature passes a bill permitting the marriage of blacks and whites) and present them so that audiences will see them that way. Gus is the ungrateful slave set free; instead of remaining on the plantation like the Faithful Retainers, he becomes a Union soldier and begins to develop ridiculous ideas about living a life independent of his white masters. He tells Flora that now that he has become a captain, he intends to marry, and Flora is clearly the intended object of that proposal. For Dixon and Griffith, and for many in the audience, it would make little difference whether Gus wed Flora before having sex with her or simply raped her. Both possibilities are viewed as equally horrific, as Flora's expressions of dismay and panic, and ultimately her suicide, convey. Gus is no proper husband for a white woman, and he is depicted as subhuman, an ape and not a man. To be physically linked to such a being would be the foulest disgrace.

Silas too loses control of himself in the presence of his victim, Elsie. The central moment when he grabs her like a gorilla seals our perception of him as inhuman. His inability to control his desire or his movements also seems to stamp him as less than human. Silas too wants to marry and has chosen Elsie to be his bride. At first she cannot believe him, and then she suggests that he should be horsewhipped "for his insolence." When Silas tells Stoneman he wants to marry a white woman, Stoneman approves, but when Silas says he wants to marry Elsie, he reacts with horror. At long last it is borne home for Stoneman, who has supported equality, and who has told Silas that he is the equal of any man present, that blacks and whites are not and can never be equal. It has taken personal involvement, the thought of his beloved Elsie wed to this black monster, but he has finally seen the light. Black men—and mulattos—are brutes, beasts who lust after white women, and they must be put in their place, violently if necessary.

This is a sexual myth that, as Billie Holliday would sing, has borne strange fruit. The wave of lynchings that lasted from the late nineteenth century well into the twentieth was often prompted by accusations of rape or sexual attention by black men against white women. *The Birth of a Nation* depicts one such lynching and implied another. Gus, of course, is captured by the KKK and killed, his body prominently displayed by Griffith as a reminder of what will happen to black men who accost white women. Silas Lynch—and surely this name was chosen ironically with the character's ultimate fate in mind—is taken off screen in the arms of the KKK, but there is little doubt what will happen to him, and in Dixon's novel, he is lynched by the Klan. The Buck who dares to touch a white woman will die, not least so that other hypersexual black men will know the cost of such actions.

The film's dramatic depiction of racial violence committed against black men in punishment for their sexual interest in white women almost certainly contributed to later acts. *BlackKklansman* had its history correct: Waco, Texas, where *The Birth of a Nation* was shown repeatedly and received a rave review in the local newspaper, was the site of one of the most horrific lynchings in American history. In 1916, after being found guilty of raping and murdering a white woman, Jesse Washington was pulled from the crowded courtroom, tortured, castrated, and burned alive in front of an estimated ten thousand spectators. A professional photographer captured the event, and postcards of the lynching were later sold as souvenirs. Those attending also claimed or bought parts of the slaughtered man's body as keepsakes, a common practice after public lynchings. Amy Louise Wood, in her study of racial violence, argues a definite correlation between the film's popularity in Waco and the lynching that shortly followed it.[31] As *The Guardian*'s Jamiles Lartey and Sam Morris reported, "lynchings were a method of social and racial control meant to terrorize black Americans into submission, and into an inferior racial caste position."[32]

Mammy and Jezebel, Mulatto and Coon, Tom and Buck: *The Birth of a Nation* employs all of these stereotypes in the service of its racial and political ideologies. A myth embedded in a story is a powerful thing, and this well-told story resonated with many white audience members. As Bogle put it, "Griffith presented all the types with such frightening force and power that his film touched off a wave of controversy and was denounced as the most slanderous anti-Negro movie ever released."[33] These stereotypes are identifiable, demonstrably false, and answerable, but they continue to resonate today, coloring the way white people view people of color, challenging us not to reduce them to simple stereotypes and false myths and challenging people of color to recognize and reject these simple and odious versions of themselves.

Slavery and Religious Tradition

Dixon and Griffith's mythology matches up to other American master narratives about the identity of white people, the inferiority of people of color, and the Manifest Destiny of white Americans to spread from sea to shining sea and beyond. It can be combated purely on a humanist basis, for to believe in the inferiority of another enslaves the one who embraces that prejudice. Hatred and bigotry are their own prison. As Baldwin told his nephew in *The Fire Next Time*, "We cannot be free until they are free."[34] Article Four of the United Nations Universal Declaration of Human Rights promulgated an uncompromising condemnation of slavery seventy years ago without the need of citing a religious text: "No one shall be held in slavery or servitude; slavery and the slave trade shall be prohibited in all their forms."[35] But we expect our wisdom traditions to offer potent counternarratives and healthy myths in opposition to the harmful ones our culture sometimes presents us. How might religious teaching help us understand slavery and wrestle with our American heritage—for we cannot ignore it—in which millions of humans were treated as the property of other people?

First, it is important to note that slavery is normative in the Bible, encompassing different types of slaves. In addition to those taken in battle, the Hebrew Bible talks about those who have sold themselves into debt slavery for economic reasons, and conjugal slavery. (Different rules applied to Hebrew and non-Hebrew slaves; Hebrew slaves were supposed to be freed after six years—like indentured servants in early America, perhaps—and blessed by parting gifts from their masters. Foreign slaves were slaves for life.) But the formative story in Jewish life is a story of slavery and exodus. Among the major characters of the Hebrew Testament who are slaves during at least part of their lives we find Hagar, slave to Abraham and Sarah and mother of Ishmael; the patriarch Joseph, sold into slavery by his jealous brothers; and of course Joseph's descendants, who become the slaves of Pharaoh in Egypt.

Slavery was normative among the Children of Israel and persisted into Jesus's time and indeed all the way to the present. However, this does not mean that the Bible—let alone God—approves of slavery or the ownership of other human beings. In Exodus and Deuteronomy the Bible is trying to offer some guidance for the humane treatment of slaves, and to suggest that while their owners might have charge over them, they are not their all-powerful masters. Exodus 21 decrees that if a slaveowner strikes a slave down dead, he will be punished (although not if the slave lingers for several days after the attack; for some reason the lawgiver believes that this exempts the owner from punishment), and if he maims or disfigures a slave, the slave will be set free in compensation. The fact that slaves are accorded protections suggests that they are seen as fellow humans. In Exodus 12:44 it is even ruled that foreign slaves who have been circumcised may partake of the Passover meal. While they are still subject to those who own them, this is a recognition of shared humanity, an offering of the most sacred event in Jewish life.

In addition to these calls for fairness toward the slave, the larger narrative of the Hebrew Testament is centered on slavery, freedom, and full flowering, and God's care is revealed to be drawn to the oppressed, not to the powerful. The voluminous work of theologian Walter Brueggemann shows how slaves are God's favored ones who, though held captive in an imperial system, are freed, invited to holiness, and entered into covenant with God.[36] What God seeks for those in bondage, Brueggemann would tell us, is liberation, and those forces that stand against human freedom—the enslavers—stand against the expressed will of God. Truly, Exodus tells us that God is the one who hears the cry of the suffering and comes to their aid. The situation of the Hebrews in Egypt seems very much like slavery as it is represented in *The Birth of a Nation*:

> Therefore they set taskmasters over them to oppress them with forced labor. They built supply cities, Pithom and Rameses, for Pharaoh. But the more they were oppressed, the more they multiplied and spread,

THE BIRTH OF A NATION 47

so that the Egyptians came to dread the Israelites. The Egyptians became ruthless in imposing tasks on the Israelites, and made their
lives bitter with hard service in mortar and brick and in every kind
of field labor. They were ruthless in all the tasks that they imposed on
them.[37]

But God heard their distress and called Moses to be the instrument
of their deliverance. "Then the Lord said, 'I have observed the misery
of my people who are in Egypt; I have heard their cry on account of
their taskmasters. Indeed, I know their sufferings, and I have come
down to deliver them from the Egyptians, and to bring them up out
of that land to a good and broad land, a land flowing with milk and
honey, to the country of the Canaanites, the Hittites, the Amorites, the
Perizzites, the Hivites, and the Jebusites.'"[38] God hears the cry of the
slave, observes the misery of the oppressed, and brings them out of
slavery into abundant life. This experience of slavery in the past (for
both Jews and Christians) not only privileges slaves as those most
needing and most worthy of God's notice but evokes what Rabbi Barry
Schwartz calls "historical empathy," recognition that a people once
enslaved should react with sympathy to slaves, yes, but also to all those
who are poor and displaced, including refugees.[39] At least thirty-six
times in the Torah Jews are reminded that they were once slaves or
strangers in a strange land; their experience then should make them
advocates for those in bondage now.

Rabbi Oliver Sacks argues that "To be a Jew is to be a stranger." Jewish
belief thus places the believer in solidarity with the slave, making the
righteous Jew a counterweight against hate and injustice for, as Rabbi
Sacks says, we and they are one:

Why should you not hate the stranger?—asks the Torah. Because you
once stood where he stands now. You know the heart of the stranger
because you were once a stranger in the land of Egypt. If you are
human, so is he. If he is less than human, so are you. You must fight
the hatred in your heart as I once fought the greatest ruler and the
strongest empire in the ancient world on your behalf. I made you
into the world's archetypal strangers so that you would fight for the
rights of strangers—for your own and those of others, wherever they

are, whoever they are, whatever the colour of their skin or the nature of their culture, because though they are not in your image—says G-d—they are nonetheless in Mine. There is only one reply strong enough to answer the question: Why should I not hate the stranger? Because the stranger is me.[40]

Some Christians used the Bible to justify American slavery and weaponized Christianity as a tool to keep their slaves under control, but these shameful ideas and practices have been thoroughly discredited. Christian tradition, building off this Jewish teaching of human solidarity, likewise inveighs against slavery and oppression because of our common humanity. N. T. Wright argues, on the basis of the Letter to Philemon, that we are seeing a "profound and profoundly revolutionary" shift in the world in which all people, slaves and free, are brothers.[41] In Galatians 3, the Apostle Paul articulates the definitive leveling: "There is no longer Jew or Greek, there is no longer slave or free, there is no longer male and female; for all of you are one in Christ Jesus."[42] Austin Stoneman is in fact echoing Paul when he describes Silas as equal to anyone in the room, and even though *The Birth of a Nation* fiercely resists the idea of equality, this is the central message offered by Judaism and Christianity in response to the ideology of white supremacy.

As Brueggemann puts it, the Torah message and the Gospel message are equally assertive about human dignity: "The confession of Christian faith is that all of God's human creatures are made in the image of God . . . We are all one in Christ. And what we know in the gospel is that God's love reaches toward all of God's creatures. To sort them out in terms of who are the deserving and the qualified and who are not is imposing a judgment on human reality that simply cannot be done."[43]

The Birth of a Nation would tell us that some of us are deservedly placed in power based on the color of our skin; that we are more or less human based on the color of our skin; that some of us are beasts with uncontrollable sexual urges, again based on the color of our skin; and that, finally, America will never truly be America until Aryans unite against the dangers posed by Africans and African Americans and resolve to do whatever is necessary, even stepping outside the laws of our country to commit acts of terror and violence, to keep black people repressed and afraid. This is the marchers of Charlottesville, shouting "You will not replace us!"

Against this racist ideology, still being spouted by modern white supremacists and neo-Nazis today, we find the Jewish and Christian teaching that God loves and values all, regardless of skin color or genesis; that God, in fact, has a preferential option for the poor and the oppressed; that all of us, black and white, men and women, slave and free, are recognizably part of the same family; and that we are called to love and respect all of God's children. It is a message that will apply to many of the films we discuss in upcoming chapters. This message not just of tolerance but of engagement and active compassion must first be a potent antidote to the hateful teachings of *The Birth of a Nation*.

Why should I not hate the stranger?

Because the stranger is me.

3

Best Supporting Actors

Casablanca, Friendship, and the Beloved Community

World War II and the New Negro

After spending the fall 2018 semester reading works dealing with race and prejudice, my Baylor University student Kennedy Stovall wrote on her American Literature final exam that "[r]acism is a part of our history, but it doesn't have to be a part of our future." Things, she believed, could change, and thankfully we have seen changes in Hollywood film that may lead to a less racist future, although the steps along the way were slow and long in coming. The blatant racism of *The Birth of a Nation* represented one form of prejudice in Hollywood film; another, in its own way as bad as feckless misrepresentations, which continued, is a failure of representation. In the decades that followed *The Birth of a Nation*, as John Silk writes, blacks were generally excluded from feature films, with white characters not only privileged but almost universally the sole culture represented.[1] A decade after the depiction of blacks as brutes and sex fiends in Griffith's Civil War epic, for example, Buster Keaton released *The General*, a comedic epic also set in the Civil War–era South, in which black characters are conspicuous by their absence. I have taught the film on several occasions but still cannot say with certainty if any black actors appear in it; certainly none are characters. This absence of people of color is typical of mainstream Hollywood features in the 1920s and 1930s. However, the failure to even acknowledge racial difference in a Southern setting where historically there were substantial numbers of black men, women, and children invites social, psychological, and theological investigation.

In January 1944, the U.S. Army released *The Negro Soldier*, a film produced by Frank Capra as part of his mandate to make propaganda films in support of the war effort. The movie was originally intended to be shown to black soldiers but was ultimately screened for white soldiers as well and in theaters across the country. Its message was simple and powerful: Black soldiers were an important part of the war effort, just as black people were an important part of America. As Sean Axmaker has noted, although the film depicted black soldiers in segregated units, it was notable for its embrace of black characters as human beings: "In an era when African Americans on the big screen were invariably subservient stereotypes or caricatured comic figures, it presented black men with dignity and respect as everyday Americans no different than white men."[2] In 1942's *Casablanca* Humphrey Bogart's Rick responds to a question about whether he will sell Sam (Dooley Wilson), who plays the piano in Rick's café: "I don't buy or sell human beings." Racism might still exist in Hollywood, but people of good conscience had begun to see people of other races as fellow children of God and to depict them as fellow human beings. This is a second phase in Hollywood's history of race and racism; while people of color are not yet lead characters, and while they continue to be written by white writers and filmed by white directors, there is an attempt to reckon with their existence and to depict them as more human and more complicated than hateful cardboard caricatures.

So from the bad beginnings of *The Birth of a Nation*, by the early 1940s we had reached a point where Hollywood film could now, on occasion, depict African American characters in less stereotypical ways and acknowledge our common humanity. *The Negro Soldier* did not catalyze this development. Rather, it reflected social changes, some caused by the coming of World War II. It's important to note that Hollywood's progress toward significant black characters was also encouraged by earlier depictions of black characters with dignity and human reality. James Baldwin, born in 1924, wrote about how through much of his youth he looked in vain at the silver screen for a character who represented his life in some way. The actors Stepin Fetchit, Willie Best, and Mantan Moreland and their stereotypical roles he loathed: "It seemed to me that they lied about the world I knew and debased it, and certainly I did not know anybody like them—as far as I could tell; for it is also possible that their comic, bug-eyed terror contained the truth concerning a terror by which I hoped never to be engulfed."[3]

Critic Donald Bogle identifies the first truly sympathetic black character in Hollywood film as Clarence Brooks's Howard University-educated doctor Dr. Marchand in John Ford's *Arrowsmith* (1931). He found another such character in Mervyn Leroy's *I Am A Fugitive from a Chain Gang* (1932).[4] Baldwin himself remembers the black janitor played by Clinton Rosewood in Leroy's *They Won't Forget* (1937) who discovers the body of a murdered white girl, is brutally questioned about her death, and then is persuaded to lie on the witness stand to help convict another innocent man lest he be charged himself. "The role of the janitor is small, yet the man's face hangs in my memory until today," Baldwin wrote, "and the film's icy brutality both scared me and strengthened me."[5]

These smaller gains were cemented by two major supporting roles in monumental films, Mammy (Hattie McDaniel) in *Gone with the Wind* (1939) and Sam in *Casablanca*. While both bear traces of earlier stereotypes, both also are strong characters and are depicted as recognizably human. They are written with sympathy and play important roles in their respective films. As Bogle told Turner Movie Classics, Mammy may support the values of white culture, but McDaniel plays her with an angry edge, and she is "all-knowing, all-seeing, all-understanding."[6] Although she is literally "Mammy," and thus bears surface similarities to Aunt Jemima and Mammy from *The Birth of a Nation*, McDaniel's character is constantly trying to influence Miss Scarlett (Vivien Leigh) toward wiser courses of action, often standing up to her. She is a strong character, and McDaniel wrings the most out of her part.

McDaniel in fact became the first African American to win an Academy Award, appropriately enough, for Best Supporting Actress, and she often spoke of the distance she felt African Americans had traveled. Her father had been a slave, after all. Admittedly the journey was not complete; McDaniel still faced considerable prejudice. She was not invited to the film's opening in Atlanta. The Oscar ceremony was held at the Roosevelt Hotel, which at the time still did not admit blacks. McDaniel was not allowed to be seated with her fellow cast members and had to be given special permission just to attend. Later in life, she was one of thirty-one black property owners involved in a landmark court case prohibiting discrimination against minorities. Things in the larger culture remained challenging. But her grandmother had worked on a plantation, and she had won an Academy Award for portraying a plantation slave. McDaniel's mother and sisters worked as maids, and she had done so herself before becoming an actress. Responding to accusations that she allowed herself to be typecast as a domestic servant, McDaniel often retorted that she would rather play a maid onscreen: "Why should I complain about making $700 a week playing a maid? If I didn't, I'd be making $7 a week being one."[7]

Sam also bears a resemblance to earlier stereotypes: As a singer and entertainer, he connects to the singing and dancing Coons. He might also be seen as an early version of the Magical Negro (or at least the Black Best Friend), a character who seems to exist only to make the journey of a white character possible. Certainly *Casablanca* contains some problematic thoughts on race. But given the distance traveled between *The Birth of a Nation*'s black characters and his, Sam looks like a paragon. The part of Sam offered Dooley Wilson, as Noah Isenberg observes in his bestselling *We'll Always Have Casablanca*, "greater emotional depth and complexity, and far more substantial dialogue" than previous roles he or other black actors had assayed.[8]

The depiction of Sam in *Casablanca* was shaped by social forces, changes taking place in American society in reaction to past prejudice and violence against people of color. We must understand the context of the film. The racially motivated lynchings that began in America around 1877 continued until the 1950s; the Ku Klux Klan was revived following *The Birth of a Nation*; and in 1921 white mob violence in Tulsa, Oklahoma, decimated the thriving black community of Rosewood. Many black people began to relocate away from areas associated with racist violence, to organize, and to push back against institutional racism. At the same time, some whites began to work against the persecution and oppression of African Americans. The tide of racism slowly began to shift. As people of color became more integrated into the culture, whites began to recognize that the oppression of black people was un-American and un-Christian, that it stood against our professed national and religious values.

Between 1910 and 1920, half a million African Americans fled the South to industrial cities in the North and Midwest in what for many of them was the only form of protest possible. As Yale scholar John Dollard wrote in 1937, "Oftentimes, just to go away is one of the most aggressive things that another person can do, and if the means of expressing discontent are limited, as in this case, it is one of the few ways in which pressure can be put."[9] More recently, Isabel Wilkerson summed up six decades of migration from South to North: "They did what human beings looking for freedom, throughout history, have always done. They left."[10] The Great Migration did not end racial violence. In the 1940s, for example, in Detroit, Michigan, competition between whites and the rising black population over housing and jobs led to rioting. Racism and prejudice were potent features of the landscape in the North even without Jim Crow laws like the South's to institutionalize. But the Migration did remove many from the most dangerous section of the country for black people and, in the process, changed American cities, American language, and American culture.[11]

White legislators and American presidents called for federal anti-lynching legislation. Between 1882 and 1968, some two hundred such bills were introduced in Congress. The majority of Americans supported such legislation, but Southern senators stood in the way, even filibustering a bill in 1937 as Eleanor Roosevelt sat in the gallery in silent protest.[12] Black writers, pastors, and activists spoke up in response to racial violence, and in 1939, the NAACP created its Legal Defense and Educational Fund to work against institutional racism. Under Thurgood Marshall, the fund would launch momentous antidiscrimination cases in the 1940s and 1950s, leading ultimately to 1954's *Brown v. Board of Education* Supreme Court decision overthrowing the segregation of public schools.

Other momentous events in the culture began to shift racial attitudes in the years leading up to *Casablanca*. In 1939, the great contralto Marian Anderson sang on the steps of the Lincoln Memorial, a watershed event in civil rights history, and according to Susan Stamberg one of the most important musical events of the twentieth century.[13] Although Anderson had sung with the New York Philharmonic and at Carnegie Hall, although she had sung across Europe to enthusiastic audiences, the Daughters of the American Revolution (DAR) denied her request to book Constitution Hall, the largest concert venue in Washington, DC, for a performance. Eleanor Roosevelt resigned from the DAR in protest, and Franklin Roosevelt gave permission for Anderson to offer a public concert at the Lincoln Memorial. Interior secretary Harold Ickes introduced Anderson to the 75,000 people gathered on the National Mall and millions more listening on the radio: "In this great auditorium under the sky, all of us are free. Genius, like justice, is blind. Genius draws no color lines."[14] The listeners were awed by her performance, and many, according to Robert L. Harris, Jr. and Rosalyn Terborg-Penn, recognized the irony of Anderson's having to perform out of doors "because of racial bigotry and discrimination at a time when the United States criticized Nazi Germany for its doctrines of Aryan supremacy."[15] Anderson's concert marked a significant moment when America confronted its own bigotry and repented of it. She went on to be the first black performer to sing at the White House and reprised her appearance at the Memorial in 1963 at the March on Washington for Jobs and Freedom that featured Dr. Martin Luther King, Jr.

In 1940, Richard Wright's Native Son was published to great critical acclaim and popular success; in three weeks, it sold 215,000 copies.[16] It marked another sea change in American culture. No longer could Americans pretend that black writers were minor figures, nor would the plot and themes of Native Son permit its many readers to ignore the history of black oppression. In its depiction of Bigger Thomas, an impoverished black man who commits horrific violence, there is the suggestion that this violence is in some sense caused by the society that formed him and insisted he was no more than a brute beast. Critic Irving Howe famously remarked in Dissent that "The day Native Son appeared, American culture was changed forever. No matter how much qualifying the book might later need, it made impossible a repetition of the old lies. In all its crudeness, melodrama, and claustrophobia of vision, Richard Wright's novel brought out into the open, as no one ever had before, the hatred, fear, and violence that have crippled and may yet destroy our culture."[17] Whatever its literary faults—and they are many—Native Son foregrounded racism for a wide audience and helped further discussion.

In 1941, several momentous events expanded opportunities for African Americans. The first all-black combat air unit, the 99th Pursuit Squadron, was established at Tuskegee Institute. Some in the armed forces thought black men didn't have the intelligence or courage to train as pilots, let alone fly into combat, but the Tuskegee Airmen distinguished themselves, winning respect from other servicemen and the general public. One of them, Col. Charles E. McGee, went on to serve in Korea and Vietnam and flew more combat missions—409—than any other pilot in U.S. military history.[18] The Tuskegee Airmen have since become a legendary part of our culture; witness their appearance alongside American icons Teddy Roosevelt (Robin Williams), Amelia Earhart (Amy Adams), and General George A. Custer (Bill Hader) in *Night at the Museum: Battle of the Smithsonian* (2009).

The year 1941 was also notable for the threatened March on Washington organized by A. Philip Randolph, the labor organizer and civil rights advocate who led the powerful Brotherhood of Sleeping Car Porters union. Pullman porters were essential to the nation's transport and made up a strong and influential sector of black middle-class life. Randolph, with the backing of the NAACP, New York mayor Fiorello La Guardia, and Eleanor Roosevelt, announced a massive march intended to end discrimination in the armed forces and in military contractors and began to organize with the intention of bringing tens of thousands of African Americans to the National Mall. A week before the projected march, President Roosevelt agreed to the integration of war industries and the march was called off. The armed forces would not be integrated until after World War II, but Roosevelt's Executive Order 8802 banned "discrimination in the employment of workers in defense industries or government because of race, creed, color, or national origin" and established the Fair Employment Practice Committee to enforce this action, which led to increased prosperity for people of color, many of whom found good jobs that continued after the war.[19]

By the early 1940s, then, in many ways black people had become a more visible and more thoroughly integrated part of the national fabric, and the Oscar win for Hattie McDaniel and the important role of Dooley Wilson's Sam in *Casablanca* might be seen as reflections of that. They also reflect, perhaps, a greater sensitivity to the depiction of people of color; whether intentionally or not, the writers and filmmakers seemed to be correcting some—if not all—harmful old stereotypes and being more responsible to their black actors and their white audiences. Howard Koch, the *Casablanca* screenwriter credited with writing the line recognizing Sam's humanity, was a writer with a liberal political bent, and the finished film—while still exhibiting racism in some ways—represents a quantum leap in Hollywood representation of people of color, part of a second wave in which films attempted to portray characters outside the white mainstream as recognizably human. As film critic Richard Corliss writes, "Sam is one of the few beings in Casablanca whom Rick would consider human."[20]

"He's Worth It": Sam in *Casablanca*

Although his is a supporting role, structurally that of past Faithful Retainers, Dooley Wilson's Sam is an essential character in the movie, and from his first appearance, he is depicted as strong and sure and integrated into the film's action. Critics and black audiences alike noted this from the film's debut. In the black-owned *New York Amsterdam News*, reviewer Dan Burley wrote that every black person should see *Casablanca*, "since no picture has given such a sympathetic treatment and prominence to a Negro character . . . There's not the slightest resemblance to the objectionable Uncle Tomming that characterizes most of Hollywood's output."[21] *Variety*'s review of the film lauded the actor and his role: "Deserving of special mention among the lesser characters is Dooley Wilson, making his film debut. A Negro, he appears as the devoted friend and confidante of Bogart, as well as the piano player at Rick's. He sings with great effectiveness 'As Time Goes By,' the theme song of the Bogart-Bergman affair."[22] Bosley Crowther, writing in the *New York Times*, also singled out Wilson's performance "as Rick's devoted friend," which "though rather brief, is filled with a sweetness and compassion which lend a helpful mood to the whole film," and he described Wilson himself as "a real find."[23]

Sam as a character has many strengths, one of them being that he is represented, as Burley noted, without stooping to negative stereotyping. In earlier films, his character might have been depicted simply as a Coon, laughing it up and serving only as entertainment; he might have been, as Burley lamented, an Uncle Tom, bowing and scraping for his white master. These stereotypes are not completely dead in the film—when Sam sings "Shine," with its lyrics "'Cos my hair is curly/'Cos my teeth are pearly," runs his hand across his scalp, and flashes his pearly whites, we get a hint of how the role could have gone badly wrong. The fact that Sam takes commands from both Rick and Ilsa (Ingrid Bergman) could have made him look servile. In truth, however, although Ilsa once refers to him as "a boy," he is treated as an equal (Corliss notes that Rick treats him with much more courtesy than he treats the rest of the staff), and he and his music are essential to the first two acts of the film.[24] If there is a tinge of racism in the depiction of Sam's character—and the film does have more than a tinge of racism in it—it comes because Sam's character is suddenly dropped from the film, and his roles as Rick's friend and mentor are pushed over to white actors. And certainly there was more than a tinge of racism in the fact that Dooley Wilson was paid substantially less for his supporting role than the white actors. But on the whole, the piano player was a substantial character in the movie's source material, the unproduced play *Everybody Comes to Rick's*, and, as Isenberg reports, the studio and writers "were generally supportive of its underlying theme of racial integration and interracial friendship."[25] We can clearly see this in the way Sam is written and filmed—at least in the opening half of the film (and perhaps his disappearance in the final section of the film owes as much to the slapdash nature of the writing and filming as to any conscious slight to the actor).

Casablanca's opening titles are projected over a map of Africa. While French Morocco, where the city of Casablanca is located, is located on the continent of Africa, most audience members would have had other associations with the continent. It might seem that we are subliminally prepared for Sam's presence in the film well before we meet him, which happens, in a sense, before we meet any of the major characters. The camera shows the sign over the door of Rick's, then tilts down to enter the door, and we hear music coming from inside—Sam, singing and playing "It Had to Be You." The camera dollies in close to Sam as the song changes to "Shine," a song that introduces and glories in Sam's black identity. Subsequent lyrics of this song, unheard in the film, make clear the speaker is black and content in that identity:

Just because my color's shady
Makes no difference, baby
That's why they call me "Shine."

The lyrics of the original 1910 introduction to the song make it clear the protagonist is a black man:

When I was born they christened me plain Samuel Johnson Brown
But I hadn't grown so very big, 'fore some folks in this town
Had changed it 'round to "Sambo" I was "Rastus" to a few
Then "Chocolate Drop" was added by some others that I knew
And then to cap the climax, I was strolling down the line
When someone shouted, "Fellas, hey! Come on and pipe the shine!"

"Shine" had been recorded earlier by Louis Armstrong and Ella Fitzgerald, and like other music that Sam "plays" in the film (a drummer by training, Wilson does not actually play the piano with which he is so closely identified), it would have been familiar to *Casablanca*'s audience and in keeping with his role as nightclub entertainer. But the inclusion of it when Sam first appears onscreen helps to tell us that Sam is secure in his identity, as well as secure in his position at the center of Rick's Café Américain. He continues to play as the camera takes in a sampling of the refugees gathered in Rick's and we get a sense of their desperation and danger; it is no exaggeration to say that Sam's music is the soundtrack to most of what happens in the film and is connected to major plot moments and the film's most central themes.

After Ugarte (Peter Lorre) gives Rick stolen letters of transit for safekeeping, Rick hides the letters in Sam's piano as he plays "Knock on Wood." These letters are emblematic of freedom in a movie about escaping Casablanca, and their connection with Sam marks his importance, as does the scene immediately following when Signor Ferrari (Sydney Greenstreet) enters, offers to buy the café from Rick, then asks "What do you want for Sam?"

"I don't buy or sell human beings," is the answer, a blunt rebuke to all those who over the centuries did buy people like Sam and who did not see their common humanity. To reinforce Sam's humanity and his agency, the scene continues with Ferrari suggesting that they ask Sam if he would like to make a change. Rick agrees—Sam is his own man and can make his own decisions. When Sam says no, Rick points out that Ferrari will "double what I pay you." Rick knows Sam's value, and Sam knows that he has choices—and he chooses to remain with his friend, whom, we discover, needs him.

When Ugarte is taken away by the gendarmes, Rick proclaims that he sticks his neck out for nobody, his announcement of his lack of interest in helping others and a clear reference to the isolationist undercurrents of the times that had tried to keep America out of World War II despite the clear moral distinctives calling for involvement. Here is Rick's major theme, spoken out loud: Because he has been hurt by previous involvement, he has decided to cut himself off from the world; only when he learns again that he must be a part of something larger than himself will he be truly whole. After Ugarte is carted away screaming, Sam is called on to play something and calm the crowd; in contrast to Rick's distance, he has to confront the emotions that the arrest has stirred up.

Even this early in the film, Sam has been associated with the film's themes of refugees, a melting pot, isolationism (as they are crossing the club to speak to Sam about making a change, Signor Ferrari tells Rick that isolationism such as he practices is no longer practical), and the dangers of authoritarianism. Now, he is about to become the instigator of the film's great love story between Rick and Ilsa. When Ilsa and her husband Victor (Paul Henreid) enter the club, Sam makes eye contact with her and she smiles. Clearly they know each other from somewhere. She asks for him to come over, greets him, and asks him about Rick, and he lies—obviously and nervously—to try and protect his friend. At last, he pleads, "Leave him alone, Miss Ilsa. You're bad luck to him." In response to her questions, he pushes back, and there is sad wisdom in his plea. He best knows what a shell of a man Rick has become since Ilsa left him at the station in Paris.

But, against his better judgment (and, we discover, Rick's direct prohibition), he begins to sing and play "As Time Goes By" for her, prompting one of the film's most astonishing cinematic moments, a long held close-up of Bergman's face in which she is sadly transported by the music and her memories—until Rick hears the music, storms over, and sees Ilsa. In both cinematic and story terms, Sam's character brings the movie's main characters together, and his music, particularly "As Time Goes By," will continue to be an important device in building plot, character, and theme. This scene, incidentally, takes place about a half-hour in and could correspond to what Syd Field calls the Act One plot point, the moment when the story is spun in a new direction and into Act Two. In other words, Sam is the agent of the plot turning in its new and true direction—toward the reuniting of Rick and Ilsa.

Like Mammy in *Gone with the Wind*, when we next see Sam he is nudging his heartbroken boss to do the wise thing:

"Boss, ain't you going to bed?"

"Not right now."

"Ain't you planning on going to bed in the near future?"

"No."

"You *ever* going to bed?"

"No!"

"Well, I ain't sleepy either."

While Rick sits and drinks and moons over Ilsa, Sam says he's staying there with Rick and offers some alternatives to this destructive (and probably familiar) behavior. "Let's get out of here," he says, and he tries to distract Rick with the idea of a fishing trip: "We'll take the car. We'll drive all night. We'll get drunk. We'll go fishing and stay away until she's gone." When Rick tells him to go home, Sam refuses, and, instead, sits at the piano and begins playing.

Like Ilsa, Rick wants to hear "As Time Goes By," and as with Ilsa, Sam at first avoids playing it, knowing it will bring painful memories. But he accedes when Rick says, "If she can stand it, so can I. Play it!" As he plays, the camera dollies in on Rick, Sam's piano is joined by a full orchestra, and suddenly we are in the past—in Paris. Sam's music has bridged the years, and we are suddenly in Rick's consciousness, remembering what he remembers.

One of the most inclusive scenes in the film, showing Sam's partnership and friendship with Rick and Ilsa, respectively, comes during the flashback. At La Belle Aurore, the three are drinking champagne as though there's no tomorrow, since the Nazis are preparing to enter Paris. Rick pours for the three of them and they toast each other, Sam a full participant. There is no inkling of anything less than full equality, a startling move for 1942. Isenberg agrees, telling me "when he, Rick, and Ilsa toast Chez Henri in the flashback sequence this is truly radical—not only because they all raise glasses together, but especially because Sam and Ilsa toast."[26] After they drink, Sam tells Rick that he will be in danger when the Nazis come, and he and Ilsa convince him they should all leave. But Ilsa does not show up at the appointed time, and Sam brings the note that tells Rick that she cannot join them and can never see him again.

Here is where Sam has his most important moment, the top of his character arc, and the most certain marker of his equal humanity. The script says that "Sam pulls a stunned, reluctant Rick to the train," but the script does not dictate all that happens next in the finished film. Sam does steer the crestfallen Rick onto the stairs of the train as it prepares to depart, and then as the train pulls away, he puts his hand on Rick's shoulder to comfort him. Again, think of the effect of seeing this in 1942, when the image of a black man touching a white man offered a radical contrast to the segregation encountered in everyday life. It is in these scenes, and in this moment particularly, that Sam demonstrates his humanity and his value to Rick. Sam is, as Isenberg has noted, "a genuine friend to Rick" and "his sole traveling companion."[27] If Rick's drunken behavior at the table in the café is any indication, he was probably of little use—and very difficult—in the days following. This suggests that Sam, in the words Rick will use to Ilsa, had to do the thinking for both of them. Without Sam, it is safe to infer, Rick would not have escaped Paris and might be in a Nazi concentration camp—or dead. We can see here that Sam has not only offered comfort to his friend but most probably saved his life.

It is important to note this amazing departure from the stereotypes normally seen for black roles, since it is Sam's last important action in the film, and almost his last appearance. When the flashback concludes, Sam stops playing and comes over to Rick's table to pick up his glass and a fallen chair, and then Ilsa enters. One moment, Sam is in the right edge of the frame. But when we cut to Ilsa and back to Rick, Sam is missing, as if he has vanished into thin air. The script offers no guidance—it too forgets to exit Sam. One minute he is standing at the table with Rick. Then he's not in the shot. After this, for all practical purposes he is no longer in the film, and his roles are subsumed by Victor and the French prefect Louis Renault (Claude Rains).

It's not that we don't at least see Sam again, but he will never again serve as Rick's confidant and ally, nor will he be central to the movie's plot and themes. His last appearance is at the piano when Ilsa and Victor enter the café and, at Rick's bidding, he begins playing "As Time Goes By." The music is strangely muted emotionally now after we have heard it performed by sweeping strings during the flashback, but it is a bridge to what comes next: Rick goes back into the casino and rigs the house's roulette game so that a young Bulgarian husband wins the money he needs to purchase exit visas for himself and his wife—and so she does not have to sleep with Captain Renault. It marks the moment in the story when Rick sticks his neck out for someone, the beginning of his return to the idealist we know he was before Paris.

But we do not see Sam again, and the screenwriters miss a chance to underline his importance in the film at the stirring moment when Victor leads the patrons of the bar in singing "La Marseillaise," the French national anthem, to drown out a Nazi drinking song. In the script—and in the film—members of the orchestra look to Rick, who nods and allows them to play, and of course it leads to one of the movie's most emotional moments. The actors playing refugees in Rick's bar were almost all themselves refugees from Nazi violence and oppression, and their genuine emotions seem to flavor the scene, which is the movie's emotional highpoint. Strangely, Sam is not part of it. In the play *Everybody Comes to Rick's*, the Sam character is directed to strike up "La Marseillaise." Why did the screenwriters make this change?

And that night, after Ilsa comes to the café and she and Rick strike up their intimate relationship again, Rick asks another minor character to take Ilsa home. Admittedly Sam would have to be given a reason to be present—the old waiter is returning with Victor from a resistance meeting that the Nazis raided—but this would have been another way to keep Sam as relevant in the last half of the movie as he had been in the first. Instead, Victor goes on to offer Rick challenges and wisdom, and it is Renault with whom Rick exits at movie's end en route to their beautiful friendship. Perhaps Sam doesn't appear because he is no longer needed; Rick's transformation is clearly under way before he makes his noble decision at the airport to send Ilsa away with Victor. Perhaps he doesn't appear because the writers forgot about him. And perhaps he doesn't appear because he is black, and, as we saw at the beginning of this chapter, the default position for blacks in film of that era was absence, but in this case it is a strange absence. Isenberg tells me, "All three credited writers—Julius and Philip Epstein as well as Howard Koch—were principled men of the Left, more FDR liberals and popular front fellow travelers (in the case of Koch) than card-carrying [Communist] party members, who were surely sympathetic to the cause of racial equality. As Jews, all three were also perhaps a bit more attuned to the Nazi menace than others." It is strange that these three, of all the writers in the world, forgot about Sam, and perhaps we'll never know precisely why.[28]

Absence marks the film in other ways, sadly. First, for a film set in French Morocco, no significant Arab characters appear. The major characters are American, French, German, and refugees from across Europe. The only discernible Moroccans are, like Abdul, stage dressing, there to open a door for the café's clients. It certainly seems like cultural elitism. Brian T. Edwards describes the film as "the paradigmatic example of 'American Orientalism'"—that is, a depiction of the exotic Orient from a white perspective of cultural superiority.[29] Edward Said, whose *Orientalism* is the classic study of this phenomenon, described Orientalism as a way of seeing or speaking that "displaced the Oriental as human and put in his place the Orient Orientalized as a specimen."[30] We Westerners are fascinated with the "exotic East" but what we want to consume is a theme park version, and of course this Casablanca we see is created on the Warner Brothers backlot and soundstages rather than showing the actual place and its actual people. The closest we get to Morocco might be the character of Signor Ferrari, the Italian bar owner and organized crime figure who in his dress and manner seems to have appropriated native practice (in the derogatory language of British colonialism, he has "gone native"). But this too is racist cultural imperialism. Ultimately, we are forced to ask: Is the appropriation and subjugation of a people by "good" white characters such as Renault, Ferrari, and Rick less oppressive than the subjugation threatened by the "bad" white characters such as Major Strasser (Conrad Veidt)?

Edwards notes the missed opportunities in the film for dialogue about race, servitude, and identity: "the complex yet readily apparent ways in which *Casablanca* brackets or suppresses concerns of gender and race . . . are a way of distracting viewers from a more potent possibility repressed by the film: that Sam . . . might enter into a conversation with the colonized Moroccan subjects who are relegated to the film's background."[31] Of course *Casablanca* is not Sam's film, and such criticisms are often a way of saying, "I wish the film had been about this." The movie is, most assuredly, about the relationship between Rick and Ilsa and Rick's reclaiming of purpose, not about Sam and his experience of racism.

Finally, for a film that talks often about German concentration camps and centers on the problems of refugees, *Casablanca* is strangely devoid of Jews. On the surface, this might seem like a typical failure to represent people outside of the white Christian mainstream who made up the majority of the moviegoing public. But the truth is that *Casablanca* is a deeply Jewish film, even though no one is depicted in a prayer shawl or wearing a yarmulke.

In *An Empire of Their Own: How the Jews Invented Hollywood* (and the documentary film made from the book), Neal Gabler argues that the Jewish studio heads found a way to appeal to a white mainstream audience while still telling stories about alienation and seeking a home, and *Casablanca* is clearly an example of this. "It was bought for Warner Brothers," David Robson writes for the *Jewish Chronicle*, "by the producer Hal B. Wallis (born Aaron Blum Wolowicz), directed by Michael Curtiz (a Hungarian-born Jew), the screenplay was written by three Jewish scriptwriters with a music score by a Jewish composer."[32] Although the leads were certainly white Gentiles, the majority of the supporting cast, many of them actually refugees from Central or Eastern Europe, were Jews. Carl, the head waiter (S. Z. Sackall), had fled Hungary in 1940. His three sisters remained behind and died in concentration camps. The most prominent of the many Jewish actors in the film was Peter Lorre, who plays Ugarte. Born Laszlo Lowenstein, he fled Germany, where he had been a star, when Hitler came to power.

Not surprisingly in a film directed, written, and acted by a number of Jews, Jewish themes of the day emerge, even though they are not explicitly recognized as such. Would the battle against the Nazis be more powerful if we understood the ultimate stakes, the core evil we now call the Holocaust? Robson notes that the *New York Times* advertised the release of *Casablanca* on November 25, 1942, and on the same day, deep in the newspaper, there was a story headlined "Slain Polish Jews Put at One Million."[33] Now, of course, we think this makes the story that much more poignant, the fight against Hitler and the Nazis that much more urgent, but at the time this was not a compelling concern for most Americans. As David Mikics writes in *Tablet*, the reason the word "Jew" is never mentioned in this film about European refugees fleeing Nazi atrocities may be that "America's war effort depended on Americans not thinking that they were fighting, even in part, on behalf of European Jews. Indeed, in 1943 a substantial number of Americans still blamed the Jews for the war, just as Hitler did."[34] American anti-Semitism, then, may account for the invisibility of Jews in *Casablanca*. The Jewish experience is there in the film, deeply coded for Jewish viewers, but non-Jewish viewers can—and do—remain blissfully unaware of any Jewish connection.

So Sam is not the only ethnic vacancy in the film, which nonetheless represents a quantum leap forward in its depiction of race and difference. After the flashback, Sam basically vanishes as though he has not been an important character; one is tempted to say that perhaps it has something to do with race. Would Ugarte or Ferrari or any other supporting character have been forgotten in the same way? But the fact is that a number of screenwriters had a hand in the writing of the script. In his look at the production history of the film, Isenberg remarks on "the many at the commissary writers' table asked to sprinkle pixie dust" on the script and notes that how after initial work by Julius and Phillip Epstein, producer Hal Wallis "put the script into a number of different hands."[35] It could be that in the rush and bustle of drafting and redrafting and shooting the film, no one noticed that Sam was left in the shadows of the Café Américain.

But in his time onscreen, Sam serves essential functions in the film. His music ties together the love story at the heart of the story and has a role in other important themes. Most important, Sam represents a thoughtful, intelligent, and talented black man whose presence in the life of the movie's main character helps Rick achieve a worthy goal—returning to the fight against evil. We discover, in this interracial friendship, an essential spiritual truth: that we need each other in order to become the people we are called to be. Friendship is a spiritual as well as emotional relationship, and our ability to be part of a community is an essential part of our discovering who we are and what we are supposed to live for.

Beautiful Friendship, Diversity, and the Beloved Community

"This is the beginning of a beautiful friendship." That famous closing line, contributed by producer Hal B. Wallis, is delivered by Rick as he and Louis Renault walk away into the airport fog. It is more than just a brilliant ending; it is also an indication of the importance of friendship in helping to shape Rick Blaine, of making him a hero worthy of a story. For all our focus on race and representation, *Casablanca* is Rick's story (in the same way that, regardless of our interest in Hattie McDaniel's Mammy, *Gone with the Wind* is Scarlett O'Hara's story). Sam is a supporting character as, ultimately, is every other character in the film. But he plays an essential role, even though he recedes from view by the end. Rick requires a friend (a whole village full of friends) to open up again to the risk of the paralyzing loss that comes with caring deeply about something or someone besides ourselves. If Rick's character arc is to move from being unwilling or unable to stick his neck out for others to the man who can renounce the woman he loves and take up the fight again, Sam is an essential part of that journey. As we have seen, Rick might not have survived without him. But we discover that a diverse community—everyone comes to Rick's—is also instrumental in Rick's transformation. In contrast to the purely transactional and deeply hierarchical relationships between black and white characters in *The Birth of a Nation*, this relationship is illustrative of the possibilities when we move from racial antagonism to human respect, of what reconciliation might make possible for us and for our society.

Friendship and community are necessary for all of us, whatever our race or culture, if we are going to achieve our truest selves.

Thinking about the friendship between Rick and Sam, we should acknowledge two contemporary tropes about friendship between black and white characters in film: the Magical Negro and the Black Best Friend. Spike Lee popularized the term "Magical Negro" in a talk at Yale in 2001. It describes a black character whose primary function in a film is to mentor the white lead. Tambay Obensom, writing about the film *Green Book*, says that this archetype is typically rooted in a white screenwriter's ignorance of any genuine African American experience. The Magical Negro is "typically patient, sometimes wise, and often has some sort of magical power. His primary function is to help the white protagonist overcome some major character flaw."[36] The writers of *Casablanca* were not black and were not steeped in genuine African American experience, and Sam is certainly patient and wise and has the power to evoke memory and soothe violent emotions with his music. He is a rounded character, but (like most of the supporting characters in *Casablanca*) he does not have a distinctive story arc.

The Black Best Friend character likewise stands in the shadow of the white lead character. According to Eric Deggans, writing for the *Washington Post*, Black Best Friends display "a devotion to helping their white friends achieve, sometimes to the detriment of their own circumstance. And despite the BBFs often having an amazing pedigree, with cool jobs, prestigious careers, or intriguing personal history, viewers rarely see their lives away from the lead character."[37] Again, Sam could fit this description, and some critics cite Sam and Rick as an early example of this stereotype. Sam's life away from Rick is not described, and while he certainly merits his own story, *Casablanca* is not the place where we would find it. Sam could be considered both a Magical Negro and Black Best Friend. It is important, however, not to impose Twenty-First Century mores and critical judgments on a 1942 film, particularly one that does so many things right compared to those that had gone before, particularly when the mere presentation of interracial friendship—and the clear affirmation of the humanity of Sam and every other diverse member of *Casablanca*'s community—represents such a positive step forward.

The response of that day was that Sam represented the most sympathetic portrayal of a black character audiences had yet seen, that black viewers could see themselves in him, and he is indeed written with strength and dignity and a sense of reality that set him apart from the stereotypes of his day. Perhaps we might hope for more, but it does not seem a stretch to argue we can learn from Sam what it means to be a friend, even if today we might hope his character would have an independent life of his own. If friendship is essential—and many wisdom traditions argue that it is—Sam is offering Rick, and us, essential knowledge about what it means to be human. For sages and teachers from Jesus to Maimonides to Augustine of Hippo to the present, friendship is the state that allows us to become our best selves, and Rick is allowed not just to survive but to thrive because of Sam's steadfast friendship.

Rabbi Hillel says, in *The Mishnah*, "If I am only for myself, what am I?" That is, if all I have is a healthy self-interest (and Hillel agrees that we ought to have a healthy self-interest), then I am incomplete. This is a teaching upon which many wisdom traditions insist. The notions of friendship, community, and conversation between equals matter as we try to achieve our fullest potential and escape the prison of our own solipsism. In the Jewish tradition, friendship is depicted as a relationship in which we are offered support, challenge, and unconditional love, and a respite from human loneliness. In the creation narrative found in Genesis 2, God looks at Adam, the man he has made, and recognizes that it is not good for him to be alone.[38] From the beginning, then, human beings were intended to be in relationship, and the Hebrew Bible describes deep friendships between David and Jonathan ("When David had finished speaking to Saul, the soul of Jonathan was bound to the soul of David, and Jonathan loved him as his own soul") and Naomi and Ruth ("But Ruth said, 'Do not press me to leave you or to turn back from following you! Where you go, I will go; where you lodge, I will lodge; your people shall be my people, and your God my God'") as models of the importance of relationship.[39]

Jesus is represented as a person with deep friendships. The "disciple whom Jesus loves" is mentioned six times in the Gospel of John, while Jesus's relationships with Mary, Martha, and Lazarus are also important to him. John 11:5 tells us that "Jesus loved Martha and her sister and Lazarus," but Lazarus is especially dear to him. When he draws near the tomb after Lazarus's death, he meets Mary and the other mourners and is powerfully affected by their grief. Deep human connection is depicted in the life of Jesus as a valuable thing.[40]

The medieval Jewish scholar Maimonides (Moses ben Maimon) taught about virtuous friendship—friendship for the good of the other, not simply for one's own good—and thought of it as the fulfillment of the Torah. "It is well known that friends are something that is necessary for man throughout his whole life," he said, and added that they are called to "love one another, help one another, and have pity on one another, and the attainment of these things is the greatest purpose of the Law."[41]

Within the Christian tradition, Augustine offers us perhaps the most developed wisdom teachings on friendship and its transformational value. In his biography of Augustine, Peter Brown shows that none of the church's formative minds thought so much about—or of—friendship as Augustine did.[42] Certainly Augustine knew that friendship, broadly defined, is capable of pulling us away from our tendency toward self-love and selfishness, and toward God. Love of our neighbor is the surest path toward God in what Augustine called the Two-Fold Commandment of Love (Love God; Love your neighbor). Friendship is also essential to our living as healthy, fulfilled human beings. From a life spent mostly in community Augustine knew that friends make laughter deeper, joy broader, and sadness bearable. "If such people are with us," he wrote of true friends, times of grief or trouble become "less bitter, the heavy burdens become lighter, perceived obstacles are faced and overcome."[43]

Donald Burt has written that Augustine saw friendship as "the highest expression of a person's social nature; it is also the solid foundation for any society. The more a society becomes a society of friends, the more perfect it becomes as a society."[44] It is here at the notion of friendship as the basis for society that we move from Rick's friendship with Sam to the numerous and diverse cast of characters who live in German-occupied Casablanca and filter through Rick's life. Augustine wrote in *City of God* that "[f]riendship . . . is the glue that forges our human ties, it binds husband and wife, brother and sister, friend to friend, citizen to citizen, even in the limited and flawed realm of earthly life."[45] It is not just Sam, but Victor, Ilsa, Renault, Carl, and others who shape Rick and make his progress possible. If everybody comes to Rick's, then everybody is in some way a part of that experience. Many critics have remarked that Rick's is a little America, a microcosm of our own strength derived from difference. Unlike *Birth of a Nation*'s call to Aryan unity, diversity is an essential part of *Casablanca*, and community a vital force for Rick's transformation and for our own.

In November 2018, I traveled to Ellis Island to visit the portal through which, from 1892 to 1954, millions of immigrants entered the United States. While Ellis Island didn't see the passage of African slaves to the United States, or of Asians through West Coast ports, or Hispanics across the southern border, almost half of Americans can trace their ancestry to someone who entered America through Ellis Island.[46] For some, Ellis Island was a place of welcome and hope, the beacon of liberty and opportunity seemingly promised by the sight of the Statue of Liberty and by "The New Colossus," Emma Lazarus's poem on the statue: "Give me your tired, your poor,/Your huddled masses yearning to breathe free."[47] But for others, it was a place of fear and uncertainty. Russians, Irish, Poles, and others met with less welcome and more contention. The debate about who could become an American has often been as angry, dismissive, and demeaning as it is in the present moment. Despite this, as Vincent J. Cannato has remarked, Ellis Island became a symbol of something essentially American, a "new Plymouth Rock," but also clearly a symbol of America's multicultural and varied composition.[48]

Ellis Island is a reminder of nativism and the regulation of immigration, and also a reminder that America is a nation of immigrants, a beautiful mixture of races and cultures and faiths. When we gather together—or offer ourselves in friendship—we enter into something larger than ourselves. And in a culture that constantly argues for the importance of our individuality—that like Rick sticks its figurative neck out for nobody—it's important to be reminded that there are others who matter, important for others to remind us that they matter, so that ultimately we may reach the point where we can, with Rick, realize that the problems of three little people don't amount to a hill of beans in a world full of suffering.

How do we begin to achieve the renunciation of living solely for self that true friendship and community require? Rabbi Hillel's version

of the Golden Rule—treat others as you yourself wish to be treated—
is one of many such formulations that lead us in the right direction.
Charles Kimball says that "[a]t the heart of all authentic, healthy,
life-sustaining religions, one always finds this clear requirement,"[49]
and we find other versions put forward by Jesus, Confucius, and
Socrates. Compassion and empathy are at the heart of a love that is
transformational—the *caritas* that Augustine opposes to *cupiditas*, the
misplaced love for the things of the world that will ultimately wither
and fade. We are told to love our neighbor, but who, exactly, is that?
The parable of the Good Samaritan teaches—and Augustine wrote—
that we are all neighbors: "Friendship begins with one's spouse and
children, and from there spreads out to strangers. But given that we
all have the same father (Adam) and the same mother (Eve) who can
be a stranger? Every human being is neighbor to every other human
being."[50] Thus we are called to extend compassion out in a larger circle,
beyond those in our immediate vicinity, and to be friends with more
than just our friends.

Christians are taught that they are meant to be in community because human beings are made in the image of a God who lives in community. Even before the first human, Adam, was created and God
mused that it was not good for the first man to be alone, God existed—
and God's existence was in Trinitarian community, Father, Son,
and Holy Spirit living in self-giving and ever-returning love. It was
Augustine who did much of the heavy lifting for our understanding of
the concept of Trinity; we are made in the image of a God who is ever
in communion, which suggests that fellowship is our rightful place as
well. "The triune God is community, fellowship," Jürgen Moltmann
writes, and in this way God "makes himself the model for a just and livable community in the world of nature and human beings." Christians
believe that the Church is the Trinity lived out in human lives and that
the eternal love of the Trinity is reflected by the mutual love within and
between the members.[51] We are formed within loving communities
oriented toward God, and because we are made in the image of a God
oriented toward loving community, we are most fully alive within such
communities.

After Rick and Ilsa have rekindled their love from Paris, he is in a
dangerous place. We wonder if and how he will adapt to the changes

taking place in his life. Having regained Ilsa for the moment, Rick does not seem to be moving toward altruism. When the young Bulgarian woman Annina (Joy Page, one of the only Americans acting in the film) comes to him to ask for his help, she intimates that she intends to sleep with Captain Renault in order to get exit visas for her husband and herself. She makes a heartrending speech about doing a bad thing to make certain the happiness of the one she loves, and Rick's response to her is curt: "Go back to Bulgaria." He surreptitiously arranges for her husband to win enough at the roulette wheel to pay for their visas but shrugs off credit for it when others try to celebrate him. When Victor comes offering a fortune for the letters of transit, Rick refuses. Victor's work for the Resistance is essential; Rick has admitted this on their first meeting. But rather than help him escape to continue it, Rick cannot let go of his grievances against Ilsa for abandoning him. He prefers his isolation to involvement. Here, not even Sam can do the work of helping him move past it, although a number of the people who come to Rick's offer the lessons he needs.

Saint Anthony, the third-century founder of Christian monasticism, was a man who fled into the desert to seek isolation, but he came to understand that the spiritual life required more than solitude. He concluded, "Our life and death is with our neighbor."[52] Augustine codified this in his Rule, calling for the brothers to live harmoniously together, to be of one mind and heart, and to forgive, come what may.[53] The Church still recognizes the spiritual necessity of community; in Pope Benedict XVI's encyclical *Caritas in Veritate* we find him restating it for the twenty-first century:

> One of the deepest forms of poverty a person can experience is isolation. If we look closely at other kinds of poverty, including material forms, we see that they are born from isolation, from not being loved or from difficulties in being able to love. . . . As a spiritual being, the human creature is defined through interpersonal relations. The more authentically he or she lives these relations, the more his or her own personal identity matures. It is not by isolation that man establishes his worth, but by placing himself in relation with others and with God. Hence these relations take on fundamental importance.[54]

Remember Rick, drunk and sitting alone at a barroom table in the Casablanca night. Remember Sam trying to engage him, trying unsuccessfully to involve him in something besides his solipsistic grief. Rick has been presented in isolation throughout the film. The first time we meet him, after the camera has traveled the length of Rick's, he is sitting alone, playing chess against himself. When a patron inquires, the waiter Carl tells her that Rick does not drink with customers: "I have never seen it." Many of the iconic images from *Casablanca* are of Bogart, splendid in his isolation (think back on those generations of Bogart posters hung on dorm room walls, the French New Wave heroes emulating Bogart, the lonely Bogie character offering existential wisdom in Woody Allen's *Play It Again, Sam*).

Isolation is a dangerous state, as Pope Benedict knew, spiritually and emotionally. Frank Griswold, former presiding bishop of the Episcopal Church, wrote that if Saint Anthony and the Church, since, are right, "then it is God's intent that we rub against one another, confront one another with the truth of our lives, and break one another open to deeper levels of awareness that take us beyond ourselves."[55] This spiritual value of community is affirmed by Barbara Brown Taylor, who notes that it is chiefly in our lives together that God has chosen to be with us: "Our life together is the place where we are comforted, confronted, tested, and redeemed by God through one another. It is the place where we come to know God or to flee from God's presence, depending upon how we come to know or flee from one another."[56]

It is not simply that we know God from our interactions with each other, although that is vitally important. We also know who we are because of our relationships with others. Desmond Tutu, former Anglican archbishop of South Africa, has taught the West about the African concept of Ubuntu. In contrast to our individualistic orientation in the West and particularly in America, Ubuntu teaches that we need others, that we are who we are only in relation to others: "We can survive only together. We can be truly free, ultimately, only together. We can be human only together."[57] In fact, to be locked in isolation, to be completely self-sufficient (or think one is), Tutu argues, is to be something less than human: "You cannot be human on your own."[58]

A few years ago, at the National Cathedral in Washington, DC, Tutu discussed Ubuntu with the dean of the cathedral, Samuel Lloyd. Lloyd concluded from their talk that Ubuntu is actually the most basic element of Christian practice: "We need each other. I can't be me without you. That is the heart of what Christians mean by being the body of Christ, the church."[59] This is a reason that diversity is essential. If I can't be me without you, and if everybody around me walks like me and talks like me and looks like me, then how am I to grow and be challenged and change? What will break me out of my isolation? How will I become the person I am called to be?

Stories as well as life teach that we must rub against one another, confront one another with the truth, and break one another open. That is precisely what happens in *Casablanca*. The challenge of Annina's devotion and courage, Ilsa's love, Victor's idealism, and of course Sam's steadfast friendship, begin to work on Rick. Perhaps the most important incident in Rick's progression comes in a true community moment. A bar filled with refugees, each with their own problems and histories, comes together as one to remember who they are. Yvonne (Madeleine Lebeau), who has come to Rick's with a German soldier, is sitting and staring into her drink. When Victor calls on the orchestra to play "La Marseillaise," the French national anthem, in answer to the singing Nazis, Rick nods his assent, but he does not perhaps expect what happens next. Victor begins singing, is joined by the cabaret singer, and then by others. Major Strasser tries to rally his troops, to rouse them to greater efforts, but it is not enough. "Finally," the script says, "the whole café is standing, singing, their faces, aglow. The song is finished on a high, triumphant note."[60] Among the best-remembered shots from the film are those that show Yvonne with tears running down her face as she sings—and then, when the song ends, when she shouts, "Vive la France! Vive la démocratie!"

It is a moment sparked by a catalyst, but it is also a moment that takes a village. Victor on his own could not have drowned out Major Strasser and the German soldiers. It requires all of them, all these people on the run from their past and toward an uncertain future, to stand up and sing and remember what they're fighting for. It is a moment that Victor might be speaking of later in the film when Rick questions what he's fighting for: "You know how you sound, M'sieur Blaine? Like a man who's trying to convince himself of something he doesn't believe in his heart. . . . I wonder if you know that you're trying to escape from yourself and that you'll never succeed."

Victor does more than model political heroism; he also models unselfish love. When Rick refuses to give him the letters that would allow him to escape with Ilsa, Victor asks Rick to use them to take Ilsa to safety, even though he himself would be left alone and at the mercy of Major Strasser in Casablanca. It is the same as the situation with Annina, and Rick's response to Victor echoes his earlier words to Annina: "You love her that much?" Rick has been thinking of his own happiness and how Ilsa is a necessary part of it, self-interest that is just as selfish as his misery when she left him. When Ilsa reproaches him for refusing to hand over the letters of transit, she says, "You want to feel sorry for yourself, don't you? With so much at stake, all you can think of is your own feeling. One woman has hurt you, and you take your revenge on the rest of the world." It may pain him to hear these words, like Victor's, but Rick needs to be challenged and stood up to, just as Sam has stood up to him, if he is going to change.

Rick hides his plans from Sam, Victor, Renault, Ilsa, and everyone else, so it's difficult to say at what point exactly he decides what he is going to do, but I would argue that it happens shortly after this exchange with Victor, who is taken captive by the French police. The next day, Rick arranges for Renault to release Victor, sells the café to Signor Ferrari (and, in one last grace note, insists that Sam get 25 percent of the profits, as well as that Ferrari keep on the rest of his staff), and engineers the conclusion that is opaque to every first-time viewer until the moment it unfolds, when, like any satisfying ending, we recognize it as the only possible one that makes sense for his character.

Practical considerations dictated that the filmmakers could not have Rick simply steal away with Victor's wife; the Motion Picture Production Code would not have permitted this illicit relationship to be rewarded. More important, narrative convention demands that Rick renounce his selfish and isolated former self and be transformed into a selfless hero. Rick can only become a hero when he gives up the things he loves, as Victor was willing to do, and indeed, Victor welcomes him back to the fight, sure that this time they will win.

The connection between heroism and community is organic. Perhaps the most famous expert on the hero is Joseph Campbell, who studied cultural and literary hero myths all over the world to construct what we now know as the archetypal Hero's Journey. Campbell noted, first, that "[t]he hero is the man of self-achieved submission. But submission to what?"[61] Campbell argued that the "what" to which heroes submitted their own desires was service to the greater needs of others. Truly mythic heroes helped to achieve something like a new society— or even a new creation. A mythic hero returned from his adventures bearing "the means for the regeneration of his society as a whole," not simply the spoils of victory for himself.[62]

Elsewhere, Campbell wrote: "The hero is the one who comes to participate in life courageously and decently . . . not in the way of personal rancor, disappointment, or revenge."[63] So, self-sacrifice, courage, decency, and a new world, of sorts, emerge from the hero's actions, actions that are the result of a community's support.

Sam keeps Rick alive, challenges him, and loves him. The institution that they have helped form together, Rick's Café Américain, brings together a transformative community with the power to help Rick overcome his self-centered bitterness and participate in life courageously. *Casablanca* is the story of a white hero whose black friend plays an important role in his rehabilitation. Hollywood had another step to take. What would it look like if instead of sympathetic minor characters, people of color began to play major roles? In our next chapter, we'll explore what has changed—and what hasn't—a few decades on as black actors appear with white actors above the title, and black people are coming to dinner.

4

"That's the Glory of Love"

Guess Who's Coming to Dinner and the Power of Love

Setting the Stage: The Civil Rights Movement and *Guess Who's Coming to Dinner*

On June 12, 1967, the U.S. Supreme Court handed down a landmark decision in the case of *Loving v. Virginia*, concerning whether mixed-race marriages were protected under the equal protection and due process clauses of the Fourteenth Amendment. Seventeen states, most of them in the South, had legislation that barred blacks and whites from marrying. Mildred and Richard Loving had been arrested, tried, and convicted in Virginia, where miscegenation was illegal. At their sentencing, the Lovings were sentenced to a year in prison, although the trial judge ruled that he would suspend the sentence for twenty-five years if the Lovings left Virginia and did not return together during that time. His ruling was based on the myth of white superiority and on the supposed divine edict against racial mixing, familiar to us by now from *Birth of a Nation* and elsewhere: "Almighty God created the races white, black, yellow, malay and red, and he placed them on separate continents. And, but for the interference with his arrangement, there would be no cause for such marriage. The fact that he separated the races shows that he did not intend for the races to mix."[1] The Supreme Court disagreed with the Virginia court and the reasoning of this judge. A third of the states had laws on the books forbidding blacks and whites to marry, but the Court found these statutes to be unconstitutional, because marriage was one of the fundamental rights guaranteed by the Fourteenth Amendment.

This decision was announced two weeks after production had wrapped on a new movie called *Guess Who's Coming to Dinner* and just two days after its star, Spencer Tracy, had died. Throughout the writing, preproduction, and shooting of the film, marriage between blacks and whites had been illegal in one-third of the United States. The film's subject matter—the proposed marriage of a black man and a white woman—was both timely and shocking, an important fact to remember when we look back on the film from our vantage point of more than fifty years. Mark Harris reports that earlier in the 1960s, the pilot for the innocuous ABC situation comedy *Bewitched* was held up for more than a year by Southern affiliates who complained that the show's depiction of a marriage between an ad executive and a witch, both played by white actors, was "a veiled argument for racial intermarriage."[2] In the summer before *Guess Who's Coming to Dinner* was released, Dean Rusk (Secretary of State under both John Kennedy and Lyndon Johnson) debated whether he ought to resign from the Cabinet because his daughter intended to marry a black classmate from Stanford, who worked for NASA.[3] The wedding, held in September, made the September 29, 1967, cover of *Time* magazine. Interracial marriage was anything but settled and accepted when the film appeared two months later.

For its time, in fact, *Guess Who's Coming to Dinner* was a radical movie that pushed the envelope of what was permissible. If today it seems dated to us, and its treatment of race passé, we should remember that *Loving v. Virginia* was not decided until after the movie was shot. The writer and director of *Guess Who's Coming to Dinner*, William Rose and Stanley Kramer respectively, were making a movie that some considered outrageous. They were trying to represent the black experience with sympathy and good will, things that were not usual in earlier films. They were, however, both white men, and in their writing of African American characters, they were writing not from experience but from sympathy and observation. In the process, despite their good intentions, some negative stereotypes and damaging racial myths sneaked into their storytelling, and in some ways they could not help affirming the social structure of which they themselves were a part. Nonetheless, *Guess Who's Coming to Dinner* was and remains an important movie milestone dealing with race and prejudice. Lyndon

Baines Johnson screened the movie at the Western White House in Texas, just as Woodrow Wilson had screened *Birth of a Nation* in the White House, and it offers us an opportunity to see where the film lands on questions of race and prejudice, and how far we have come.

The film is stylistically old-fashioned compared to some of its contemporaries, those movies identified with the New American Cinema (also called New Hollywood or the Hollywood New Wave). However, while *Bonnie and Clyde* (1967), *The Graduate* (1967), *The Wild Bunch* (1969), *Easy Rider* (1969), and other films of the time portrayed violence, sexuality, and countercultural values in ground-breaking ways, none of them deals with race. *The Graduate*, for example, doesn't feature a single African American in a speaking role, while the most important contribution to *Easy Rider* made by African Americans was Peter Fonda's iconic Captain America chopper, which was designed and built by Clifford Vaughs and Ben Hardy. Vaughs himself asked, "Why is it that we have a film about America and there are no negroes?"[4] With the exception of *Night of the Living Dead* (1968), Hollywood films of the era largely did not seem to be aware of race. It remained for more stylistically conservative films like *Guess Who's Coming to Dinner* and *In the Heat of the Night* (1967) to tackle race and prejudice as central subjects.

Guess Who's Coming to Dinner fits securely into the third phase of Hollywood's representation of characters outside the white mainstream. Unlike *Birth of a Nation*, which represented black characters as negative stereotypes, or the vast majority of American films from the 1920s and 1930s, which simply ignored people of color, and unlike *Casablanca*, which features a strong African American in a supporting role, *Guess Who's Coming to Dinner* has four major African American characters. Sidney Poitier, as Dr. John Prentice, is listed above the title with the megastars Spencer Tracy and Katherine Hepburn. While people of color are not, ultimately, the film's most important characters, there is an attempt to render them as human, partaking, like Dooley Wilson's Sam and Hattie McDaniel's Mammy, of the same essence as the white stars, and, presumably, as the still largely white audience.

What identifies this as a third-phase movie is that, while it is well-intentioned and features Poitier in a leading role, the film is the product of white storytellers telling myths about black characters. These are, on the whole, new myths, and most of them are more positive. It seems clear at times, however, that the filmmakers may empathize with the experience of their characters but do not necessarily know their lives from the inside. The Magic Negro (or "Wonder Doctor," as James Baldwin calls the Sidney Poitier character) is still a limiting myth that doesn't encompass full humanity.[5] The fourth phase, when ethnic and nonwhite groups get to tell their own stories in the Seventies and Eighties, offers new versions of racial myths and, often, more realistic looks at racial issues.

Stanley Kramer, director of *Guess Who's Coming to Dinner*, was a filmmaker with a passion for exploring cultural issues. His *New York Times* obituary describes him as a maker of message movies who tackled "tough themes and social issues . . . insisting on making movies that daringly raised the sensitive subjects that a prosperous postwar America frequently preferred to ignore."[6] As a producer and then producer/director, Kramer took on issues such as McCarthyism (*High Noon*, 1952), racism (*Home of the Brave*, 1949; *The Defiant Ones*, 1958), juvenile delinquency (*The Wild One*, 1954), nuclear war (*On the Beach*, 1959), and fascism (*Judgment at Nuremberg*, 1961). While later critics were to find his films sentimental and Kramer himself an old-fashioned filmmaker (as indeed he was; Ronald Bergan of *The Guardian* summarized Kramer's direction as "heartfelt but rather heavy-handed"), some of his films were incredibly popular, and *Guess Who's Coming to Dinner* continues to be watched and enjoyed fifty years after its release.

In the film, Joey Drayton (Katharine Houghton, Hepburn's niece in real life) returns to the home of her parents in San Francisco with her fiancé, Dr. John Prentice (Poitier). They met while vacationing in Hawaii, fell in love, and now have flown back together to the States before John leaves to take up his position with the World Health Organization in Switzerland. Joey has always been taught by her parents, Matt (Tracy) and Christina (Hepburn), that all people are equal. Matt himself is a famous liberal, the editor of a San Francisco newspaper, so she does not expect any resistance when she tells them that she and Prentice are in love and want to get married.

While Christina is momentarily shocked by this revelation, she quickly recovers and accepts their decision when she sees how happy her daughter is. Dr. Prentice's mother (Beah Richards) also moves past her initial surprise to acceptance. Not everyone makes that easy leap; the Drayton family's maid, Tilly (Isabel Sanford), believes John is seeking to marry above his station, and John's father (Roy E. Glenn) disapproves. Most important, Matt Drayton cannot seem to accept their love, ostensibly because of the social stigma they will face.

The movie is sometimes thought of as a romantic comedy (its destination, of course, is a wedding, and there are certainly funny moments along the way), but perhaps it more closely resembles the genre of drawing-room comedy. It takes place primarily in the Draytons' apartment, it revolves around entertaining a series of guests, and like other drawing-room plays, it sets up a set of artificial conventions that raise the level of complication and tension. Benedict Nightingale said the drawing-room genre could be recognized by its "carefully manufactured tension, its deftly placed revelations and surprises, its climactic curtain-lines, its near and sometimes trite denouements."[7] The tensions in this film all revolve around artificial constructs that viewers must accept, at least during the film's running time, as necessary for the story.

In *Guess Who's Coming to Dinner*, the manufactured tension comes from two conditions the story sets for itself. John is leaving after dinner on a plane for Switzerland, and Joey expects to fly with him so that they may be married in Europe. The clock is ticking for Matt Drayton's decision. His decision is essential because of the film's second condition: John has told Matt that without his enthusiastic assent to their union, he will not marry Joey. It is fruitless to argue that these are ridiculous and artificial elements; despite its radical subject matter, *Guess Who's Coming to Dinner* is less a social justice film than a drawing-room comedy exploring the possible ramifications of throwing such disparate people together in one salon. Look at earlier examples of the genre. Why will Mrs. Cheveley, in Oscar Wilde's *An Ideal Husband* (1895), threaten to reveal to the world the misdeed Sir Robert Chiltern committed in his youth if he does not encourage the House of Commons to vote for her fraudulent canal scheme posthaste? Because it lends every moment in the play urgency, constitutes what dramatists sometimes speak of as the "ticking clock." The ticking clock set up for us in *Guess Who's Coming to Dinner* is that Matt Drayton must change his mind about approving the marriage—and do so within hours—or disaster will ensue.

The film carries more weight than it might have had this story been cast with lesser actors. (For evidence, you have merely to look at the 2005 remake, *Guess Who*, starring Bernie Mac as the father and Ashton Kutcher as the white beau brought home by Zoe Saldana.) Hepburn and Tracy were appearing in their ninth movie together and, as was well known in Hollywood, had been a couple for over twenty-five years, although Tracy remained legally married to his wife. The complicating factor for this film was that Tracy was dying of congestive heart disease, and Hepburn had to keep a close eye on his time on set and his energy, often deciding when he needed to stop for the day. In the last years of his life, she had quietly moved in with him to take care of him but would not attend his funeral or even make their life together public for many years. The fact of Tracy's impending death, however, lends extraordinary heft to their final work together, as we will see.[8]

Poitier, meanwhile, was the top box office star in the world in 1967, appearing in *To Sir, With Love* and *In the Heat of the Night* in that year as well as *Guess Who's Coming to Dinner*. He had become the first African American nominated for an Oscar for *The Defiant Ones* and won Best Actor for 1963's *Lilies of the Field*. He carried an incredible weight on his shoulders as the only person of color appearing as a lead actor in Hollywood. Poitier was deeply involved in the struggle for civil rights. Along with his friend the actor and singer Harry Belafonte, he carried cash to the Freedom Riders in the Deep South, was chased and shot at by the Ku Klux Klan, and helped organize the 1963 March on Washington and the memorial for Dr. Martin Luther King, Jr. after his assassination. His presence in films was an inspiration to many black Americans, and *Guess Who's Coming to Dinner* became an occasion in the black community. In Chapter 1 we learned how Kelly Brown Douglas reacted to the vision of Poitier onscreen, and hers was a typical reaction. Filmmaker Cornelius Moore saw the film with his mother and her friends when he was thirteen years old. He remembers that it was shown at the nicest theater in town and recalls the simple fact that the film was a significant moment for the black community.[9]

As we think about the film, it is crucial to place it against the backdrop of the late Sixties: war in Vietnam; changes in sexual, cultural, and religious mores; unrest on campuses; and, most significantly for this film, the civil rights movement. Even if this film is old-fashioned in genre and style, it is of the moment in its depiction of race in 1967.

Until the mid-1960s, it was possible—and accurate—to speak of America as a white Anglo-Saxon Protestant nation. Indeed, as David A. Hollinger notes, not only was the population of the United States still overwhelmingly white and Protestant in the middle years of the twentieth century, but "[m]embership numbers in the major, classical denominations were at an all-time high. Persons at least nominally affiliated with these denominations controlled all branches of the federal government and most of the business world, as well as the nation's chief cultural and educational institutions, and countless state and local institutions. If you were in charge of something big before 1960, chances are you grew up in a white Protestant milieu."[10]

In ways that feel very similar to the state of things in the United States as I write in 2019, the tension between the way things have always been and the specter of change marked the decade of the 1960s as a seminal moment in the racial history of our country. Although in some ways the civil rights movement can be dated back to the post–World War II return of black sailors and soldiers to a nation that claimed to respect all human beings but did not, in the 1960s the movement galvanized the entire country. Violence against the Freedom Riders in 1961 and against protestors on the Edmund Pettus Bridge in Selma, Alabama, in 1965 outraged people throughout the nation and opened their eyes to the scope of the problem. In 1964, Dr. King received the Nobel Peace Prize, and we realized that the eyes of the entire world were on our struggle.

But while there had been progress, moments of great emotional power like the March on Washington, and legislative achievements as President Johnson shepherded landmark voting and housing acts through Congress, in 1967 Americans still remained bitterly divided, not because they did not witness the violence and economic distress that racial prejudice caused, but perhaps because they faced changes that were difficult to countenance. Dr. King spoke at Stanford University in April 1967 about how the battle for civil rights had moved beyond a desire for simple decency: "It's more difficult today because we are struggling now for genuine equality. And it's much easier to integrate a lunch counter than it is to guarantee a livable income and a good solid job. It's much easier to guarantee the right to vote than it is to guarantee the right to live in sanitary, decent housing conditions. It is much easier to integrate a public park than it is to make genuine, quality, integrated education a reality."[11]

Even for people of good conscience in 1967 and 1968, the problem of racism seemed intractable, and when Dr. King began to link race, economics, and opposition to the war in Vietnam he not only lost the support of many who agreed with him on race but aroused further suspicions among those who wondered why he would question a war being fought by the United States of America. While a link clearly existed between racism, poverty, and war, the combination seemed too much. In an editorial, the *Washington Post* called his April 1967 sermon at New York City's Riverside Church denouncing the Vietnam War "a tragedy" and argued that it had "diminished his usefulness to his cause, to his country, and to his people."[12]

In 1967, Dr. King and the Southern Christian Leadership Conference began to talk about a "Poor People's" march on Washington; the march, slated for May 1968, stirred up even more fear and anger. The Lyndon Baines Johnson Presidential Library holds countless letters and telegrams from this period sent to the president, decrying Dr. King as a threat to America and its way of life. A telegram from Ventura, California, to President Johnson advised, "You had better lock up Martin Luther King or we will have a revolution." An Episcopal priest from Florida asked LBJ, "Can it be possibly be true that rabble-rousers, hippies, and scatter-brained clergy, professors, and their ilk are free to violate any law they do not like? . . . Martin Luther King is the most dangerous man in America today." A letter from Montebello, California, advised the president to "put a scare into Martin Luther King and have him stop all of these marches . . . those black devils breaking and destroying everything on both sides of the streets they march down." A letter from Birmingham, Alabama, offered the president this wisdom: "The only way to control a negro is with force." And a letter from Hollandale, Florida, opined that "Mr. King has outlived his usefulness and I think is bringing about his own downfall . . . Please order the march on our capitol stopped. We look to you, our president, to solve this dilemma. There will be bloodshed." These are representative of a multitude of letters, telegrams, and other communications received in the president's office right up to the day that Dr. King was assassinated in Memphis.[13]

It is a startling evidence of the divisions in the nation in 1967 and 1968. The civil rights movement, of which King was the most visible leader, was at the center of a tumult. While many people of good will vocally affirmed their willingness to move toward equality, other people of good will stood silently by. Dr. King often said that when historians looked back on the era, they would not remember the actions of the bad people but the strange inaction of the good. Some were genuinely torn between compassion and fear, and some resisted these changes with all their might. To read *Guess Who's Coming to Dinner* from the perspective of the present is to badly misread it, because we are not understanding the audience for whom the film was made, the culture that produced it, and the headlines that gave it additional resonance.

The story itself references Dr. King, and the characters at the heart of it, particularly Spencer Tracy's character, embody this conflict at the heart of American culture. The movie doesn't simply take racists to task; it also tasks white liberals with standing to one side and failing to act as they know they should. When Monsignor Mike Ryan (Cecil Kellaway), Matt Drayton's best friend, shows up for the titular dinner, Christina breaks down and tells him, "We're in terrible trouble," because Matt cannot—or will not—approve the marriage.

"Where is he?" Monsignor Ryan asks.

"He's upstairs changing," she says, in what may be a conscious reference to Matt's seeming inability to change. "He's—he's not himself."

What follows is one of the movie's most poignant scenes. Monsignor Ryan confronts Matt in his bedroom as he dresses for dinner. Ryan tells him that what he is doing—keeping Joey from marrying John—is wrong, and that his great anger has an unexpected reason:

I think I know why you're angry too. Not with the doctor, whom you
    obviously respect.
Not with Joey or Christina, not even with me.
You're angry with yourself . . .
You're angry because all of a sudden, and in a single day, you've been
    thrown.

You're the last man in the world I would have expected to behave the
    way you are.
You're not yourself. You're off balance.
You don't know who you are, what you are, or what you're doing.
    That's your trouble.
You've gone back on yourself, Laddie, and in your heart you know it.

In very simple terms, Monsignor Ryan, who is both Matt's dear
friend and an official representative of the Church, is saying that Matt
is angry because he knows deep down that he is not living up to the
standards he has set for himself as a fighting liberal and, more important, that he is not living into his full humanity. In Dr. King's terms, he
represents the appalling silence of the good people in a time when the
bad people are numerous and vocal. Can he come to his senses and do
the right thing? Or will he remain silent—or even disapproving—on
this most important issue of the age?

Baldwin said that perhaps the best scene in the film was the one in
which Christina tells off her assistant Hilary (Virginia Christine), who
"is horrified at the news of this impending disastrous marriage and is
full of sympathy for the mother."[14] Indeed, every time I have shown
the film, this scene has drawn applause and hoots of approval, for it
represents a white liberal standing up to a white bigot and presenting
her with real consequences for her prejudice. But the responses from
Matt, from Dr. Prentice's father, and from the Draytons' maid, Tillie,
to the possible nuptials remain troubling. Each, in their own way,
complicates our reaction to the film and its efforts to be a force for racial reconciliation.

Types and Stereotypes in *Guess Who's Coming to Dinner*

Unlike my friend the Very Rev. Dr. Douglas, who was enraptured
with the depiction (finally) of a strong, intelligent black lead actor
on the screen, Baldwin was critical of *Guess Who's Coming to Dinner*
for its continuing use of types and stereotypes. It should be admitted
that stereotypes are the very stuff of comedy. The dumb blondes in

Gentlemen Prefer Blondes (1953) and *Three's Company* (1977–84), the officious butlers in *The Importance of Being Earnest* (1895) and *Arthur* (1981), or, for that matter, the tippling Irish clergymen, represented by Father Jack (Frank Kelly) in *Father Ted* (1995–98) and of course Monsignor Ryan in *Guess Who's Coming to Dinner*, are all character types played broadly for humor. Audiences see familiar characters, and part of the humor comes from our awareness and expectation. But when racial stereotypes are caught up in a story, even in a comedy, what we must ask, finally, is whether these stereotypes are allowed to seem something more than two-dimensional. Do we see these characters as truly human, fully human, despite their resemblance to stock characters? In some cases, characters who are types can also be rounded. Monsignor Ryan is one of the most human characters in the film, a moral center as the question of race swirls all around him.

But Baldwin's reaction to the film, and specifically to the character of the maid Tillie, is that she remains a racial stereotype and a disturbingly familiar one. In *The Devil Finds Work*, Baldwin told of seeing *The Birth of a Nation* and *Guess Who's Coming to Dinner* on the exact same day, which must have shaped his reaction, but his observation that Tillie resembles Mammy in *The Birth of a Nation* carries weight: "In *The Birth of a Nation*, the loyal nigger maid informs the nigger Congressman that she don't like niggers who set themselves up above their station. When our black wonder doctor hits San Francisco, some fifty-odd years later, he encounters exactly the same maid, who tells himself exactly the same thing, for the same reason, and in the same words."[15] And while audiences find this scene funny, and her conservatism is a useful counterpoint to the white racists, Tillie is still a stereotype. She remains a servant to the white family with no reality of her own. In our conversation on the film at the National Cathedral, the Very Rev. Dr. Douglas asked, "I wonder why it was necessary in the making of that movie for a white audience to have a Tillie character, and to have that character making the speech that she made to John?"[16]

The Faithful Retainer is a consistent type, in service from nineteenth-century popular culture and *The Birth of a Nation* down to the modern day. The domestic helper who is so attached to the white household that we don't know about her or his own household appears in *Gone with the Wind* and continues to appear in contemporary films like *Driving Miss Daisy* (1989), *The Help* (2011), and *Get Out*. Typically, these stereotypical figures are actually and dramatically in service to white characters, and while Tillie is a relatively minor character in the movie—her confrontation with Dr. Prentice represents one of her only big moments—she largely exists to facilitate (or complain about preparing) the evening's meal. Many other such characters exist only to serve white characters, and, perhaps, to make possible some essential realizations on the story function of those white characters, as Keli Goff argues looking at recent Hollywood history:

> The black servants of *The Help* needed a perky, progressive Emma Stone to shed light on their plight; the football bruiser in *The Blind Side* couldn't have done it without fiery Sandra Bullock; the black athletes in *Cool Runnings* and *The Air Up There* needed the guidance of their white coach; and in *12 Years A Slave*, Solomon Northup, played by Chiwetel Ejiofor, is liberated at the eleventh hour by a Jesus-looking Brad Pitt (in a classic Deus Ex Machina).[17]

The White Savior motif is at the heart of many of Hollywood's most memorable films, including several that precede *Guess Who's Coming to Dinner*. In *To Kill A Mockingbird* (1962), however well written both novel and screenplay might be, the ultimate fate of Tom Robinson (Brock Peters), the black man unjustly accused of rape, rests entirely on the eloquence and empathy that his white attorney, Atticus Finch (Gregory Peck), can generate. Atticus and his family are the primary characters in both novel and film, and Tom's fate, while the catalyst for the story, is not the focus of it. In *Up the Down Staircase* (1967), a white teacher (Sandy Dennis) comes into a multiracial public high school in New York City (the film was shot in Harlem) and tries to balance the administrative demands of her job with the personal challenges of her students. Her ability to find a way to reach them is the core of this story, and the students' dramatic dilemmas pale in comparison to whether or not she will succeed as a teacher. These are films about white characters made for white audiences.

More recent examples of the White Savior appear in *Glory* (1989), in which Matthew Broderick plays Colonel Robert Shaw of the

Union Army, who leads an African American regiment against an unassailable Confederate target during the Civil War; *Amistad* (1997), in which a group of Africans who overcome their captors onboard a slave ship are defended in court by white lawyer Robert Sherman Baldwin (Matthew McConaughey) and later by John Quincy Adams (Anthony Hopkins) before the Supreme Court; and *Free State of Jones* (2016), another Civil War tale in which Newton Knight (Matthew McConaughey again!) commands a group of ex-Confederate soldiers and runaway slaves in capturing a "free state" territory in the South.

The White Savior stereotype is potent. Perhaps it exists because white audiences want to feel themselves in some way exonerated from the racism of their ancestors—and their own—by watching good-hearted white protagonists fight against racism. Perhaps, as in *Guess Who's Coming to Dinner*, they enjoy seeing racially ambivalent white characters transformed in some way during the course of the story. In either case, the black characters, however well drawn, exist primarily to further the journey of white characters. While this in and of itself may not be shameful (in any telling of my life story, for example, I will be the prime character, however compelling the supporting cast might be), a steady diet of White Savior narratives both reduces the possibility of understanding the stories of people of color and elevates white characters into prominence above them, as though their stories are always the ones that matter.

In a widely read and cited article for the *New York Times* in 2019, Wesley Morris explored the popularity of the racial reconciliation fantasies represented by the White Savior. He argued that, like audiences, the Academy Awards are also drawn to such stereotypical fantasies:

> Any time a white person comes anywhere close to the rescue of a black person the academy is primed to say, "Good for you!," whether it's "To Kill a Mockingbird," "Mississippi Burning," "The Blind Side," or "The Help." The year "Driving Miss Daisy" won those Oscars, Morgan Freeman also had a supporting role in a drama ("Glory") that placed a white Union colonel at its center and was very much in the mix that night.[18]

As Morris notes, over the years the Academy, whether with *Gone with the Wind, Driving Miss Daisy, Crash* (2005), *The Help*, or *Green Book* (2018), has been drawn to racial reconciliation fantasies, many oriented around a person of color who is paid to be companion to a white person and leading to that white character's greater racial enlightenment. In *Guess Who's Coming to Dinner*, Tillie is paid to be a part of the Drayton family. Although she features more as comic relief than a transformative figure, other black characters in the film do serve Matt's growing racial enlightenment By coming into Matt's life and confronting him with his dignity and achievement, and his blackness, John Prentice forces Matt to grapple with his own hidden prejudice. Mrs. Prentice, John's mother, confronts Matt with the accusation that he has forgotten what it means to love. Mr. Prentice, John's father, shares Matt's reluctance to accept the marriage of their children—and perhaps leads him to reflect on what it means that he and this African American father think alike about the matter. But however capable John may be, the entire film ultimately rotates around whether Matt Drayton will or won't grant his blessing to the relationship between his daughter and John. For all of John's achievements, however voluminous his *Who's Who* entry might be, if Matt does not approve the marriage, he will fly off to Europe alone and unfulfilled.

In dramatic terms, Matt Drayton is the main character of the film, for he is the character who moves; he begins in one place—resistant to the marriage—and ends it in acceptance after experiencing an epiphany in the film's final act. Audiences have always reacted positively to this late movement (although not all; Baldwin wondered why the Draytons were making the decision instead of the Prentices, given that John seems light-years more advanced than Joey), and Matt's closing speech is, as we will see, a significant concession and confession of wrong. But it remains true—if Matt does not change his mind, the film ends unhappily, and no one is saved.

What may to some small extent redeem the White Savior trope in this film is that this particular Savior is Spencer Tracy. George Clooney—himself a famous Hollywood liberal—has said that Tracy was by far his favorite actor. Tracy's moral rectitude was such, he said, that you don't just want to watch him; you want to be like him.[19] So yes, it's unfortunate that this movie is largely concerned with whether or not a Great White Father will change his mind about mixed-race marriage and give his consent, but because it is Tracy, perhaps white viewers may progress from admiration to imitation. Perhaps when they see this actor who so strongly projects a sense of moral rectitude changing his mind about this emotionally charged issue they consciously or unconsciously feel, "I see that. And maybe I could do that too."

Guess Who's Coming to Dinner doesn't stop with the stereotype of the White Savior, of course; it contains plenty of others. Its depictions of young people in their teens and twenties, for example, are reductive and played for simple humor—most of them seem like be-bopping fun seekers who can't be taken seriously. Even the young African American man whose hot rod is smashed by Matt's car as he backs out of a drive-in is stereotyped in this way. Matt offers him a sum of money to make up for the damage, and the young man's passionate attachment to the car that he has built is played for laughs. This reduction of young people is even carried over to Joey, who is treated as more akin to the other flighty teens than as a peer to her startlingly competent fiancé.

The younger generation is seen as more enlightened in one way, however, and that is in their attitude toward race. The young white delivery driver (Skip Martin) does not see the young African American Dorothy (Barbara Randolph) across a racial divide when he drops off food for the titular dinner; they immediately connect and dance their way out to his van. When John and Joey meet Joey's white friends Peter (Tom Heaton) and Judith (Grace Gaynor) for drinks, the other couple is enthusiastic about the relationship, their attitude standing in stark contrast to those of the older generation. Even in the easy mixture of races among the young patrons at the drive-in we see a future in which, we hope, the question of race will be less important than it seems to be to Matt and Mr. Prentice.

In one of the film's most challenging scenes, John confronts his father about his resistance to the marriage and casts their contrasting worldviews in terms of their respective generations:

> You don't even know what I am, Dad, you don't know who I am. You don't know how I feel, what I think. And if I tried to explain it the rest

of your life you will never understand. You are 30 years older than I am. You and your whole lousy generation believes the way it was for you is the way it's got to be. And not until your whole generation has lain down and died will the dead weight of you be off our backs! You understand, you've got to get off my back! Dad . . . Dad, you're my father. I'm your son. I love you. I always have and I always will. But you think of yourself as a colored man. I think of myself as a man.

Critics have pointed out the difficulty of this scene, the movement from the calm, cool, and collected character of Dr. Prentice to a son who is angry and dismissive. Roger Ebert's 1968 review noted that the speech is inconsistent with Poitier's character: "Contrasted to Poitier's awe of Tracy, it seems to establish the older Negro as a second-class father."[20] The Very Rev. Dr. Douglas said at the National Cathedral that she was troubled by how and why John made this speech. She suggested that "he perhaps should have given it to Spencer Tracy," but because of the way the film constructs white patriarchy, he could not.[21] My suspicion is that Poitier wanted a scene in which he could finally emote rather than sit waiting for a decision to be handed down. In terms of the character, John's frustration with the situation boils over onto the only person it can without damaging his prospects—his own father. It might also be that the writer didn't foresee how this scene would play onscreen; in any case, the racial dynamic and the dismissive way John talks of his father and his experiences before the civil rights era often causes audiences real discomfort.

John's nobility throughout the rest of the film, his noble perfection, is a final stereotype worth considering. For Baldwin, this "magic" depiction made it impossible for him to connect with Poitier's character; for the Very Rev. Dr. Douglas, Poitier's dignified existence onscreen was a small miracle to be celebrated. Both of these realities bear consideration. First, we should note that a movement away from racist and insulting depictions should be lauded; it is not unusual for thoughtful white filmmakers to go overboard in creating characters who stand in stark opposition to racist stereotypes (as Kevin Costner did, for example, with Native American characters in *Dances with Wolves* [1990]).

If black men have been depicted as lazy, stupid, and shiftless Coons for generations, then, yes, it is some sort of victory that John Prentice has a résumé of accomplishments longer than my arm. Matt's attempt to dig up dirt on him only showcases his many virtues, his hard work. If black men have often been depicted as violent and oversexed Bucks, then it is some sort of victory that—with the exception of the scene with his father—John is depicted as calm, respectful, and sexually restrained. When Christina asks Joey how deeply they are involved, Joey responds: "How deeply involved? Do you mean have we been to bed together? I don't mind you asking me that. We haven't. He wouldn't. I don't think he could've been in much doubt about my feelings, but he just wouldn't."

John's nobility and seeming perfection are necessary story elements, since they mean the only possible reason for objecting to him would have to be the color of his skin. Matt, even though he's adamant that John should not marry Joey, unfailingly treats him with respect, addressing him by his title, "Doctor," rather than his given name, as Christina does. It is no wonder that for the Very Rev. Dr. Douglas and many black members of the audience, seeing Poitier's performance in this film and his treatment by two of Hollywood's iconic stars was a powerful and formative experience.

But although we should certainly celebrate the movement away from negative cultural stereotypes, which we began to observe with Sam in *Casablanca*, we must also note that this narrowing of human possibility, this whitewashing of the black lead, makes John Prentice less human than if he were allowed the normal quotient of foibles and flaws. Like Jackie Robinson, who integrated Major League Baseball in 1947, like Dr. King's nonviolent protestors, Poitier's John is called to perfection, to be above the fray, to represent his race by refusing to lose his cool or stooping to the level of those who attack or resist him. And while it is, indeed, more than right to show that African Americans are not brutes or imbeciles or animals, it is unfair to ask them to uphold standards that transcend human nature. Human beings are complex and contradictory. A villain can love his mother or his cat. A heroine can fail at an important moment to do the right thing. In more recent American films, particularly those that begin to be written by and star the ethnic groups they feature, we will see more complex characters. In *The Godfather*, an Italian American family can be both loving and murderous. In *Do the Right Thing*, a neighborhood oracle can dispense loving wisdom and then call for a mob to burn down a local business. The Latin writer Terence wrote, "*Homo sum, humani nihil a me alienum puto*," and in recent years Maya Angelou introduced countless people to this quotation: "I am a human being. Nothing human can be alien to me." All of us have a right to our imperfections and our complications, and a character rendered inhuman by perfection is in a way as racist as one rendered inhuman by denigration.

In my conception of this book, I resolved to identify the failings of the films we discussed, to celebrate the achievements, and to strike a balance, neither automatic condemnation nor automatic affirmation. Whatever its failings, we have to think of *Guess Who's Coming to Dinner* as momentous, an achievement for its time, even though it falls short of granting its lead black character his complete and complex humanity. That it took on the contentious issue of miscegenation, that it depicted people of color in major roles, and that it depicted a white liberal icon, Spencer Tracy, wrestling with his own prejudice must be claimed as progress, especially for 1967.

Most important, though the film derives its currency from race, it asks us to think about one central issue that transcends race and marks all of us as human. In its much-repeated theme song, *Guess Who's Coming to Dinner* asks us to consider the power of love. Love is not simply a fuzzy emotion that magnetically pulls together potential partners but a transcendent emotion that can bring together potential enemies. The song "The Glory of Love" (originally made a hit by Benny Goodman) tells us that

> You've got to give a little,
> Take a little,
> And let your poor heart break a little.

This story—give and take and, sometimes, sacrificial heartbreak—is the story of love, the power of love, and the transcendent value of love, and it is the primary spiritual lesson that the film imparts to us.

The Glory of Love: Love and Do What You Will

On May 19, 2018, the Most Rev. Michael Curry, the first African American presiding bishop and primate of the American Episcopal Church, stepped to the lectern in St. George's Chapel at Windsor Castle in England. He proceeded to bemuse the guests at the royal wedding of Prince Harry and Meghan Markel and to captivate the rest of the world. He began by quoting Dr. King—"We must discover the power of love, the redemptive power of love"—and went on to preach on the power of love. "We were made by a power of love," Bishop Curry said. "Our lives were and are meant to be lived in that love. That is why we are here. Ultimately the source of love is God himself. That is why we are here."[22]

Bishop Curry's sermon swept across traditional and social media; the passion of his delivery and his sure confidence that love is the answer (Bishop Curry's ongoing initiative for the Episcopal Church is called "The Way of Love," and the Church offers a number of resources to help long-chilled Episcopalians reconnect with the concept) brought invitations for him to appear on TV and radio programs around the world, and he became an Internet meme.

Bishop Curry tells us that his insistence on the Way of Love grows out of the life of Jesus himself: "In the first century," he writes, "Jesus of Nazareth inspired a movement. A community of people whose lives were centered on Jesus Christ and committed to living the way of God's unconditional, unselfish, sacrificial, and redemptive love."[23] At the heart of this movement, the meaning of the movement, was love. The medieval English saint Julian of Norwich expressed it this way: "Do you wish to know your Lord's meaning in this thing? Know it well, love was his meaning. Who reveals it to you? Love. What did he reveal to you? Love. Why does he reveal it to you? For love."[24]

Ah, but what kind of love was Bishop Curry speaking of—or Julian—or Augustine of Hippo, who wrote, simply if somewhat confusingly, "Love, and do as you will . . . Nothing but good can come from this root."[25] As you no doubt suspect, when we speak of this emotion, we often do not mean the same things and may not be thinking of the sort of expression these theologians most closely associate with the life of Christ and the Way of Love. There is love in *The Birth of a*

Nation—familial love, romantic love, love between bosom friends—although hatred and bigotry are revealed as far stronger forces. How can we argue that love is more powerful when these examples do not reveal that good of which Augustine spoke?

Music, which reminds us that love is the central issue of *Guess Who's Coming to Dinner*, can help us offer some distinctions. Some songs center on the more juvenile expressions of love—take, for example, the Beatles' "She Loves You." As Bishop Curry insisted at the wedding, love is not simply a flighty emotion, a passion or ardor felt by lovers. It is that, of course, but it can be so much more. It can be expressed in songs like the Beatles' "All You Need Is Love," or Carole King's "You've Got a Friend," or Todd Rundgren's "Love Is the Answer."

Ultimately, love makes it possible for us to act ethically and unselfishly, to sacrifice something big for something good, to be transformed from creatures centered on ourselves and our own ideas and opinions, and redirected outward to the lives and needs of others. As Thomas Aquinas wrote, "Our actions, habits, and dispositions must be formed by love if we are to grow into what God intends us to be."[26] Love makes service and unselfishness possible. It makes all things possible, including the recognition that all human beings are part of the same family.

If love is the answer, what is the question? *Guess Who's Coming to Dinner* suggests that love helps us answer these questions: How do we live together? How can I be a true friend? How can I treat others with human dignity? How should I make good choices? How can I act with justice? And how can I acknowledge the centrality of love in human experience?

C. S. Lewis wrote a classic study, *The Four Loves*, in which he investigates four central understandings of love: Affection, Friendship, Eros, and Charity. In the film we first see Affection, or *Storge*, represented. It is, Lewis argues, the least discriminating of loves, the humblest, but it makes love possible for people from widely different backgrounds and provides an important backdrop for deeper and more sacrificial kinds of love. Affection is what grows up between people who are acquainted with each other, live together, and do not necessarily choose each other or regard themselves as "made for each other."[27] In *Guess Who's Coming to Dinner*, this may be Tillie's place in the Drayton family. Like many such characters in films over the years, who serve the white family and are known by them primarily in that role, they are accepted and valued, and the differences between them are minimized. Often, as Joey says of Tillie, they are treated as one of the family—although Tillie has a family and others she loves outside of her loyal but paid service to the Draytons.

My family had an African American maid during my childhood years in Charlotte, North Carolina. I knew that she cooked and cared for us, but I did not know until my mother told me recently that our maid had lost several babies, and that consequently she thought of us as her own. I didn't know anything about her except that she was there to make a snack for me after school, and that she was lovely and loving; as a child, it would not have occurred to me that she had a life outside of her time in our presence, that she existed independently when she was not sitting in our kitchen. But now, as an adult, it is clear to me how sadly imperfect my knowledge of her as a human being was and is, and so it is with many of these Faithful Retainers whom we may nonetheless regard with affection in film, from Mammy in *Birth of a Nation* to Mammy in *Gone with the Wind*, from Tillie in *Guess Who's Coming to Dinner* to Maria (Yomi Perry) in *Crash*. There is shared affection in relationship, but outside of that relationship much is mysterious.

One of Lewis's central insights about affection is that it resists change and can react jealously to it. Tillie's most dramatic scene comes when she confronts John Prentice about his courtship of Joey, and it demonstrates some of the hallmarks of this aspect of affection. Tillie does not want to see her relationships in the house change, does not want additional people at dinner, and does not want Dr. Prentice around, period:

JOHN: How do you do, Miss Binks?
TILLIE: I got somethin' to say to you, boy. Just exactly what you tryin' to pull here?
JOHN: I'm not trying to pull anything. I was lookin' to find me a wife.
TILLIE: Ain't that just likely! You wanna answer me somethin'? What kind of doctor you supposed to be, anyhow?
JOHN: Would you believe horse?

TILLIE: Oh! You make with witticisms and all, huh? Well, let me tell you somethin'. You may think you're foolin' Miss Joey and her folks, but you ain't foolin' me for a minute. You think I don't see what you are? You're one of those smooth-talkin', smart-ass niggers, just out for all you can get, with your Black Power and all that other troublemakin' nonsense. And you listen here. I brought up that child from a baby in her cradle, and ain't nobody gonna harm her none while I'm here watchin'. And as long as you are anywhere around this house, I'm right here watchin'. You read me, boy? You bring any trouble in here, you just like to find out what Black Power really means! And furthermore to that, you ain't even all that good-lookin'!

Lewis speaks of how Affection is threatened by the feeling of desertion, how when one partner in affection is moving on to someplace new and does not bring the other along, the one left outside reacts bitterly: "How if the deserter has really entered a new world which the rest of us never suspected? But, if so, how unfair!"[28] Affection is a love that needs to be needed, and a love so shot through with need doesn't reach the higher levels of sacrificial love to which Bishop Curry referred. But affection does at least enter us into relationship and show us how our lives might be enriched by contact and communion with people who are within our orbit, as well as with those who might otherwise be outside of it by virtue of race, caste, or clan. Imagine a world in which, say, Tillie and Christina consciously choose to be in community; it would have to have a very different shape and intention, wouldn't it? It would probably, at least, look more like Friendship, or *Amity*.

Friendship, as we saw in our discussion of *Casablanca*, is a love with significant virtue, a love that allows us to be accompanied by others and to be of service to them. It is, as Lewis points out, a relationship freely chosen and utterly free of Affection's need to be needed.[29] Friendship plays a part in a number of the relationships in *Guess Who's Coming to Dinner*, but it is expressed most perfectly in the relationship between Monsignor Ryan and Matt Drayton, the Catholic clergyman and the agnostic newspaperman. Their relationship is marked by affection; certainly they are different enough that they might not naturally fall together. But it is also a relationship in which there are shared interests and perhaps even a shared worldview, a seeking of the same truths.

Monsignor Ryan can be so hard on Matt because he hasn't just become accustomed to his face; he knows Matt's heart.

Four Loves, which appeared in 1960, is of course very much shaped by Lewis's own life and situation. He spent a great deal of his time with Oxford companions who, like him, taught and wrote and drank pints and wanted to understand why we are here. To read of the Oxford Christians now is to see a certain kind of friendship writ large, to see Lewis and J. R. R. Tolkien, for example, conversing as they walk to the Perch or the Trout for a drink or dinner, to see the members of the circle delivering their latest writing and awaiting pungent but also valuable criticism. The fact that Lewis primarily limited his conception of friendship to men with men and women with women does not change the value of his insights; there remains wisdom for us here.

As we saw in *Casablanca*, friendship offers us support and challenge simultaneously; in a strong friendship, our friends can take us to task at the same time that their clear *philia*/friendship love shines through. So it is in the scene in which Monsignor Ryan takes Matt to task for falling short of their shared vision of what justice looks like. Only a real friend could rake someone over the coals like this, with love and the expectation that however unwelcome his words might be, they are necessary for the hearer.

We will not take seriously the admonition "you're not yourself" from anyone who doesn't truly know us; while affection may bring people together, it does not grant deep knowledge. Friendship, romantic love, and charity may be accompanied and deepened by the bonds of affection, but they all seek a deeper knowledge of Friend, the Beloved. In Eros, we are preoccupied with the Beloved. We may be blinded to the Beloved's true self in defective versions of Eros, preferring our own version of her or him. But rightly given, romantic love is purely about the Beloved. One version of Eros we see in the film is embodied by the Prentices, long married and mostly opaque to us; it is as if writer William Rose and director Stanley Kramer couldn't imagine the shape of love between a black man and woman. Nevertheless, they knew it had to have shape, and one of the most important moments in the film comes when Mrs. Prentice laments to Matt that both he and her husband have forgotten the power and transformative value of love.

John and Joey represent a second version of love, new love, affectionate and longing, willing to do anything for the other. For John, that includes the dubious but dramatically necessary offer to give up his future with his Beloved if her family doesn't approve. Lewis, not much of an expert on romantic love in his own life but an authority on the literary depiction of love throughout the ages, wrote that transcendence of one's self and willingness to sacrifice one's own happiness is a vital ingredient of true Eros.[30] Certainly it is an essential element of great cinematic love stories. Rick must be willing to give up Ilsa for a noble cause in *Casablanca*; in *Titanic* (1999), Jack (Leonardo DiCaprio) must be willing to sacrifice his life in the frigid North Atlantic so that Rose (Kate Winslet) might be saved (even though it looks like there's plenty of room for both of them on that particular piece of floating debris).

But the great romantic love in *Guess Who's Coming to Dinner* is the one between Christina and Matt (and, if Hollywood history and our own eyes are to be believed, between Hepburn and Tracy). It's a love with history and shared purpose, a love not perhaps currently charged with romance and passion, but comfortable and at the same time *necessary* for both of them. Tracy was dying during the making of the film, and his hours on set were closely and carefully managed by Hepburn. His final speech was his last work on the film, the last scene he ever filmed, and our awareness of it now is shaped somewhat by our sense of the awareness that he and Hepburn must have had while he was filming. When you watch Tracy's final sequence again, pay close attention to Hepburn's reaction in the background—she is crying throughout the speech, for she is watching a great actor offering his last speech and, perhaps, hearing the love of her life telling her goodbye.

All of which highlights for us how love is at the heart of this story. We began by talking about interracial marriage, and the film certainly made its way in the culture by framing itself as being about this particular manifestation of love, an affirmation sharply at odds with *The Birth of a Nation*'s panic over miscegenation. The movie's one-sheet poster features Poitier and Houghton arm in arm alongside the caption: "A love story of today." But a different kind of love story is at work in this climactic moment. During the course of the evening, John has talked to Matt, and Monsignor Ryan has talked to Matt, and Christina has talked to Matt, and Mrs. Prentice has talked to Matt, and at last, in his garden, Matt has an epiphany. "I'll be a son of a bitch," he says, and while we don't yet know what he's realized, it is evident that something has become clear to him that has not been clear before. He calls the company together to announce his decision, and while his announcement foregrounds romantic love, it grows out of all the varieties we have noted and one we have not:

> Now Mr. Prentice, clearly a most reasonable man, says he has no wish to offend me, but wants to know if I'm some kind of a nut. And Mrs. Prentice says that, like her husband, I'm a burned-out old shell of a man who cannot even remember what it's like to love a woman the way her son loves my daughter. And strange as it seems, that's the first statement made to me all day with which I am prepared to take issue . . . 'cause I think you're wrong, you're as wrong as you can be. I admit that I hadn't considered it, hadn't even thought about it, but I know exactly how he feels about her and there is nothing, absolutely nothing that your son feels for my daughter that I didn't feel for Christina. Old, yes. Burned-out, certainly, but I can tell you the memories are still there: clear, intact, indestructible, and they'll be there if I live to be 110. Where John made his mistake, I think, was in attaching so much importance to what her mother and I might think. Because in the final analysis it doesn't matter a damn what we think. The only thing that matters is what they feel, and how much they feel, for each other. And if it's half of what we felt—that's everything.

At its best, Eros can show us some of the elements of love at its highest, its ability to privilege others, its willingness to diminish the self, to risk heartbreak, and Matt's speech may begin in Eros, but it actually moves us in the direction of Charity/*Caritas*/*Agape*, that sacrificial love based not on need but on gift. In his "I'll be a son of a bitch" epiphany, Matt has had his own Garden of Gethsemane moment: *I have to give up what I want, painful as that is going to be, for the sake of those I love.* Lewis notes that true love does place us at risk. We may not get what we want, or keep what we desire. Our beloved friend may die, as Augustine's Nebridius does in *The Confessions*. We may not be able to protect our charges or our children from being hurt by the uncertain future (as with Tillie and Matt). In love, Lewis argues, true love, "there is no safe investment. To love at all is to be vulnerable. Love anything and your heart will certainly be wrung and possibly be broken."[31]

But in this, like Jesus in the Garden of Gethsemane, we are aligning ourselves with God as God loves. God loves with the awareness that this love may not be returned. God, in the person of Jesus, loves the whole world, knowing it will cost him his life. It is no wonder, then, that in the Johannine community (the Christian community that held the Gospel and various Epistles of John as their formative texts), we hear Jesus repeatedly speaking of love as the organizing principle of what it means to follow him. In the Gospel of John, he offers a Great Commandment: "This is my commandment, that you love one another as I have loved you. No one has greater love than this, to lay down one's life for one's friends."[32]

The Johannine community saw love as the transcendent value that identified its members as God's:

> We know that we have passed from death to life because we love one another. Whoever does not love abides in death. All who hate a brother or sister are murderers, and you know that murderers do not have eternal life abiding in them. We know love by this, that he laid down his life for us—and we ought to lay down our lives for one another. How does God's love abide in anyone who has the world's goods and sees a brother or sister in need and yet refuses help?
>
> Little children, let us love, not in word or speech, but in truth and action.[33]

How does love lead us to truth and action—if the action we are speaking of is more than buying our Beloved roses, or helping a friend move to a fifth-floor apartment? How does it move Matt from his recalcitrance to acceptance? The love of which these writers are speaking is more than affection, more than friendship, more than romantic love, and certainly more than sappy claptrap. This love, Dr. King wrote, "is not to be confused with some sentimental outpouring. Love is something much deeper than emotional bosh."[34] This at last is the highest form of love, *caritas* or, to use the New Testament Greek, *agape*, which Dr. King defined as a love that is "understanding and creative, redemptive goodwill for all men. An overflowing love which seeks nothing in return, agape is the love of God operating in the human heart. At this level, we love men not because we like them, not because their ways appeal to us, nor even because they possess some kind of divine spark; we love every man because God loves him."[35] This highest form of love, at its best, is to love as God loves.

When we look at Dr. King's life and death, we can see that Love was not for him a static emotion, not simply a feeling. It prompted action but, perhaps more important, it made action possible. As Aquinas put it, love forms us. This sort of love makes it possible to love the unlovable, to forgive the unforgiveable, to do the right thing when the wrong thing would be so much less costly, to risk being hurt. Yes, one kind of love brought two people together across the color line in *Guess Who's Coming to Dinner*. But ultimately it was another sort of love that allowed a father to step back from his fear and his prejudice, to think about the bond that he was proposing to break, the happiness he was preparing to take, and, most important, to recover himself and his sense of what was just, how you are supposed to act if you are a person of good will.

Loving in some small fashion as God does doesn't just place us in right relation to our neighbors and ourselves; it also, somehow, allows us to do the right thing.

The Christian ethicist Scott Bader-Saye wrote that "[i]f love is just a good feeling, it will do little to help us live well. But if love is the energy of gift that made the earth and stars, if it is the force of connection that moves us into common life, if it is the very nature of a God who exists as three persons in an eternal dance of reciprocating charity—then love is exactly the place to start when we think about Christian ethics."[36]

Love is the most important force in the universe, the power that animates it, and the power that animates us. If we love sacrificially and as God does, then, as Augustine says, all our actions will bear good fruit. But if we don't, then we will create systems that oppress, we will personally harbor hate instead of good will, and we may ultimately do some sort of violence to each other. Thus, the struggle between Love and Hate: "If I love you, I love you," Radio Raheem says in *Do the Right Thing*. "But if I hate you . . ."

Birth of a Nation movie poster *The Birth of a Nation* (1915) shaped filmmaking and culture and prompted the rise of the modern Ku Klux Klan (KKK) and the resurgence of the National Association for the Advancement of Colored People (NAACP).

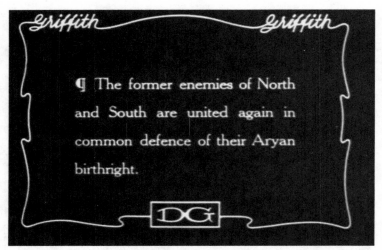

Birth of a Nation **title card** The "nation" being born in *The Birth of a Nation* is not the United States, emerging from the cauldron of the Civil War, but the "Aryan nation" that will emerge when white people of the North and South come together to again put black people under their heels.

Birth of a Nation Gus, a "renegade slave," is killed for daring to desire a white woman. This murder is one of several lynchings shown or suggested in *The Birth of a Nation* as a way of imposing (or reimposing) white power over black men. Courtesy of the Schomburg Center for Research in Black Culture, Photographs and Prints Division, The New York Public Library

14959-A

Jesse Washington lynch mob In 1916, 10,000 people gathered in downtown Waco, Texas for the public torture, burning, and dismemberment of Jesse Washington, accused of raping a white woman. Before this violence *The Birth of a Nation* had shown regularly in Waco to great acclaim, and may have helped to spark this lynching. Courtesy of the Library of Congress.

Casablanca Rick (Humphrey Bogart), Ilsa (Ingrid Bergman) and Sam (Dooley Wilson) toast each other in *Casablanca*'s flashback to Paris. Sam is treated as a valued equal both in this scene and throughout the movie.
© Photo 12 / Alamy Stock Photo

Guess Who's Coming to Dinner screening poster *Guess Who's Coming to Dinner* was shown at the Texas White House, Lyndon Baines Johnson's Johnson City ranch, on March 16, 1968. This parallels Woodrow Wilson's White House screening of *The Birth of a Nation*.

Do the Right Thing After Radio Raheem (Bill Nunn) has been killed by the police and hustled away, pizzeria owner Sal (Danny DeVito), his sons, and their deliveryman, Mookie (Spike Lee) face off against an angry mob hungry for vengeance in *Do the Right Thing*.

Crash The day after he has sexually assaulted her on a routine traffic stop, Officer Ryan (Matt Dillon) climbs back into a burning car to rescue Christine (Thandie Newton), confounding him, her and audiences of the film *Crash* who have previously written him off as a racist.

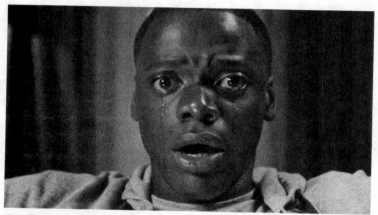

Get Out Early in the film *Get Out*, during a visit to the home of his white girlfriend and her family, Chris (Daniel Kaluuya) is hypnotized and sent into the "Sunken Place," where he can watch everything that is happening to him but is powerless to stop it.

BlacKkKlansman poster The poster for Spike Lee's *BlacKkKlansman* invites comparisons to the poster for *The Birth of a Nation*, and the film itself makes numerous references to Griffith's film, including images from the film and Griffith's signature cross-cutting editing technique to build suspense at its climax.

James Baldwin photo As a child, writer and cultural critic James Baldwin began seeing and thinking about movies, race, representation, and how film can broadcast harmful or helpful myths about identity. He remains one of America's most important voices on racism and reconciliation. Courtesy of Allan Warren.

Washington National Cathedral photo A crowd fills the nave of
Washington National Cathedral in Washington, D. C. for a screening of
Spike Lee's *BlacKkKlansman* and conversation about race, reconciliation,
and justice in February 2019. Courtesy of the author.

5

Do the Right Thing

"Together Are We Going to Live?"

Racism, Reaction, Riot

In May 1989, Spike Lee's new film, *Do the Right Thing*, premiered at Cannes. It was widely expected to win the Palme d'Or, the top prize at the festival, and certainly the audience was stunned by the power and audacity of the film. Roger Ebert recalled that screening as one of the most powerful moviegoing experiences of his life: "Most movies remain up there on the screen," he said. "Only a few penetrate your soul. In May of 1989 I walked out of the screening at the Cannes Film Festival with tears in my eyes. Spike Lee had done an almost impossible thing. He'd made a movie about race in America that empathized with all the participants. He didn't draw lines or take sides but simply looked with sadness at one racial flashpoint that stood for many others."[1] It was not only a magical moment for Ebert, but a major moment in film history.

The action of *Do the Right Thing* is familiar to many by now: Lee sets his story during one hot summer day in Brooklyn, a day that builds slowly toward violence that will scar the neighborhood forever. After being tossed out of Sal's Famous Pizzeria (Sal is played by Danny Aiello) for complaining about the fact that no photos of African Americans appear on Sal's Wall of Fame, neighborhood gadfly Buggin' Out (Giancarlo Esposito) tries to organize a boycott of Sal's. His friend—and Sal's delivery man—Mookie (Spike Lee) is one of many who try to talk him out of it, but Buggin' Out continues to militate for action, and at the end of the long hot day, he pushes his way into Sal's at closing time with Radio Raheem, whose boombox is, as always, playing Public Enemy's "Fight the Power" at oppressive volume. The day's tensions spill over into racist words and violent actions.

Sal has earlier confronted Raheem about bringing his boombox into the restaurant, but now he destroys it with a baseball bat. Raheem drags Sal out from behind the counter and begins choking him. In the melee that follows, the entire neighborhood gathers, yelling, fighting, and then the police arrive, including two officers we have seen in the neighborhood throughout the day. The police pull Radio Raheem off Sal and in the process choke him to death. After they flee with Raheem's body, Mookie shatters the restaurant window with a garbage can, the angry mob rushes in, and Sal's Famous Pizzeria goes up in flames. The next morning, Sal and Mookie confront each other across every gulf there seems to be in contemporary America—and yet, despite their anger and sadness, they manage to have some kind of conversation in the midst of the ruins before they turn away.

Jason Bailey wrote in *The Atlantic* that *Do the Right Thing* "is one of the few truly great films of the 1980s: an intelligent, matter-of-fact examination of race in America and also a vibrant, funny slice of New York life."[2] I agree. I think of it as one of the most challenging— and most entertaining—great films ever made. I have taught it in universities and churches and seminaries, have shown it in the nave of Washington National Cathedral. Like Ebert, I value the movie's fairness, its open-endedness, the way Lee puts art in the service of his outrage but doesn't insist on offering us a solution. Ebert wrote from his perspective as a white man that at the time of the film's release, "it comes closer to reflecting the current state of race relations in America than any other movie of our time," and, sadly, that remains true thirty-plus years later.[3] Vann Newkirk, who writes about race, politics, and culture for *The Atlantic*, recently told me that he grew up attending black schools and was blown away by Lee's depiction of interethnic conflict; seeing blacks, Puerto Ricans, and Italian Americans fighting and living together in Brooklyn was a new experience. The movie felt, Vann said, like an honest appraisal of the times, and it opened up a new world for him.[4]

That authenticity and artistry has brought plenty of recognition over the years. *Do the Right Thing* received the Best Picture Award from the Los Angeles Film Critics Association; cinematographer Ernest

Dickerson was named Best Cinematographer by the New York Film Critics Circle. Lee appeared on the cover of *American Film* (dressed in his Jackie Robinson Dodgers jersey) with the suggestion that black filmmakers were crossing a new color line and Lee was in the forefront of that movement. The Library of Congress named *Do the Right Thing* to the National Film Registry in 1999, the first year of its eligibility, recognizing it as a national artistic treasure.

[handwritten margin note: Library Congress]

Still, not everybody has been so moved by the film—or even the concept of the film. Lee's original studio, Paramount, decided not to fund the movie. They were hoping for something lighter in tone, something perhaps more like Lee's comedic *She's Gotta Have It* (1986) than this slice of urban racial drama. The studio's notes betrayed their concerns with the violent ending, which Lee refused to change: How would audiences feel leaving the theater? Will blacks want to go on a rampage? Will whites feel uncomfortable?[5] Lee responded to the studio's fear with the observation "TOO BLACK AND TOO STRONG," and he lamented that the executives "are convinced that Black people will come out of the theaters wanting to burn shit down."[6] Lee found another studio, Universal, that believed in his vision, and the film was profitable for them. Filmed at a cost of $6.5 million, it earned an initial $27.5 million.

[handwritten margin note: Paramount Notes Lee reply]

Even after the film was funded, produced, and released, others devalued it. The 1989 Cannes jury, chaired by German filmmaker Wim Wenders, gave the Palme d'Or to Steven Soderbergh's *Sex, Lies, and Videotape*. Wenders complained that *Do the Right Thing*'s lead character, Mookie, was unheroic. Others actively feared it. At the Cannes press conference, Ebert sat behind a critic who expressed her belief that the film would cause rioting, and she was far from the only writer to suggest this possibility.

[handwritten margin note: Cannes riot concern unheroic]

Joe Klein was one of the many white journalists who decried *Do the Right Thing* as sure to set off race riots and increase racial tension in the United States. In an op-ed in *New York Magazine*, he lamented the depiction of violence against white property that follows Radio Raheem's murder: "It is Spike Lee himself—in the role of Sal's deliveryman—who starts the riot by throwing a garbage can through the store's window, one of the stupider, more self-destructive acts of violence I've ever witnessed (if black kids act on what they see, Lee may have destroyed his career in that moment).["7] Lee has been asked often over the past thirty years if Mookie did the right thing in initiating this destruction; he notes that the questioner is never a black person.

[handwritten margin note: 7 never, black person.]

Other white writers derided the film as a messy, needless provocation. Film critic David Denby, writing in the same issue of *New York Magazine*, called the movie's ending an incoherent shambles (that is, the audience isn't told what to think or believe) and argued that "if Spike Lee is a commercial opportunist, he's also playing with dynamite in an urban playground. The response to the movie could get away from him."[8] Jack Kroll, writing for *Newsweek*, also employed the dynamite metaphor and said that there was no way to know how "young urban audiences—black and white—[would] react to the film's climactic explosion of interracial violence."[9] These responses showcased the fear and lack of understanding on the part of white critics, their sense that black audiences might be unable to separate the film and their own emotions.

To this day, Lee continues to think of those reviews from white writers as straight-up racism:

[handwritten margin note: Lee response to white critics]

> It was such a condescending [thing] . . . to think that black moviegoers don't have the intelligence to discern what is on screen, and that they would duplicate what Mookie was doing, was ludicrous. If you have some time, please, please, please Google those articles by Jack Kroll, David Denby, and Joe Klein. To me, it was pure, uncut, unfiltered racism. Those articles basically said to white moviegoers, please don't go. If you are in the same theater with black people, it's not going to end well.[10]

Jason Bailey parsed Lee's response to Klein's article as "What he's saying is, 'Pray to God that this film doesn't open in your theater, (because) niggers are gonna go crazy.'" And while it's never assumed that white audiences are going to "go crazy" over violent action films, black audiences are "such mental midgets that we can't tell the difference between what's on screen and what's in real life?"[11]

For his part, Ebert wrote, "Some of the advance articles about this movie have suggested that it is an incitement to racial violence. Those articles say more about their authors than about the movie. I believe that any good-hearted person, white or black, will come out of this movie with sympathy for all of the characters. Lee does not ask us to forgive them, or even to understand everything they do, but he wants us to identify with their fears and frustrations."[12] In other words, the movie sets out not to solve the problems it identifies, but to illuminate them out in a thoughtful way, and to invite the audience to respond by solving these issues for themselves.

Gregg-Ebert Summary

In his book-length study of the film for the British Film Institute, Ed Guerrero notes that the attacks on *Do the Right Thing* represent a typical conservative response from those in a position of privilege. However well intended, it is ultimately an expression of the fear of the black Other, the continuance of hundreds of years of stereotypical vision of people of color as violent, bestial, and uncontrollable. To suggest that a film depicting the sort of violence that actually takes place is "inflaming and exacerbating the very problem that it seeks to expose, engage, or change" mistakes artistic reactions and responses to violence for actual causes of it.[13] Lee's character Mookie may have initiated the destruction of Sal's Famous, in the film, but Lee didn't light the fire of racial injustice in America, and *Do the Right Thing* did not fan those flames. In that summer of 1989, people of color in America did not require a push from Lee to incite them to rise up in anger and frustration. They had plenty of other provocation.

"Black Other"

Finally, although the film received a great deal of positive acclaim, and many critics believed it deserved consideration for Best Film and Best Director at the Academy Awards, Lee's film received only scant recognition at the industry's biggest party. Danny Aiello was nominated for Best Supporting Actor, and Lee was nominated for Best Original Screenplay. (Lee would not, amazingly, win a competitive Oscar until 2019, sharing Best Adapted Screenplay for *BlacKkKlansman*.) To add insult to injury, the Best Picture winner that year was *Driving Miss Daisy*, one of the racial reconciliation fantasies Wesley Morris decries as Oscar-bait feel-good films. Morris writes that *Driving Miss Daisy*'s one-sheet told audiences exactly the sort of heartwarming experience they might expect: the poster is "a warmly painted rendering ... [a] vague nuzzling of Norman Rockwell Americana. And its warmth evokes a very particular past. If you've ever seen the packaging for Cream of Wheat or a certain brand of

Oscar noms

Driving Miss Daisy

rice, if you've even seen some Shirley Temple movies, you knew how Miss Daisy would be driven: gladly."[14] That film's approach to racism is oblique, mediated largely through the question of employment we've previously considered; Morgan Freeman's Hoke is a lovely and wise man—but he is also, perhaps, first and foremost a Magical Negro and a Faithful Retainer.

What New York City—and America at large—needed in 1989 and 1990 was not a *Driving Miss Daisy*, a genteel fantasy about how an elderly and wealthy white lady could gently and gingerly gain a modicum of racial awareness through decades of close proximity to a black domestic. What they needed—and what Lee gave them—was a film that wrestled explicitly with the biggest issues in American life. "He wanted to make America look in the mirror," Matt Haber writes.[15] Guerrero notes that *Do the Right Thing* tackles a number of issues related to race, prejudice, and systemic injustice: police brutality, racial profiling, neighborhood colonization and gentrification, gender and family relations, identity politics, nonwhite immigration and interracial relations, and systemic racism.[16] Yolanda Pierce, dean of the Divinity School at Howard University, grew up in the neighborhood depicted in the film and has spoken about how that place where she lived no longer exists. Her own roll call of issues dealt with in the film begins and ends with displacement: "Gentrification, climate change, violence, not just physical violence, not just racialized violence, but the violence of displacement, the displacing of people, the displacing of communities and histories and traditions."[17]

Lee's film is so filled with issues because it needed to be, for in New York City, and across America, 1989 was a time fraught with peril, particularly for people of color. The initial inspiration for *Do the Right Thing* was an occasion of racial violence in Howard Beach in Queens in 1986, when a black man, Michael Griffiths, was chased down and murdered by white men after asking for directions in a "white" pizza parlor. As those who have seen the movie know, however, the list of black victims of racial violence is longer: Eleanor Bumpers, Yusuf Hawkins, and Michael Stewart are among those memorialized in the film. New York City had also been shaken by racially charged incidents like the April 1989 rape of a white female jogger in Central Park, supposedly by five young black men (the so-called Central Park

Five, whose convictions were later vacated), and false allegations of rape and kidnapping by a black teenager, Tawana Brawley, against four white men, including members of the law enforcement community. The city was moving toward a watershed mayoral election, in which the sitting mayor, Ed Koch (whom Lee considered responsible for the racially charged atmosphere in the city), was opposed by an African American candidate, David Dinkins. Guerrero concludes, "In the summer of 1989, New York City, along with many other urban combat zones, could not have been more tense and divided along racial lines, and judging from the social and material inequality of their lived relations the social dynamite was already in place—black people hardly needed the pretext of a movie to explode."[18]

Lee himself—as a filmmaker and as a media personality—was at the forefront of important movements at the time. While the end of the 1980s brought the fall of the Soviet Union (and the elimination of an often-demonized external enemy), it also brought the rise of the culture wars. Those in a position of power and privilege inevitably pushed back against those seeking their day in the sun: women, gays and lesbians, people of color. Historian Jill Lepore has written, "In the waning decades of the twentieth century, liberals and conservatives alike cast the lingering divisions of the 1960s less as matters of law and order than as matters of life and death."[19] In some communities, they literally were matters of life and death. Perhaps we no longer feared atomic death at the hands of the Russians, but death or oppression at the hands of fellow Americans continued to be a daily issue for many people outside the white mainstream; Lee's job was to show that.

Lee's ongoing cinematic project has been, he says, to represent "how entrenched racism is . . . It's sewn into the flag by Betsy Ross. It's part of the DNA of this country." It's the job of the artist, Lee notes, not to show how we heal, but to show audiences what's happening—to be that mirror held up to the nation."[20] In *Do the Right Thing* and *Malcolm X* (1992), *Four Little Girls* (1997), *Bamboozled* (2000), *When the Levees Broke* (2006), and *BlacKkKlansman*, Lee has held up a mirror to racism and prejudice in America, showing the ways individuals contribute to the brokenness we all witness and exploring the ways that our systems are complicit in the ongoing oppression of black people.

He has been portrayed as an agent provocateur, but truth be told, he is simply a filmmaker trying to get his productions watched, to tell the truth about a badly broken system. Jason Bailey reminds us that *Do the Right Thing* did not cause riots in American cities; a few years later a different film, a home video of the police beating of Rodney King in Los Angeles, did. Ultimately, "Lee was not a provocateur; he was a prognosticator. But the image that was crafted early that summer and disseminated on the pages of *Newsweek, New York,* and *Time,* of Spike Lee the bomb-throwing race baiter, not only held, but became common wisdom. A notorious 1992 *Esquire* cover story announced the widespread perception, then and now, in the plainest language imaginable: 'Spike Lee Hates Your Cracker Ass.'"[21]

Cracker ass

Fortunately for him—and for us—Lee was more than just a strapped-for-cash independent filmmaker making a movie about race in America; he was also a national celebrity. His commercial work with Michael Jordan for Nike, appearing as Mars Blackmon in Air Jordan commercials, had made him a household name and an emblem of hip-hop cool. Mars was a character first played by Lee in *She's Gotta Have It,* a Brooklynite, a passionate sports fan, and a guy who wouldn't take off his Air Jordans even to have sex with the girl of his dreams. Nike's public relations agency Wieden + Kennedy caught *She's Gotta Have It* and saw it as ripe for promotional opportunity. They developed a series of commercials featuring Lee and Jordan, with Jordan exhibiting basketball wizardry and Lee insisting, "It's gotta be the shoes." In a 1988 commercial, for example, Mars hangs from the rim and talks about how the shoes make it possible for him to get such game, to be "way above the rim"—and as the camera pulls back, it reveals Mars standing on the shoulders of Michael Jordan—who steps away and leaves him hanging. In these commercials, Jordan displays incredible tolerance for Mars, even permitting him to claim him as "my main man."

So at the time that *Do the Right Thing* came out, not only was the film front and center in the culture wars, with equal numbers of people appalled and engaged by Lee's treatment of race and prejudice, but it also played off the image of Lee as alternative filmmaker, racial gadfly, and Madison Avenue icon, roles that Lee has continued to occupy in American culture ever since. Some of this was necessary. As Lee has known forever, to be on the outside of the Hollywood studio system means that he must stand up and help promote his films, bringing attention to them any way he can. Studios have relegated him and, traditionally, other black directors to second-class status, so in that quest, all publicity is good publicity. "Consequently," as Guerrero notes, "self-generated promotion and publicity leading to any media attention—good or bad, just not indifferent—has always been recognised by him as a winning gambit."[22]

It's not enough, then, to be a great filmmaker; in order to keep making money, getting paid, Lee has had to wrangle attention to his films, to be provocative as well as thoughtful, visible as well as artful. With *Do the Right Thing*, the story itself generated so many different angles worthy of discussion that Lee didn't have to drive the media conversation; the movie did that. By exploring race relations in America in 1989—and, sadly, still in 2019—Lee has created plenty of space for conversation.

Fight the Power: Confrontation, Collision, and Synthesis

Lee's artistic and philosophical strategy for the film is revealed to us from the outset: It is a strategy of confrontation and collision in the hopes of creating some new, powerful, third meaning. Before the movie's opening credits run, the soundtrack for *Do the Right Thing* brings us into the space we are going to occupy for the next two hours, this place of engagement and confrontation. First, Branford Marsalis begins to lyrically play "Lift Every Voice and Sing," the so-called Negro national anthem, with lyrics by the black poet James Weldon Johnson. Maya Angelou wrote about the emotional power of this anthem in her memoir *I Know Why the Caged Bird Sings*; I was exposed to that power often in St. James Episcopal Church, my community of faith in East Austin, Texas. St. James was a historically African American church, and music in our parish was a mix of traditional hymns and African American spirituals. "Lift Every Voice and Sing" was an invitation to remember where we had come from and to hope for something better, if we could only remain faithful: "Thou who hast by thy might, led us into the light, keep us forever in the path, we pray."

In the film, that traditional black gospel hymn is then interrupted and confronted by Public Enemy's "Fight the Power," and by Tina (Rosie Perez), who dances, boxes, and assaults the audience to that music throughout the opening credits. The conflict between these two visions of race and progress is instant; there is faith and patience on the one hand and angry rejection of those qualities on the other. "Elvis was a racist/Tried and true," Public Enemy proclaims. "Motherfuck him, and John Wayne too!" Which of these musical visions—or versions—of reality and resistance should we follow. Either? Neither? Or is it possible that somehow from the cognitive dissonance of this collision we may imagine a third way?

Lee's strategy thus reveals itself from the first minutes of the film. He intends to confront us with diametrically opposed alternatives. This movie is also going to be combative, and our reaction as viewers is going to have to include the fact that the film is going to push back against us, hard. He is not offering us answers, but options. In this musical introduction, moving from traditional to contemporary music, "we are ready," Guerrero observes, "for combat as the political and aesthetic gauntlet is thrown down. This is straight-up cultural war voiced in the raw street vernacular of today's urban black, hip-hop youth."[23]

There are no easy answers. Anyone who says there are is a demagogue of the left or the right. Ebert understood this in 1989, writing in his initial review of the film that "[o]f course some of the characters are sympathetic and others are hateful. And of course some of the likable characters do bad things. Isn't that the way it is in America today? Anyone who walks into this film expecting answers is a dreamer or a fool. But anyone who leaves the movie with more intolerance than they walked in with wasn't paying attention."[24] Nothing has changed in the decades since. Lee told *Politico* in 2019 that "I will not sit in front of this microphone staring at the Capitol Building and tell you that Spike Lee has an antidote to cleanse the world of hate, and racism. I won't do that. It'll be a lie. I don't have the answer."[25] But like any great artist, Lee can pose questions and offer us choices, even if they're not intended as definitive answers. In a recent conversation with past Archbishop of Canterbury Rowan Williams about how storytellers work, he and I agreed that sometimes the job of the writer is simply to point toward the things that concern him or her. "If you find this a problem,"

Williams says, "be assured I find it one as well. If you would like to know if there's a way through, here's a thought. Here's a possible way of walking with it, or walking into it."[26] In *Do the Right Thing*, Lee poses alternatives for us to walk through and allows us to choose from those alternatives. What is the right thing? What is the wrong thing? We'll explore those questions in more detail in our next section, but first let's see how Lee sets up those dilemmas for us and how his film offers us opposing images, characters, and themes for us to try to reconcile.

After Tina's battle dance in the opening credits, we hear the voice of Samuel L. Jackson, the WE LOVE radio disc jockey known as Mister Señor Love Daddy, exhorting his morning listeners to wake up. "Wake up! Wake up! Up you wake!" This call—Wake Up!—is a recurring element in Lee's films and an essential one for the characters and audience of this film, although we cannot know how at this point in the movie. After this invitation, we meet the characters we'll revisit throughout the film. Da Mayor (played by actor and civil rights icon Ossie Davis) rises complaining about the heat. Mookie (Spike Lee) gets out of bed and starts counting his cash. Sal and his sons Pino (John Turturro) and Vito (Richard Edson) pull up in front of Sal's Famous Pizzeria in an Eldorado and get ready to open for the day. Mother Sister (Ruby Dee, spouse of Ossie Davis in real life) calls out to Mookie to take care of himself because it is going to be a hot day. Smiley (Roger Guenveur Smith) shows us the one extant picture of Malcolm X and Martin Luther King, Jr. that we'll keep viewing throughout the film. And so on, and so on. We are introduced to all these characters, who will embody the good and the bad of the neighborhood, and to the structural elements that will bookend the story—fire hydrants and fire hoses, police officers who will show up early as frightening if superficially civil outsiders and return at the end as violent betrayers, Sal's interrupting of his squabbling kids, "I'm gonna kill somebody today," and the death of Radio Raheem.

The movie presents us with various kinds of collisions throughout, starting with "Lift Every Voice and Sing" facing off against "Fight the Power" and moving into images, scenes, and all the ways we confront each other. The movement from thesis to antithesis to synthesis is known as the dialectical method. In the thinking of the eighteenth-century German philosopher Georg Wilhelm Friedrich Hegel, this process works through an initial proposition, the *thesis*, which is refuted or complicated by a competing *antithesis*, and evolves into a *synthesis*, in which the two competing ideas find some sort of reconciliation and evolve into a newer, higher, and more perfect truth. Within the film we are offered a series of dichotomies built on oppositions: Racist/ Not Racist, Love/Hate, Peace/Violence, Italian American/African American, African American/Puerto Rican, Anglo/People of Color, African American/Korean, Man/Woman, Day/Night, Martin Luther King, Jr./Malcolm X, Sal/Pino, Mookie/Sal, Mookie/Pino, Vito/Pino, Mookie/Tina, even Frank Sinatra/Michael Jackson. How can these opposites be reconciled? Is there a way forward emerging from the stark divides the movie displays?

The film's strategy of confrontation and complication is further revealed in a number of instances of breaking the fourth wall, theatrical scenes in which characters speak to us directly, breaking out of the bounds of the film. Mister Señor Love Daddy, the neighborhood DJ, is continuously in our face, from the moment he orders us to wake up to the multiple times he tells us to chill out. Smiley shows us the picture of Malcolm X with Dr. King and thus launches us into the ongoing task the movie gives us, to somehow integrate the ideas of these two great black leaders. Radio Raheem's speech on Love and Hate (taken, incidentally, from Robert Mitchum's speech in *Night of the Hunter* [1955]) is delivered to Mookie in the street, but also directly to us. And the race rant sequence, perhaps the most-remembered part of the film, is also directly in our faces, with no in-film audience suggested at all.

In this world of collision and confrontation, contradictions bedevil us, just as they do in life. Da Mayor, perhaps the closest we come in the film to a moral exemplar, can be a hero who saves a young boy from being run over by a car and, at the same time, a drunk who is taken to task by a group of teenagers for failing to take care of his family. Mookie, our protagonist, who negotiates the world between white and black, can simultaneously be "like a son" to Sal and a deadbeat employee whom Sal tells to watch himself. Mother Sister, the oracular figure who watches over the neighborhood, can call out to Mookie to be careful on this hot day but can call Da Mayor, who treats her with nothing but kindness, an old fool. Sal, whom Melissa Harris-Perry calls one of the moral centers of the film, can love the people of the neighborhood and take great pride in feeding them every day for decades and can also erupt into racial insults and personal violence at the end of this long, hot day.[27]

The bright colors of the production design (like the orange wall behind the Corner Men) and the lighted Sterno cans in front of the camera make us feel the heat of this hottest day of the year. Dickerson is constantly pitching his camera at a disconcerting angle, using a shot called a Dutch angle or "canting," in which the horizon of the shot is crooked, a disorienting device Lee says they admired from its use in Carol Reed's *The Third Man* (1949). Lee and editor Barry Alexander Brown edit point-of-view shots, using the imposing size of Bill Nunn's Raheem to emphasize confrontation between Raheem and Mookie, Sal, and the Korean shopkeepers. The breaking of the fourth wall where Raheem delivers the Love/Hate soliloquy shows him (in film terms) looking down on the shorter Mookie but in reality looming over us, just as he does in the exchange of point-of-view shots where he and Sal confront each other over the counter in the pizzeria.

Lee's strategy of confrontation and collision can perhaps best be seen dramatically and cinematically in the two most famous sections of the film, in which Lee places race and prejudice in America front and center. After Mookie has been on the pay phone with Tina, Pino complains to Sal that he is losing them business, and under his breath mutters that he hates niggers. Mookie invites him back to a conversation over the cigarette machine and asks Pino who his favorite actor, rock star, and athlete are. It turns out that all of Pino's favorite celebrities are black—not "niggers," Pino is quick to say, offering a tortured explanation of how they manage to be not quite white, but definitely not black, and certainly not niggers.

Mookie confronts him with the truth—that Pino identifies with these figures and loves them—and yet they are most assuredly black. How can he say he hates black people when his favorite people are all black? "It's different," Pino says. "Magic, Eddie, and Prince are not niggers, I mean they're not black. Let me explain myself. I mean they're black, but they're not really black. It's different."

[handwritten margin note: "Not Black"]

It's an essential conversation. At a 2016 showing of the film at Saints Andrew and Matthew Episcopal Church in inner-city Wilmington, Delaware, Bebe Coker, an elderly African American writer and social activist, reminded us that conversation—real conversation—about who we are is at the heart of reconciliation. "I have to help you understand me," she said. "See me, know me, respect me as a human being."

"You know," Mookie tells Pino, "deep down inside, I think you wish you were black." When Pino rejects this hypothesis and every theory about the worth of black people, Mookie curses him and his Italian American idols. Lee then moves us from Mookie's anger with Pino into perhaps the most important segment of the film, the sequence Lee's script calls the RACIAL SLUR MONTAGE. It offers the recognition that prejudice flows across racial and cultural boundaries, and it implicates all of us.

Mookie stands in the middle of the street, looks into the camera, and says, "You dago, wop, garlic-breath, guinea, pizza-slinging, spaghetti-bending, Vic Damone, Perry Como, Luciano Pavarotti O Sole Mio non-singing motherfucker!" His racist rant is followed by others, lots of others: Pino inveighs against black people from the counter of the pizza parlor; Steve (Luis Ramos), one of the Puerto Ricans, fumes from the stoop about Koreans; the Irish American officer Long (played by Danny Aiello's son Rick), the police officer who will later kill Radio Raheem, insults Puerto Ricans while standing in front of his police cruiser; and Sonny (Steve Park), the Korean grocer, fumes against Jews and New York City mayor Koch from in front of his store. This escalating landslide of verbal hate only stops when Love Daddy slides into the front of his radio booth and confronts us head on with the call to "cool that shit out!"

This sequence, made up as it is of working-class men, all of whom have some connection to this neighborhood, does two things thematically. First, of course, it reminds us that all of us harbor vile feelings about another group of people. Perhaps the group we vilify, the group our own inner rant would address, is Republicans or conservative Christians or hipsters or vegans, rather than Jews or Puerto Ricans or African Americans or Italian Americans. But almost all of us harbor some hidden "ism," whether it is racism or sexism or some other prejudice, that under the right circumstances might erupt into a hateful monologue. This litany of hate and disdain, does, as Guerrero puts it, "depict the danger and futility of racism at a personal level, from which no social formation is exempt" and also helps to "forecast the impending social disaster of the film's dénouement."[28] But what may *economic oppression* be even more important, these individual expressions of prejudice may make us forget about the racism and economic forces at the heart of the system that oppresses all of these groups and keeps them all down— and, simultaneously, at each other's throats.

Throughout the movie, Public Enemy calls us to "fight the powers that be," and even though Officer Long is a servant of those powers and bears their token of authority, he too is one paycheck or one crisis away from disaster. He has more in common with the people he polices. We must combat racism on a personal level, of course, but Guerrero argues that "[t]hese angry, isolated figures representing different races scapegoat and fight each other" instead of the powers that be.[29] Our *White male privilege* solutions have to be both individual and societal; it is futile for me to recognize and work on my own personal racism and not also acknowledge the institutional privilege I have as a middle-aged, middle-class white man. That too requires dismantling.

However, even dealing with individual racism and the ways we look past each other instead of seeing each other would be a significant achievement. One of the most important ways that we fail to deal with each other on an individual basis is represented by the film's almost constant noise. In that 2016 discussion at the church in Delaware, Pat Hampton, a woman then in her late seventies, called out one of the film's essential truths: "Nobody is listening to anyone!" The prime *Louder voices "Boombox"* case in this regard might be the battle of the boomboxes, where Radio Raheem and Steve compete to see whose music can be louder. The winner—and still champion—is Radio Raheem, and Steve is forced to turn his boombox off in acknowledgment that Raheem's is the louder voice. I can be louder, angrier, more vocal than you—thus I win, even if we both lose.

As Pat recognized, most of the scenes of "dialogue" are marked by noise, as people speak or shout over each other. Just a few of them: When Clifton (John Savage), a white guy in a Larry Bird Celtics jersey, accidentally steps on Buggin' Out's Air Jordans, Buggin' Out shouts at him, over him, backed up by the dissonant outrage of the neighborhood teenagers. Later, when Da Mayor tries to tell these same kids something of his life, they shout him down. Tina yells over Mookie (who may in fact deserve to be yelled at). In early confrontations in

Sal's Famous, Sal and Buggin' Out shout and curse at each other about the Italian American faces on the wall of fame and Buggin' Out's threat of a boycott. Over the sound of Radio Raheem's boombox, Sal shouts, "Mr. Radio Raheem! I can't hear myself think! You are disturbing me! You are disturbing my customers!" Late in the film, when the teenagers talk Sal into reopening the store for one more slice, Buggin' Out, Radio Raheem, and Smiley charge in to demand African American faces on the wall of fame, the screaming and loud music reach a zenith, and the silence after Sal bashes Radio Raheem's radio is shocking because of it. Finally, when Sal and Mookie meet in front of Sal's Famous Pizzeria the morning after, Sal shouts at Mookie as he throws crumpled hundred-dollar bills at him: "You're fucking rich!"

Over and over again, rather than talk *to* each other, people talk *over* each other, talk *past* each other. The few scenes of quiet dialogue register as so much more important because they stand out tonally as well. When Da Mayor stops Mookie in the street to tell him, "Doctor, always do the right thing," Mookie does not listen, but we listen. When Mookie and Vito talk about the way Pino bullies Vito, we see two human beings trying to work through a hard family situation. When Sal talks with Pino about why he loves his work, loves owning a pizzeria in a black neighborhood, we recognize his love for his son and his pride, and, at the same time, we see Pino's desperation and feeling of being trapped. When Pino and Mookie talk about race and black celebrity, there is a moment where some connection might be made. When Sal and Jade (Joie Lee) talk (and perhaps flirt) in a booth at Sal's Famous, there is a sweetness about their conversation that reminds us that the color line is optional (although a parallel eyeline cut shows that Pino and Mookie, despite being foes, are joined in agreement in disapproving of this relationship). When Sal and Mookie find a place of quiet connection over the weather the morning after, we're offered a tiny sliver of hope that despite all that stands between them, they've found something to talk about. And at the end of the film, Da Mayor and Mother Sister greet each other the morning after the tragedy, and she tells him, "We're still standing." We hear.

After our screening of *Do the Right Thing* at the National Cathedral in 2019, Vann Newkirk said, "For me, the thing that always stands out when I watch this film is number one, just how beautiful it is, how well shot it is. The cinematography is fantastic."[30] And so it is. It's beautifully filmed, and also wonderfully written, in fact conforming to the Classical unities of Time, Place, and Action, and observing Anton Chekhov's famous dramatic prescription that a gun shown hanging on the wall in the first act should go off in the final act. Lee offers us skillful foreshadowing and symmetry in dialogue, images, and events. We hear Love Daddy's call to wake up and Sal's prophetic "I'm gonna kill someone today" at the opening. "Fight the Power," heard in its entirety at the start as Tina boxes and dances, recurs throughout the film and is heard again at the end, as Smiley pins the photo of Malcolm and Martin on the wall of fame while Sal's Pizzeria burns around him. We see the fire hydrants opened up by neighborhood kids to cool off; at the film's end firefighters' hoses are connected to those same fire hydrants and used to knock down black protestors, in clear reference to 1960s Alabama. When Officer Long shuts off the fire hydrant early in the film, he shouts that if he has to come back there will be hell; we remember this when he kills Radio Raheem at film's end. We hear Radio Raheem's soliloquy on the hands that represent Love and Hate and hear Mookie shout "Hate" as he throws the garbage can through the pizzeria's plate-glass window, while at the movie's conclusion, we hear Sal talking about how "these hands" built Sal's Famous. We see Da Mayor rising to another hard day in the neighborhood at the beginning and again at the end of the film, and Love Daddy bookending the film. *Do the Right Thing* is, formally, near perfect, a thing of beauty, as Newkirk argues. The early critical judgments that the film is messy or sloppy may reflect those critics' desire for a formal ending in which all is reconciled, wrapped up with a bow, perhaps as in one of the racial reconciliation fantasies beloved by the Academy of Motion Picture Arts and Sciences, perhaps a film where a White Savior puts things back the way they were before.

But *Do the Right Thing* is about things falling apart, not being put back together. In a nation shattered by racism, perhaps the fact that we are still standing is the dramatic truth in which we have to live. It is a film in which confrontation and collision are the dramatic, cinematic, and philosophical tools Lee and his collaborators are employing, a film where we are told to always do the right thing, yet not told what that right thing might look like in a neighborhood—in a nation—where racism, hate, violence, gentrification, and institutional privilege run wild. Ebert understood that the film is an experience that asks the audience to do the hard work: "Since Lee does not tell you what to think about [the ending], and deliberately provides surprising twists for some of the characters, this movie is more open-ended than most. It requires you to decide what you think about it."[31] Ed Guerrero agrees that the film is "an open and unresolved text, meant to challenge and disturb the viewer with relevant questions, rather than provide smug, predictable answers that paper over or maintain the starkly unequal power relation between America's whites and its black and non-white others."[32] Lee has given us the tools we need, and he has asked the truly important question. How, then, might we try to answer it?

Always Do the Right Thing: Ethics and the Art of Virtue

*Theological &
Philosophical aspect*

When we consider "this question of do the right thing," Yolanda Pierce said, "It is, for those of us who do theology and religion, an ethical question. And so I've been marinating on what does it mean to do the right thing when the answer is messy and complicated and it is not black and white."[33] Our lives are shaped by our desire to do the right thing: What political party should I support? What charities are worth my resources? How should I be active in my community? Should I support abortion rights? The death penalty? What ditch should I ultimately be willing to die in—and why?

In my recent conversations with Rowan Williams, one of the finest theologians of our time, we talked often about the connections—and the differences—between what art and story try to do, and what theology or philosophy try to do. As a novelist, I feel called to ask hard questions, as Lee does in *Do the Right Thing*, but not necessarily to provide a tidy answer—that's not the task of art, to moralize—while as a theologian, I feel more asked to offer some provisional answers, some possible ways forward. As we talked in his study in Magdalene College, Cambridge, I expressed the thought that

Here [in story] is one of the ways it might be lived out in the form of a human life. And you can see what is successful about it and what is unsuccessful about it, and gauge your own response to it.

RW: So I think all that we've been saying is that the imaginative and the theological alike focus on that agenda. That both attempt for the writer to feel his or her way into a tangle of emotion, perception, narrative, and move through, and for the writer to say, "This matters" and there's more than one response to how it matters. The imaginative and the theological are both responses to how it matters and at what level it matters. But they're not divisible.[34]

Narrative is an essential way that we understand our lives and the lives around us. "What do you know about me?" Da Mayor asks the kids who are tormenting him. "What do you know about my life?" What do you know about my story? Unless you hear my story, how can you leap to judgments about whether I am right or wrong, good or evil, a hero or an old drunken bum? "Stories," the ethicist Stanley Hauerwas tells us, "are not substitute explanations we can someday hope to supplant with more straightforward accounts. Precisely to the contrary, narratives are necessary to our understanding of those aspects of our existence which admit of no further explanation—i.e., God, the world, and the self."[35] Because we live our lives through stories, we need them to know what we're supposed to do, how we're supposed to live, and in a world where racism is pervasive, stories about race and prejudice can be of real service.

Lee thus offers us the question "How do you do the right thing?" in a series of human stories and asks us to judge whether any of them comes close to answering the question in a form that makes sense to us. For that reason, I propose an exploration of the major characters of the film, asking how their actions can be read as a response to the film's central question, and interrogating these stories by asking how my wisdom tradition, Christianity, understands ethics. I agree with Hauerwas that maybe our question should be less about knowing the right thing to do in a given circumstance and more about how we become the kind of person who does the right thing without having to deliberate over it. Scott Bader-Saye writes, "When we learn an instrument, a sport, or a craft, we are often told that we need to practice. But unlike the popular saying 'practice makes perfect,' I was told 'practice makes permanent' . . . To practice is to engage in a repeated, structured activity that develops particularly skills, habits, and dispositions."[36] In *Batman Begins*, Batman (Christian Bale) says, "It's not who I am, but what I do that defines me." When we make a practice of doing the right thing, it becomes less necessary to agonize over what the right decision might be. But it is hard. In 2016 on BBC Radio, British theologian Linda Woodhead remarked that our first and easiest human instinct is not to put others first: "We are naturally tribal. We naturally want to protect our own little group and our own narrow interests. And we have to be schooled and socialized and educated into actually believing every human being counts for something, because it does not come naturally to us."[37]

Movement away from self-interest is hard. Of course we hope for a world in which we—and others—who have been doing the wrong thing might finally do the right thing. We do believe that people are capable of change, and we long for it, both in our lives and in those of others. The New Testament Greek word *metanoia*, often translated as "repentance," is at the heart of some of our most fundamental stories and may inform *Do the Right Thing*. But a habit of virtue—of always doing the right thing, as Da Mayor counsels Mookie in the early minutes of the movie—will perhaps serve us better over a lifetime.

Ed Guerrero argues that the three most reliant personas in the film are Mister Señor Love Daddy, Malcolm X, and Dr. King. While I appreciate what he's saying in terms of their moral authority, these are lives that offer obstacles to our easy appropriation of them.[38] First, Malcolm and Martin, are, well, martyrs, killed for their persistence in doing the right thing. While Dr. King is one of my greatest heroes, and I long to live a life of such sacrifice, I consistently fall short; Malcolm X's insistence on revising his faith and tolerance outward predictably led to his assassination. There is much I can learn from these stories, from these lives, as I can learn from the lives of Moses, or the Blessed Virgin Mary, or the Gautama Buddha, or Jesus of Nazareth, or Mother Teresa, or Archbishop Romero, but I cannot emulate them consistently, and although I argue here for a life of virtue, I like to think that this failure doesn't make me a bad person. More—like Eleanor Shellstrop on *The Good Place* (2016–20), maybe—a medium person, or, like the Apostle

Paul who, in his Letter to the Romans writes that he doesn't understand himself, since he knows what he ought to do and yet—like almost all of us—consistently falls short of doing it. "I do not do the good I want," he laments, "but the evil I do not want is what I do."[39]

Love Daddy, while he says all the right things and is an oracular voice, does not take part in the action of the story. He comments on it and corrects it, and when water from the firehoses ricochets off his studio window, he takes off his shirt and throws it in anger. But he is not a true character in this story; he is in some way above the events and choices of this film. His reactions to it can't be taken as a human story we enter into. This does not mean that we ignore his story. He issues the important calls to wake up and for tolerance, extols black pride and offers the roll call of black music that celebrates its seminal place in our culture, gratefully consumes food from Sal's Famous Pizzeria, and asks the hard questions on the morning after: "My people, my people, what can I say; say what I can. I saw it but didn't believe it; I didn't believe what I saw. Are we gonna live together? Together are we gonna live?" Like Lee himself, Love Daddy is here to offer us the central questions, but we are going to have to answer them for ourselves, and his slender story (we know nothing of his life, of his past) cannot answer them for us.

Another oracular figure is Smiley, present at the beginning, middle, and end of our story, a prophet for Dr. King and Malcolm X who frames their importance for us ("They're dead now, but we still have to fight the powers of apart-hate"), the person who finally integrates the Wall of Fame, and the person whose photograph closes the film before the final credits run. Does Smiley do the right thing? Well, demonstrably no. With Buggin' Out and Radio Raheem, he completes the unholy trinity that launches the violence. He is actually the one who lights Sal's on fire, and he responds to Pino, and to an anonymous voice asking Radio Raheem to turn down his damn music, with anger and threatened violence. None of Lee's characters can be easily pigeonholed as good or bad. At our screening of the film in New York City in 2019, Kelly Brown Douglas said, "I don't think there's any one character that you can say, 'That's the right thing,' because [Lee] presents it in a more complex way." Harris-Perry concurred: "It is not only complicated, but it is a requirement for us to push back against any notion that we can be a good character or that we are exclusively an evil character, because

Smiley ✓

Victim & perp.

perp.

we are not."[40] In a well-told story—as in real life—lives are complicated and contradictory. Smiley can be both a victim of prejudice and a source of it, can be threatened with violence and threaten back. That is our human nature, for better and for worse.

Barry Jenkins

Represented

When we turn to the morality of Buggin' Out, we can see that he has a point in asking for pictures of African Americans in the restaurant where he eats every day. As Barry Jenkins observed, if you do not see yourself represented (on a movie screen or on a Wall of Fame), it is as if you don't exist. But Sal's response to Buggin' Out is also sane and reasonable: This is my place. When you get your own place, you can put up whatever pictures you like. Bebe Coker, at the screening in Delaware said, ruefully, of Buggin' Out's "request," "He didn't even say please." But she went on to place Buggin' Out's demand in the context of "the conversation they're not having about photos on the wall." This is the essential thing that does not happen in the film, and too often in our lives. Catherine Meeks, who leads the Episcopal Church's racial healing efforts, says we have to ask "what is the conversation that you don't want to have, and have it."[41]

Buggin' Out

Buggin's Out's instant response to this exchange—boycott Sal's!—is derided by almost everyone else in the neighborhood. The three men on the wall laugh about how he'd be better served boycotting the barber that messed up his hair. Neighborhood girl Ella (Christa Rivers) joins her homeboys in saying she grew up on that food, that it's good, that in fact they're on their way to get a slice right now. Jade encourages him to do something positive for the neighborhood instead of whatever this is, and Mookie, admittedly speaking with his paycheck in mind, says he is making a mess for him. Buggin' Out is repeatedly presented as a comic figure, to be ridiculed rather than listened to, although his desire to be represented is an authentic desire.

Radio Raheem

Radio Raheem is another complicated figure, whose undeserved, violent, and shocking death may cause us to forget that in life he was an intimidating figure who rarely seems to have done the right thing. As we have seen from Lee's use of point-of-view shots and editing, Raheem looms over other figures in the neighborhood, a figure whose constant music is a symbolic way of towering over others. His soliloquy on love and hate is an important character piece—he has depths of feeling and thought that we do not see in the rest of the film, and his love for Mookie endears him to us—but in the rest of the film he seems barely articulate, preferring perhaps to let his music do the talking, and, as Bebe from Delaware recognized, he doesn't say "please." To Sal at Sal's Famous: "Put some extra mozzarella on that motherfucker and shit." To Sonny and his wife Kim (Ginny Yang) in their store:

RADIO RAHEEM: Give me 20 D Energizers.
SONNY: 20 C Energizers?
RADIO RAHEEM: Not C, D.
SONNY: C Energizers?
RADIO RAHEEM: D, motherfucker, D. Learn to speak English first, all right?
KIM: How many you say?
RADIO RAHEEM: 20, motherfucker, 20.

None of this, of course, constitutes a reason Raheem deserves to die. We should and, I hope, do react with outrage to his death at the hands of the police. But he is hardly a figure we look to when we're trying to do the right thing, unless we count the constant refrain coming from his radio: Fight the powers that be.

Mother Sister might be seen by some as a potent figure of good, for as she says at the beginning of the film, "Mother Sister always watches." She is a sort of mother goddess watching over the neighborhood, and there is much to admire about her, as well as things to condemn. She looks out for Mookie and has an affectionate relationship with Jade, but she denigrates and insults Da Mayor:

MOTHER SISTER: Hey, you old drunk, what did I tell you about drinking in front of my stoop? Move on; you're blocking my view. You are ugly enough; don't stare at me. The evil eye doesn't work on me.
DA MAYOR: Mother Sister, you've been talkin' about me for 18 years. What have I ever done to you?
MOTHER SISTER: You a drunk fool.
DA MAYOR: Besides that? Da Mayor don't bother nobody and nobody no bother da Mayor but you. The Man just tends to his own business. I love everybody. I even love you.
MOTHER SISTER: Hold your tongue, you don't have that much love.

Eventually Mother Sister relents from her often-expressed disdain for Da Mayor, but when Radio Raheem is killed, she shocks us and perhaps those around her with a sudden contrast to her matronly calm. When the mob surges into Sal's, she stands in the street screaming, "Burn it down!" Now, she is not shouting for the death of Sal and his boys. Although some people may have a hard time seeing the distinction, there is a drastic difference between violence directed at people and destruction of property. Harris-Perry observes: "As much as we tend to call property damage 'violence,' it's not. Mookie's point when he's standing there talking to Sal at the end is 'Dude, you have insurance.' When we think about how we define urban unrest, when there is property damage we call it a violent protest, but when kids at Duke [where Harris-Perry teaches] burn the whole damn place down [while celebrating an athletic victory] we actually don't call it violence. We say, 'Oh, they damaged the property.'"[42] White people especially tend to regard damage to property as violence, perhaps because they feel themselves more liable to be affected by this sort of action. But while Mother Sister sees herself as a protector of the neighborhood, she fails in respect to her treatment of Da Mayor, and ultimately she is unable to stop the violence. What she does, thankfully, is to show herself somewhat changed by it. At the end of the film, she takes care of Da Mayor, greets him civilly (as he had earlier predicted), and sees the virtue in surviving to try again another day.

In contrast to Pino, who is overtly racist, Sal seems reasonable, and during much of the film he displays tolerance and affection. He offers Da Mayor money to sweep the sidewalk—as apparently he does every day—and treats him with respect, deals patiently with Smiley's constant attempts to sell him postcards, and tries to explain to Pino why there is nothing shameful about being an Italian American pizzeria owner in a black neighborhood:

PINO: I'm sick of niggers. It's like I come to work, it's Planet of the Apes.
     I don't like being around them. They're animals.
SAL: Why you got so much anger in you?
PINO: Why? I'll tell you why. My friends, they laugh at me. They laugh right in my face. They tell me, "Go to Bed-Stuy. Go feed the moulies."

SAL: Do your friends put money in your pocket, Pino? Food on your table? They pay your rent, a roof over your head? They're not your friends. If they were your friends, they wouldn't laugh at you.

PINO: Pop, what can I say? I don't want to be here. They don't want us here. We should stay in our own neighborhood, stay in Bensonhurst, and the niggers should stay in theirs.

SAL: I never had no trouble with these people. I sat in this window. I watched these little kids get old. And I seen the old people get older. Yeah, sure, some of them don't like us, but most of them do. I mean, for Christ's sake, Pino, they grew up on my food. On my food. And I'm very proud of that. Oh, you may think it's funny, but I'm very proud of that. Look, what I'm trying to say, son, is, uh . . . Sal's Famous Pizzeria is here to stay. I'm sorry. I'm your father, and I love you, I'm sorry but . . . but that's the way it is.

Harris-Perry makes a strong case for Sal as a largely moral character, and at our screening in New York City, she spoke at length about his pride in feeding the neighborhood: "I see Sal doing a lot of the right thing. . . . There's this really interesting race/gender inversion where he says 'this community grew up on my food,' and of course we know it was white people who grew up on black women's food." But when Ella and the neighborhood kids affirm it, his statement feels true. "When she repeats it, we understand that it's not just Sal doing something performative."[43]

At the end of the long, hard, hot day, however, Sal (like Mother Sister, and more meaningfully) snaps. He attacks Radio Raheem's boombox (symbolically assaulting him, since his music is so much a part of his identity) after shouting a series of racist taunts (in response, admittedly, to Buggin' Out's "Fuck you! We're closing you guinea bastards for good! For good, motherfucker! Until you get some black people on that motherfucking Wall of Fame!"). If during most of the film we have seen Sal's best self, the self with a habit of acting with virtue, now we see his worst self, and in some ways, it discounts, even destroys, the memory of what he has said and done before. (If, at the end of his life, Dr. King had said, like *South Park*'s Cartman, "Screw y'all, I'm out of here," we would remember his selfish desertion, not his selflessness in Selma and the Birmingham jail.) If our habit of virtue deserts us when we need it most, what good is it? If fear or anger gets the better of us (as it often does), how can we do the right thing?

We live in a world where we are constantly battered by anger and anxiety. Scott Bader-Saye remarks that, in the work of ethicist H. Richard Niebuhr, before we ask "What is right?" or "What is good?" we are told to ask "What is going on?" Our answer to that question will shape our answers to the other more existential questions. If we answer from a place of anxiety, then self-preservation will become our first mandate.[44] "In a culture of fear," says Bader-Saye, "the short answer to 'What is going on?' is 'We are at risk' or 'We are in danger.' Insofar as we accept that as our dominant description of the world, our lives will be shaped by that drive for self-preservation of which Niebuhr speaks. Our moral vision becomes tunnel vision. Fear becomes the ambient background to our lives rather than a proper and targeted response to a concrete and passing threat."[45] Simply put, anger and fear have a tendency to deform us ethically.

One could argue that in the lives of these characters, fear is not just a passing threat. I am willing to have that conversation, for certainly I have not known the systemic outrages most of these characters face. I recognize that in many ways I have been ridiculously privileged. But if we say that their lives are inevitably tinged by fear and anxiety, by the feelings that their lives are out of their control no matter what they might accomplish, then it means that doing the right thing, let alone living with virtue, is constantly challenged by fear of extinction. If you reflect on your own life and recall times when you have been angry or terrified, you know the truth of this: It is harder to make good decisions when you feel frightened or threatened. While I lament Sal's decision to preemptively attack, I cannot condemn it. I understand it.

During the making of *Do the Right Thing*, Danny Aiello and Spike Lee constantly argued about whether Sal is a racist. Lee said yes, undoubtedly; Aiello flatly rejected that. Certainly, Sal is a character who has a tragic shape to his story, for when the crisis came, he failed the people he had faithfully served for so long, and he failed his best self. He knows it, I think. His response to the crowd's promised violence is "Do what you gotta do"; there is something beautiful about his acceptance. I also recall an African American woman who pulled me aside after our screening at the National Cathedral and said, "There is

[margin note: fear of extinction]

[margin note: Sal fails himself]

another American family whose hearts were broken in this film," and, truly, to watch the camera pan across Sal's heartbroken face at the end of the movie when his store burns is to forgive much. This man who murdered Radio Raheem's radio loves this neighborhood and feels betrayed by it, forgives Mookie his many offenses and says he thinks of him as a son, and can't understand why his adoptive son (admittedly also an employee) would throw a garbage can through the window of his business. *Their* business.

At the end of the film, has Sal learned anything? He seems sunk in his suffering, mourning for the store that he built with his own two hands, although when Mookie tells him the store doesn't matter, that Radio Raheem was murdered, he responds that he knows: "I was there." He might rightfully turn Mookie and his demand for his wages away, but although he literally throws the money at him, Sal offers Mookie more than he owes him and refuses to pick it up when Mookie leaves it lying on the ground. After broaching the weather as a conversational gambit, he asks Mookie a question betraying some concern: What are you gonna do with yourself? Sal isn't perfect, but in a world full of flawed characters, he does the right thing more often than not, and that is something we should remember.

Mookie too is imperfect, too imperfect to be our exemplary figure. Lee has said that he is constantly asked if Mookie did the right thing at the end of the film. In the movie *Southside with You* (2016), on their first date Barack Obama (Parker Sawyers) and Michelle Robinson (Tika Sumpter), the future Mrs. Obama, see *Do the Right Thing*. After the film, they encounter one of Michelle's white law partners, who asks Barack if he knows why Mookie did what he did. Obama argues with some facility that Mookie did the right thing, directing the violence away from Sal and his family and toward the business. Harris-Perry agrees:

> I've always read that moment as him moving away from physical violence and toward property damage.... In that moment when Sal says "Do what you have to do," he's preparing for a physical fight.... And instead Mookie gets the trash can and says, "We're going to fight the store" ... So much better to fight property than to fight the people. I see that as undoubtedly the right thing in that moment, but my

God! Mookie does 800 terrible things before that, so you can't like him for doing that.[46]

That is our problem with Mookie, because, truly, he has done eight hundred terrible things before breakfast. As Lee has written and played him, he is a likeable layabout whose primary drive from the beginning of the film to the end is to get paid. He shirks his responsibility to his son and his partner, he capitalizes on the kindness of his sister, he takes advantage of his boss (he is known for his two-hour lunch breaks and slow deliveries, and, in the course of the film, breaks to take a shower and to deliver a pizza to Tina and fool around), and he looks angrily on Sal's kindness to Jade, framing it as an attempt to have sex with her.

Still, not to minimize Mookie's many offenses and his pattern of lazy self-service, if we watch carefully as Mookie, Sal, Pino, and Vito stand in front of the angry crowd, we can see that Mookie seems to make a conscious decision. In that moment, he knows what to do, and he does it. He walks away from his employer, crosses the street, takes the garbage out of a can, picks up the can, crosses the street again, and, getting a running start, shouts, "Hate!" and heaves the can through the pizzeria window. It does seem to be the right choice; Sal and his sons survive the evening, and, as Mookie points out, Sal does have insurance. And yet white audiences for thirty years have misunderstood or condemned Mookie for his action. Why does he scream, "Hate?" Is it for the fallen Radio Raheem, who told the story of Love and Hate? Or is it Mookie's acknowledgment that there is no loving way out of this dilemma? In any case, the end of the movie—the possibility of some sort of connection between Sal and Mookie, reflective of the fact that, as Love Daddy says, we are going to have to somehow live together—isn't possible without Mookie's action. Without him, many people in the neighborhood would wake up with more on their consciences than looting and property damage. James Baldwin told Studs Terkel, "It is easy for an African to hate the invader and drive him out of Africa, but it is very difficult for an American Negro to do this. He obviously can't do this to white people; there's no place to drive them. This is a country that belongs equally to us both. One has got to live together here or else there won't be any country."[47] We have to find some way to relate to each other, some way to talk to each other, even in the ashes. Or there will be no us.

It is, I believe, true that, as Bader-Saye argues, "Courage is the capacity to do what is right and good in the face of fear," that this is the core of moral virtue. It is for this reason that I believe Da Mayor may be the essential character for us to consider in terms of proper decisions and an ethical life.[48] (I also continue to think about Jade, who, while a minor character, behaves kindly and ethically throughout the film; to paraphrase Pontius Pilate, I can find no fault in her.) But Da Mayor is a major character who demonstrates a pattern of virtue throughout the film, and his reactions in times of fear, anxiety, and anger seem to be worth our attention. Richard Harries, past Bishop of Oxford, writes that if we have practiced truth-telling and courage, we are much more likely to behave with truth-telling and courage as a matter of course.[49] Like the other major characters in this film, of course, Da Mayor is flawed. He is a drunk who asks a young boy to fetch beer for him, even if he pays him, and his addiction has made it impossible for him to care for his family. So yes, Mother Sister is right, existentially he can be defined as a drunk fool. But Da Mayor is a drunk fool who asks the right questions and gives us useful answers.

Early in the film, Da Mayor hails Mookie, who responds with barely veiled impatience:

DA MAYOR: Doctor . . .
MOOKIE: C'mon, what. What?
DA MAYOR: Always do the right thing.
MOOKIE: That's it?
DA MAYOR: That's it.
MOOKIE: I got it, I'm gone.

Mookie most assuredly does not always do the right thing, even if on one occasion he does. The habit of virtue—the practice, if you will, that makes permanent—is worth extolling, and Da Mayor responds to stress, fear, and threat with consistency, doing the right thing, resisting the wrong thing. When Eddie (Richard Habersham) runs after the ice cream truck and almost gets run over, Da Mayor runs into the street and throws him out of the car's way. He admits that he was as terrified as Eddie; if he'd thought about it, he probably wouldn't have done it. This is the important thing, however: Da Mayor automatically does the right thing, without thinking about it.

When the neighborhood teenagers ridicule him, call him a pathetic drunk, ask how he can dare to call himself Da Mayor, he is naturally upset, but he doesn't attack them, physically or verbally. He tells them simply that they don't know anything about life yet, and they certainly don't know anything about his life. "How could these children know anything?" is the question Bebe asked in Delaware after we watched the film together. "You don't know yourself," she said. "You don't know how to value yourself, because you're not in the history books." And because, Da Mayor might say, *we're* not in the history books. It's a sad response, because if they don't know about his life, and although they think they know better, they might be condemned to repeat it.

When the kids use water spraying from the hydrant to soak a self-important white driver in a convertible, the driver demands justice. He informs the two police officers who arrive at the scene (as ever, Officer Long and his partner Officer Ponte [Miguel Sandoval]) that he wants the perpetrators arrested. Can he describe the kids? Yes, they were black. Then he has a thought. That guy, he says, pointing at Da Mayor, he saw the whole thing. But when the police ask, Da Mayor answers enigmatically: "Doctor, those that'll tell don't know, and those that know won't tell." What the boys have done is a minor sin, he knows, and certainly not one that merits arrest. Once a kid gets in that system, it could destroy his whole life. And so, in oracular fashion, he declines to answer a police officer's direct question.

At the movie's climax, when the police have fled with Radio Raheem's body, the angry crowd edges toward Sal and his sons, and Sal tells them, "Do what you gotta do," Da Mayor interposes himself, calls his neighbors good people, and asks them to think about what they're about to do. Because Sal and the boys did not cause Radio Raheem's death, their revenge will be particularly pointless; they will be no better and quite possibly worse than the police who killed Raheem, because they should know better. While they don't listen—only Mookie's inter-vention saves Sal—Da Mayor instantly and instinctively steps between angry people and their intended victims.

Finally, when the store is burning and people are running and Mother Sister is screaming "No" in the middle of the chaos, he goes to her. Despite her past snubs, he holds her close and pulls her off the street to safety, presumably back to her brownstone. That's where they speak the next morning:

MOTHER SISTER: Good morning.
DA MAYOR: Is it a good morning?
MOTHER SISTER: Yes, indeed. You almost got yourself killed last night.
DA MAYOR: I've done that before. Where did you sleep?
MOTHER SISTER: I didn't.
DA MAYOR: Hope the block is still standing.
MOTHER SISTER: We're still standing.

The question then really becomes, out of our brokenness, could we do any of these right things Da Mayor does? Could we call for what's right? Could we risk our lives for each other? Could we refuse to be a part of institutional injustice? Could we act in such a way that we inch our neighbors and ourselves even a tiny bit closer to Beloved Community? If courage is the capacity to do what is right and good in the face of fear, could we, in the constant refrain of Catherine Meeks, become just a half a shade braver?

If all of us are imperfect and naturally selfish, if all of us have a group, a people, a person we hold in contempt, then the example of Da Mayor is an important one for us. Inevitably we will be tested; we will crash into others, including the ones we hold in low esteem. When we do, how will we treat them? Will our best self or our worst self show up? Will we do the right thing?

6

Crashing into Each Other

Crash as Multicultural Post-9/11 Fable

Worst Best Film? Or Essential Parable?

The headlines and news stories from the 2019 Academy Awards bore a remarkable consistency. They often lauded the diversity of the awards—three of four actors winning were people of color, African American women won for costumes and production design, and Spike Lee was one of the winners of best adapted screenplay. But the winner for Best Picture, while a popular choice among audiences, was panned by many writers. Amanda Hess wrote in the *New York Times* about "The Biggest Step Backward (for Best Picture)"; David Sims's byline in *The Atlantic* appeared over the headline "The Oscars Thwarted Its Bid for Relevance by Crowning *Green Book*"; and Justin Chang's headline in the *Los Angeles Times* said in bold letters what others also said in their stories: "Oscars 2019: 'Green Book' is the worst best picture winner since 'Crash.'" Like *Driving Miss Daisy*—which was named Best Picture in the year that *Do the Right Thing* appeared and was not even nominated— these writers and many others took the Academy to task for making what they saw as a safe choice, a crowd-pleasing choice. Brookes Barnes writes that the 2019 award went to "a segregation-era buddy film. While admired by many as a feel-good depiction of people uniting against the odds, the movie was criticized by others as a simplistic take on race relations, both woefully retrograde and borderline bigoted."[1] While I will argue that *Crash* is hardly a safe or crowd-pleasing film, much less a simplistic take on race relations, it finds itself in the company of *Driving Miss Daisy* and *Green Book* in the eyes of some.

Crash, co-written by Paul Haggis and Bobby Moresco and directed by Haggis, appeared in 2005, and it has always been a polarizing film. Some few critics at the time thought it ridiculous, overwrought, overwritten. A multi-plot, multi-character film demands a reservoir of audience disbelief; how is it that these same people keep running into each other? Aren't there millions of people in Los Angeles? Its win for Best Picture over *Brokeback Mountain* was as offensive to many in 2006 as the selection of *Green Book* in 2019; the Academy had a chance to take an important stand on gay rights, many felt, and didn't, and some remain angry. When I crowdsourced on social media, several respondents told me that now—fifteen years later—they have not forgiven *Crash* for taking the prize that should have gone to *Brokeback Mountain*. One admitted she had never seen it—and didn't want to. But after the Oscars, it became especially fashionable to bash *Crash*. Scott Foundas was one of several critics calling it the worst movie of the year; Ta-Nehisi Coates, writing in *The Atlantic* in 2009, called it the worst movie of the decade.

However, many prominent critics admired *Crash*, and their praise revolved around consistent elements: the premise, the writing, the acting, and the movie's jarring relevance. Lisa Schwarzbaum's summary in *Entertainment Weekly* sets the tone: "A stunning, must-see drama about the collision of cultures—proving that words have not lost the ability to shock in our anesthetized society. Nobody gets by in this tough, at times unexpectedly funny movie without getting dented."[2] Ella Taylor, writing in *LA Weekly*, called it "not just one of the best Hollywood movies about race, but, along with *Collateral*, one of the finest portrayals of contemporary Los Angeles life period."[3] *Rolling Stone*'s review by Peter Travers (who gave the movie three and a half of four stars) found the film "alive with bracing human drama and blistering wit . . . In the style of *Magnolia*, Haggis and co-writer Bobby Moresco weave many stories (too many) into the narrative. But the rage sticks, as do the emotions underlying it . . . Despite its preachy moments, the film is a knockout. In a multiplex starved for ambition, why kick a film with an excess of it?"[4] The African-American Film Critics Association named it Film of the Year, and praised it as "a bridge towards tolerance."[5] The movie owns a 74% positive rating on the aggregate site Rotten Tomatoes, a strong showing for a film derided by some critics, and 7.8 of 10 rating by users of the Internet Movie Data Base. Time has largely swung perceptions in favor of the film.

None of these positive reviews, by the way, describes *Crash* as a feel-good movie, or a movie with a simplistic resolution, as its putative stablemates *Green Book* and *Driving Miss Daisy* are said to be. Almost all of its stories are left open and unresolved, although there has been some movement in every character's life, whether positive or negative. Some characters have done a good thing after a series of setbacks; some will be haunted forever by the things they have done or did not do. Also importantly, reviewers rarely mention 9/11 in discussing the film—one set of characters is Persian, and they are mistaken for Arabs, the father and store owner insulted as "Osama." But one of the reasons I believe the film works is that it offers us, in response to the fear and anguish of the 9/11 and 7/7 terror attacks, the reminder that for all our differences, all our bigotry, all our fear, we are all still more alike than we are different. The Persian shopkeeper, the Hispanic locksmith, the suburban housewife we meet in the film may live very different lives, but their desires are surprisingly similar: respect, security for themselves and their families, and some sense that the world makes some sort of sense.

Roger Ebert was perhaps the greatest champion of the film, giving it four stars in his initial review, later naming it his film of the year, and defending it against the offended lovers of *Brokeback Mountain* and others who thought it contrived and false. I particularly admired two things about Ebert as film critic. First, he had the gift of seeing the film on the screen, not the film he wanted to see, and several times in my filmgoing life, baffled, I went to him to teach me how to watch a particular film. Ebert's insight about *Crash* here is stunning: he thought of the film as parabolic, inviting us to watch not through the lens of realism, but suspending our disbelief that such encounters could not happen so we might learn from it: "The movie is constructed as a series of parables, in which the characters meet and meet again; the movie shows them both sinned against, and sinning."[6] The writer and editor Phyllis Tickle, of blessed memory, used to tell a story about a post-speaking encounter she had with a young woman who wanted to know if these stories about Jesus were actually true. "If they didn't happen," the young lady concluded, "they *should* have happened." Suspend your disbelief, Ebert tells us. Imagine that—as in a Dickens novel—these particular characters have to crash into each other over and over again, for their own good, and for ours.

The second thing I loved about Ebert was his facility in appreciating the spiritual elements of a film. He wrote with real insight about the dual natures of Christ in his review of *The Last Temptation of Christ* (1988) and helped me understand that *The Tree of Life* (2011) could not be understood as a narrative film; it was an act of worship. I know nothing about Ebert's own personal faith, if any, but more than any other film writer, he understood that great stories—great films— are about who we are, where we come from, and where we're going. They're about that possibility of metanoia, both for the characters in the film and for the audience watching, and he loved *Crash* partly because he believed it might make a difference in the lives of those who saw it. "Not many films," he said, in his initial review, "have the possibility of making their audiences better people. I don't expect 'Crash' to work any miracles, but I believe anyone seeing it is likely to be moved to have a little more sympathy for people not like themselves. The movie contains hurt, coldness and cruelty, but is it without hope? Not at all. Stand back and consider. All of these people, superficially so different, share the city and learn that they share similar fears and hopes."[7] It is the gift we also find in *Do the Right Thing*, the hard truth that we respond to certain people as stereotypes, and only encounter can help us know them better. But we can know them better, can learn their stories, can see our shared humanity, which was sometimes a challenge in those years just after 9/11, years when many Americans were willing to countenance preemptive attacks and extreme interrogation if they might make us feel a little safer. After all, it wasn't people like us who were being bombed or tortured. Ella Taylor noted that "Haggis has claimed that *Crash* is less about race than about the frayed nerves and mistrust that shape our public encounters in the wake of the 9/11 disaster," and while the film is certainly about race and prejudice, it also deals with the fear and distrust that was endemic to that era.[8]

Sandra Bullock's Jean complains that she is angry all the time. Why is she so angry? It's not because her maid Maria is late coming home from the store, or because the gardener keeps overwatering the lawn, although these are the things she cites. Anger is a response to fear—the fear of black men she tries to suppress on the night their car is stolen, the fear of another potential robbery she attributes to the Hispanic "gangbanger" (Michael Peña) who replaces their locks, and that loss of security that many of us felt after 9/11. The world seemed less safe, violence less distant. It is a free-floating anxiety that afflicts Jean all the time, the reason that she wakes every morning filled with anger. I dislike her character for her casual racism, but I understand her fear, and like all the characters in the film, as we will see, she is more complicated than she first appears, has more capacity for change and growth than her white privilege first suggests.

I have taught *Crash* for fifteen years, always offering Ebert's praise and critical insight to offer context, and when oriented to watch the film as he suggests, students and audiences have consistently discovered its lessons. Jean and her fellow characters are complicated human beings, more than just the prejudice they manifest. The people who have watched *Crash* with me have laughed and cried and gasped; when considered on its own terms, it is a phenomenally powerful and moving film, and the conversations about race, privilege, and our common humanity I've then had with students, parishioners, pastors, and priests have been stirring every single time.

Crash is more than just a powerful film; it is also momentous for social reasons. In its casual multiculturalism, it represents another phase of Hollywood filmmaking. Gone are the racist stereotypes and racial absences of early Hollywood, gone the thought that a well-drawn minor character or even a major role starring a person of color makes a film racially conscious. Haggis and Moresco are both white, and we have properly extolled the importance of writers, directors, and actors of color appearing in their own stories, but *Crash* is a film in which all the characters are well written and complex, and the rainbow hues represent not only modern-day Los Angeles but our own culture. Don Cheadle, who plays Graham, the central character in the film, served as a producer and may have had some influence on casting, but however it came about, the movie answers our 9/11 fears about the Other by inviting greater diversity, not by limiting it.

In this, *Crash* was a precursor of the multiracial casting in such franchises as *The Avengers*, *Guardians of the Galaxy*, and *Star Wars*, and perhaps even of the casting of people of color in dramatic roles where they would not have been previously considered (*Hamilton*, for example, or the casting of a person of color as Hermione Granger in *Harry Potter and the Cursed Child*). *Crash* does not make a big deal of its diversity; it simply accepts that this is what the world looks like, how it works, and that its story cannot be told with a monolithic cast. Why shouldn't a movie be about a Persian shopkeeper, a Hispanic locksmith, an African American detective, and a pampered white housewife? All of us are in some way implicated in personal prejudice, and all of us are necessary to properly tell the story of how we might recover from it.

Recover from prejudice

Racism and Reversal

In the "RACIAL SLUR MONTAGE" of *Do the Right Thing*, Spike Lee acknowledged the prejudice that all of us harbor for some other group of people, and race is the central prejudice that has always defined our American lives. Jim Wallis has called racism "America's original sin," and this problem resonates with people of every tradition and every background, with people of color who have been marginalized, with Anglos who see a day coming in which they are no longer Masters of the Universe, and with all people of good will who want to live in a world in which, as Dr. Martin Luther King, Jr. said, the content of our character rather than the color of our skin defines us.[9] By employing racial prejudice as its central organizing factor, *Crash* shows us a world—our world—in which everyone has a bias of some sort that emerges spontaneously in the emotionally charged collisions of our day-to-day lives. But the movie does more than simply note that we have a problem and move on. Like *Do the Right Thing*, by showing us people wrestling with this problem at the heart of American life and, mostly, resolving that they want to do better, to be better, *Crash* reveals itself, as Ebert argued, as a deeply ethical and spiritual film.

Some years ago, I had the experience of doing archival research into screenwriter Ernest Lehman's work with Alfred Hitchcock. In their conversations, and in many of Hitchcock's public pronouncements about film, the two men displayed a concern for involving the audience in the story directly, for putting them into scenes and making them experience the story alongside the characters. While the subject matter of *Crash* is dramatic enough, what we discover as we enter into the viewing experience is that, as in Hitchcock's films, we are doing more than simply watching a movie; we are ourselves being implicated in the prejudice it explores. *Austin Chronicle* critic Steve Davis, who picked *Crash* as his film of the year, argues that the film "invites you to make comfortable judgments about its myriad characters based on [your] first impressions and to pigeonhole them in uncomplicated, black-and-white terms."[10] In other words, the first appearances of characters in the film invite us to establish our own prejudices about them, to see and judge them first through our imperfect knowledge of them and, later, through the more complicated human reality. First appearances rarely give us all we need to know.

[margin note: First appearance]

While Ebert did not speak about the participatory element of the film, our own involvement in making snap judgments, he recognized that the film's characters do so:

> One thing that happens, again and again, is that people's assumptions prevent them from seeing the actual person standing before them. An Iranian (Shaun Toub) is thought to be an Arab, although Iranians are Persian. Both the Iranian and the white wife of the district attorney (Sandra Bullock) believe a Mexican-American locksmith (Michael Pena) is a gang member and a crook, but he is a family man.
>
> A black cop (Don Cheadle) is having an affair with his Latina partner (Jennifer Esposito), but never gets it straight which country she's from. A cop (Matt Dillon) thinks a light-skinned black woman (Thandie Newton) is white. When a white producer tells a black TV director (Terrence Dashon Howard) that a black character "doesn't sound black enough," it never occurs to him that the director doesn't "sound black," either. For that matter, neither do two young black men (Larenz Tate and Ludacris), who dress and act like college students, but have a surprise for us.[11]

Indeed, the movie begins with Peter (Tate) and Anthony (Ludacris) and immediately ropes us into the stereotypes and suppositions about which Steve Davis spoke. The two young men, black, smart, self-aware, funny, are talking about the terrible dining experience they have just had in a restaurant filled with white patrons. Anthony was not offered coffee, although their black waitress was pouring coffee for everyone around them. Peter reminds him, "We didn't get any coffee that you didn't want and I didn't order, and this is evidence of racial discrimination?"

We're immediately attached to these young men, incensed, even by the way society thinks of them, and then, as they're walking down the sidewalk, they see ahead Jean (Bullock), and her husband Rick (Brendan Fraser, rather improbably the district attorney of Los Angeles), and he remarks on her reaction to seeing them:

ANTHONY: Look around! You couldn't find a whiter, safer or better lit part of this city. But this white woman sees two black guys who look like UCLA students, strolling down the sidewalk and her re- action is blind fear. I mean, look at us! Are we dressed like gang- bangers? Huh? No. Do we look threatening? No. Fact, if anybody should be scared around here, it's us: We're the only two black faces surrounded by a sea of over-caffeinated white people, patrolled by the trigger-happy LAPD. So you tell me, why aren't we scared?

PETER: Because we have guns?

ANTHONY: You could be right.

And bang, the first of the many reversals that Haggis and Moreno will spring on us; we thought one thing, and we were wrong—or at least, not in command of all the information. These smart and thoughtful black men carjack the DA and his wife, stealing their black Lincoln Navigator and setting in motion a series of events that will shock us and rock us in the course of the next two hours. Haggis spoke about this as his intention, and of the construction of the film literally being from one collision to the next, one reversal to the next:

"Crash" was very different because one set of characters literally led you to the next. You followed a character until he or she bumped into someone else and then you followed that person. That was the con- struct, it was à la ronde. I was initially going to show you stereotypes and I was going to reinforce them until you believed them. We all secretly think things like that, and as soon as I reinforced them and you felt comfortable enough to laugh in the dark of the theater, then

I could turn you around in your seat. I've been accused of writing stereotypes, but in that case, that was my intention.[12]

Anthony and Peter are a throughline, beginning the flashback after Graham discovers the body that will turn out to be that of his brother, Peter. Anthony is presented during the course of the story as self-aware about race as it relates to black lives but completely prejudiced toward Asians. When he runs over a "Chinaman," he is all for driving off dragging him underneath, but Peter insists that if they do, he will die. He is also shown to be all about himself, but during the course of the film he changes. After asserting that he would never do crimes against black people, he and Peter accidentally carjack the black Lincoln Navigator owned by Cameron (Terence Howard), and at the end of a scene we will discuss in more detail on Cameron's storyline, Cameron turns to him and calls him out: "Look at me. You embarrass me. You embarrass yourself."

Sometimes we come face to face with what we have become, and what we see in the mirror does embarrass us. While it seems like a stretch that Anthony could change, at the end of the film when he tries to sell the van owned by the "Chinaman" he ran over, he and the chop shop operator discover it to be full of Thai slaves. The operator offers him a substantial sum of money for them, and we cut away without knowing what he will do. We certainly expect, based on his mercenary behavior and his prejudice, that he will take the big money. But at movie's end, Anthony pulls up in the white van and releases the Thai captives in Chinatown, gives them money for "chop suey," and calls them, with perhaps a hint of new affection, "Stupid fucking Chinamen." Yes, this is a racist insult. But instead of selling them back into slavery, he has freed them, and his face, with a sideways smile, recognizes that he can hardly believe he is doing this. It is one of the success stories in *Crash*, one of the most positive outcomes we observe in any of the storylines.

Not all the stories have such optimistic endings. Ryan Phillippe plays Officer Hanson, a young LAPD officer, and in the wake of the DA's carjacking he and his partner Officer Ryan (Matt Dillon) pull over a vehicle matching the description—but with a different license plate. Ryan has pulled them over because he has seen the light-skinned woman in the passenger seat (Christine, played by Thandie Newton) performing oral sex on the black man driving (her husband Cameron). After he pulls them over, Ryan "frisks" Christine, sexually assaulting her in front of her husband and in front of the disbelieving eyes of his partner.

This scene by itself is so rich that it deserves closer attention. How many times have we stood by silent when we should have acted? During his imprisonment in Birmingham, Dr. King wrote, "We will have to repent in this generation not merely for the vitriolic words and actions of the bad people, but for the appalling silence of the good people. We must see that human progress never rolls in on wheels of inevitability. It comes through the tireless efforts and persistent work of men willing to be co-workers with God."[13] Hanson stands by when he could have stepped in; Cameron and Christine are completely at the mercy of Officer Ryan, and his racist assault, as we will see, has seismic consequences.

Unable to accept what he witnessed but did not stop, Hanson asks his supervisor to transfer him to another car, and he accepts a humiliating compromise to get away from Ryan—and perhaps from his complicity in Ryan's act. Ryan then confronts him in the parking lot with a hard truth: "You think you know who you are? You have no idea." It is brilliant foreshadowing, although we, as the audience, are totally on board with Hanson, and in opposition to the racist Ryan. That day, Hanson responds to a call where Cameron has been observed brawling in the street with Anthony, who tried to take his car, and when he arrives, Cameron is taunting the officers who, weapons drawn, are ready to shoot him. Shattered by what Ryan has done to him and Christine, Cameron is prepared to prove his bravery in the only way he can—suicide by cop—and Hanson, who immediately understands what he is doing, steps in the middle, putting his own life on the line:

OFFICER HANSON: I know this man.

CAMERON: You don't fucking know me!

OFFICER HANSON: You see what's happening here? Do you want to die here? Is that what you want? Because these guys are going to shoot you and the way you're acting, they'll be completely fucking justified.

CAMERON: Fuck you.

OFFICER HANSON: Fuck me? I'm not the one who's fucked here. You're the one who's fucked here, because it's not going to be my head blown off and onto that man's patio.

CAMERON: What do you want from me?

OFFICER HANSON: Unless you think your wife is going to be better off with a husband who has a bloody stump for a head, I want you to sit down on the curb and put your hands on your head and do nothing until I speak with these officers.

CAMERON: I'm not sitting on the curb and putting my hands on my head for nobody.

OFFICER HANSON: Then stand where you are and keep your hands in plain sight. Can you do that?

CAMERON: I can do that.

OFFICER HANSON: I told this man to stand where he is and keep his hands in plain sight.

OFFICER HILL (BILLY GALLO): This man better be related to you by blood, because this is fucking nuts.

OFFICER HANSON: I need this favor. You can check the guy's license, he's got no priors, no warrants. I need to let him go with a warning.

It does not change what he stood by and watched the night before, but it is clearly atonement for it, and we continue to think of Hanson as a good cop, a good human being who might have done more but is trying to make up for it. And that is the place we are in when he picks up Peter, trying to hitchhike home on a cold night. In the conversation that follows, they misunderstand each other. Hanson, instead of accepting that Peter actually likes hockey and has developed an appreciation for country music, thinks he is mocking him, and when Peter reaches into his jacket, Hanson reacts in fear, shooting him as Peter pulls out not a gun, but the statue of St. Christopher we have seen earlier in the film. Hanson dumps Peter's body on the side of the road, where it will be found by the police, and investigated by Graham. He then abandons his car, sets it afire, and walks into the night, surely forever haunted by what he—one of the "good guys"—has done.

Perhaps the central storyline of the film, foregrounded in previews and the film's one-sheet poster, is that of Officer Ryan. When we first meet him, he is calling someone at his father's HMO, and when he discovers that she will not help him solve his father's health problem and that she is African American, he insults her and she hangs up on him. Immediately after this, he pulls over Cameron and Christine, assaulting her and shaming him. Rape and sexual violation are rarely sexual crimes; they typically grow out of anger, hatred, and the desire to humiliate and hurt. Before he and his partner clocked in, Officer Ryan had been trying to find help for his father, who is in agony, and he is left furious and without a solution. So his desire to humiliate this black couple—and especially this mouthy black woman—grows out of his own recent experience.

It's part of *Crash*'s strategy to show that people are always more complicated than the simple stereotypes we try to assign them. While Officer Ryan's treatment of Cameron and Christine is beyond the pale, his character is not so easy to type as he first appears. *New Yorker* film critic David Denby writes that "as we later find out, a racist can also be a good son and a good cop."[14] This is the startling and hopeful power of *Crash*; people behave at their worst and people behave at their best, and it becomes abundantly clear by watching them which it is we should choose.

After confronting Hanson in the parking lot, Ryan and his new partner drive off to work, and, encountering a line of stopped cars, they discover a serious accident, one car overturned and another car on fire. In what has become the signature scene of the film, Ryan runs head-long up the hill to rescue the motorist stranded in the overturned SUV. He gets there and finds a woman still inside (Christina, although Ryan doesn't yet know this). He—and we—see gasoline dripping steadily from the SUV's tank, but despite the danger, Officer Ryan crawls in to try and pull her out.

It's already a dramatic reversal; by this point, we have reached our conclusions about Ryan as person and police officer, and now we find him putting his life on the line. As he crawls in, as they come face to face, Ryan and Christine recognize each other, and it's hard to say who is more affected. Ryan is seeing the reminder of a degrading act he committed that he now cannot put away from him; Christine is looking at an officer of the law who violated her body and her dignity, who drove a wedge between her and her husband. She screams at him not to touch her. It's clear at that moment that she would rather die than be rescued by him.

Maybe Ryan sees that she'd rather die than be touched by him again; maybe down deep he isn't such a terrible person after all; or maybe something happens to him, something like that transformation we've been calling metanoia, something that makes him want to be a better human being.

Ryan has just told his former partner Officer Hanson, "Wait 'til you've been on the job a few more years . . . Wait 'til you've been doing it a little longer. You think you know who you are? You have no idea." It is sage but depressing advice from the jaded but streetwise cop to the idealistic rookie. Desson Thompson writes that "if 'Crash' only showed the dark side of humanity, it would barely be worth the viewing. The movie has its funny moments, its terrifying moments, its tragedies, moments of inspiration and depressing ugliness. It's about the worst in people but also the best. As soon as we think we have some character's number they turn around and do something quite astonishing. We're all so hopelessly human."[15]

And now, confronted with the horrible reality of another human being in danger—not to mention the fact it is a human being he has badly wronged—Officer Ryan is his best self. He could leave Christine to die; his offenses would burn away with her. But maybe he, too, is discovering who he is.

Christine screams at him to get away, and he tries to calm her, telling her that he's not going to hurt her. "I'm not going to touch you," he tells her. "But there's nobody else here yet, and that's gasoline there. We've got to get you out of here."

Gently—with surprising and genuine respect given the way he previously violated her—he asks if he can reach across her lap to try and undo the seat belt. He pulls her skirt down to cover her exposed thigh. She asks if he's going to save her, and he vows to her that he will, but her seatbelt is jammed. The flaming car down the hill ignites the pool of gasoline, and the SUV catches on fire. But Ryan doesn't abandon Christine. When his partner and a bystander pull him out of the car to try and save his life, Ryan crawls back into the burning SUV, and he manages to tug Christine free just before the tank blows.

What follows may be the most important moment in the film, and Haggis emphasizes it by going to slow motion. As Christina is helped away by the paramedics, she turns back for a moment to look at Ryan, and she shakes her head. *How could you?* is what she seems to be saying. How could the man who assaulted her also be the man who saved her?

And as the camera holds on Ryan, he seems to be thinking the same thing: *Who am I? What have I done? What have I become?*

As we saw with *Do the Right Thing*, the fact that Mookie may have done the right thing in a moment of crisis does not erase the multitude of his earlier sins, but it does offer us hope. As Stephen Hunter notes, "The story goes on, and suddenly this hated icon of today's culture, the brutal, racist cop, finds himself in a truly desperate emergency, and risks everything, including his own terrible death by fire, to save an African American motorist from sure death in an auto crash. So you're left with the conundrum: Which is the real Officer Ryan? Which leads to the next logical question: Which one is the real you and which one is the real me?"[16] If Officer Ryan, a certifiable racist, can reach across the racial divide, can try to mitigate past offenses, then what else might be possible?

Negative criticism of the film often centers around the character of Jean, the movie's straight-up white racist. After she and Rick are carjacked at the beginning of the film, she says, loudly, and perhaps so Daniel can hear her, that she wants the new locks replaced by someone who isn't a Hispanic gangbanger. She treats her maid Maria dismissively, and until she slips and falls on the stairs rails against her husband (who she may realize is having an affair with his black personal assistant), all her domestic help, and all her friends. She is, despite her wealth, power, and privilege, alone in the world. "Poor little rich girl," we might sneer, because even though she is played by the perpetually likable Bullock, she is cold and brittle, one of the film's least redeemable characters. But at the end of the film, we realize the depth of her loneliness. As her maid, Maria, helps her up in bed, she pulls her in for a tight embrace:

JEAN: Do you want to hear something funny?
MARIA: What's that, Mrs. Jean?
JEAN: You're the best friend I've got.

Some critics have equated this to the scene in *Driving Miss Daisy* where Daisy (Jessica Tandy) tells Hoke that he's her best friend; some have compared it to the friendship that grows up between the white and black characters in *Green Book*. This is a terrible misreading of the film. Jean's words are expressing a tragic truth; she has given up on friendship from her husband, from her society acquaintances, or from anyone except Maria, who is paid to take care of her. Maria is not Mrs. Jean's best friend; watch the scene and you will see that Maria is discomfited, not comforted by this exchange. If anything, she is thinking, "I am paid to be your best friend." As in *Guess Who's Coming to Dinner*, we see a domestic helper who is thought of as a family member, but again that vision complicates the relationship considerably. Megan Stack, a foreign correspondent for the *Los Angeles Times*, writes about the revelations she had about her own domestic help:

> Because you sort of say, well, she's here and you know we love her
> and she loves us and she loves the kids. She doesn't mind working the
> extra day off. She doesn't mind coming in even though maybe her
> family has something else to do—and you sort of impose. I think it
> often starts from a very good place and an honest place—and I un-
> derstand that place because I have definitely felt that I loved the
> women who worked in my house, like I literally loved them. . . . But
> the problem is when you put that on somebody who is actually your
> employee and who doesn't have the same power in the relationship,
> you are taking away more of their power, I think.[17]

Jean's brittle racism is a sign of her deep brokenness, and her attachment to Maria is her own projection of family and connection. This is, ultimately, not a scene of facile racial reconciliation, but of heartbreaking solitude. Perhaps as a result of this realization, Jean will change in some way; we cannot know. But it is offered here as a cry for help: I have no one.

Crash has too many storylines to represent them all, but just as we sought a moral exemplar in *Do the Right Thing*, perhaps it's important to note that the one uncompromised figure in this film is Daniel, the Hispanic locksmith. Daniel ties together the Rick-and-Jean subplot, as well as the subplot with the Persian family store. Although he's attacked by Jean as a gangbanger, when we next see him, he is pulling into his driveway and checking on his daughter Lara (Ashlyn Sanchez), whom he finds hiding under her bed because she's afraid she heard a gunshot. It turns out that they've moved into this new neighborhood from a dangerous neighborhood where someone shot through Lara's window.

Daniel gets down on the floor to talk to Lara, and he tells her a story about something that happened to him when he was her age: A fairy flew into his room and offered him a magic cloak that would protect him from all manner of harm: "You know what impenetrable means? It means nothing can go through it. No bullets, nothing. She told me that if I wore it, nothing would hurt me. So I did. And my whole life, I never got shot, stabbed, nothing. I mean, how weird is that?" And then he remembers that the fairy told him to give it to his daughter when she was that age, which he had forgotten to do until that moment. He takes off the cloak, ties it around her neck, asks if she can feel it.

No, she says.

"Pretty cool, huh?" is his response.

Haggis says that this was a classic "gun on the wall" scene; the cloak would have to be a plot element later, when the Iranian shopkeeper (Shaun Toub) comes to the neighborhood bearing a gun and seeking revenge against Daniel for his looted shop: "I knew how it was going to happen as soon as I wrote the words 'impenetrable cloak.' You can't have an impenetrable cloak and not have it tested. You can't put a gun in a scene and not end up using it somehow. Children always try to protect their parents. It is a highly emotionally charged moment that is still the stuff of life."[18]

I have never shown this film that every breath did not catch when Lara runs out to put herself and the impenetrable cloak between her daddy and this man with a gun. We discover later that the shopkeeper's daughter (Marina Sirtis) has loaded her father's gun with blanks, worried about his volatility and his perceptions of threats everywhere, but we certainly do not know it at this point in the story. No: We hear a gunshot; we see Daniel's agonized face; and we weep. Every time.

And then we hear Lara, unharmed, say, "It's a really good cloak."

It is emblematic of *Crash* that the one truly good person in the film faces the greatest heartbreak—and is rescued from it—by coincidence. Daniel's moral authority does not protect him, but in this film, which often seems to be operating from a God's-eye view, it is as if Providence steps in to rescue him and his family—and Farhad, the shopkeeper, who almost commits the most heinous crime in the story. The world is full of danger and violence, *Crash* acknowledges, and we can react with anger and fear, or with something else. Farhad tells his daughter that angels saved the little girl—and himself—and he is not far wrong. As Desson Thompson writes:

> Although the movie's fate-binds-us-all scheme (an integral compo-
> nent of these multilayered, multi-character dramas from "Nashville"
> to "Magnolia") may strike some as manipulated coincidence, the big
> picture, the passing truths and the overall suspense are too omnis-
> ciently compelling for any of that to matter. Haggis's drama is about
> much more than interlocking front-end collisions. It's about the way
> we learn, often badly, about one another and how it may take a bad
> confrontation to peel away the misperceptions.[19]

The movie ends with the camera climbing into a God's-eye view over Los Angeles, pulling back farther and farther from the concerns of humankind, and the message seems to be this: We need to crash into each other to reveal the truth about ourselves and about the Other we do not know. Fear can tempt us to remain behind our walls, in our ac-tual or symbolic gated communities, but if we give in to that fear, we will never know the true humanity of those who do not look like us, and perhaps we will never know our own. Stephen Hunter also sees the God-like quality of Haggis's storytelling and remarks that "Haggis's deity-like camera wanders indiscriminately over the landscape, lis-tening in to conversations, meeting, following then abandoning characters, and continually showing us what only God can know: how they are all linked by space, time, coincidence and blood, even if they themselves can never know. This, for some odd reason, is extremely satisfying. Briefly we know what He knows and we feel the sadness He must feel."[20]

Both Daniel and Farhad experience the shooting and its lack of consequences as a miracle, but Lara, confident in her cloak (and con-fident in her father), never thinks twice about throwing herself into harm's way. What would it take for us to imagine we had a cloak of impenetrability? How could we rush headlong into possible peril, sure that we were ultimately safe?

The Parable of the Good Samaritan: A First-Century Palestinian *Crash*

Some years ago, in the early 2000s, shortly after my divorce, I drove a series of old Volvos (stick with me; I promise this is relevant!). They were cheap, and they were reliable until they weren't, so several times in those years I found myself in the improbable position of standing beside the road with my thumb out, a long-haired college professor hoping against hope that someone who wasn't a serial killer would pick him up and move him down the road. On one occasion, driving back from a summer gig teaching at Ghost Ranch in northern New Mexico, the right rear tire on my maroon Volvo station wagon went flat. I changed it, the hot afternoon sun beating down on me, tossed the flat tire in the back, and went on my way again.

Then two miles down the road, my spare went flat too.

I was a hundred miles away from the nearest town, Roswell, in a part of the New Mexican high desert with no cell service. What could I do? I picked up my flat tire and started walking down the highway, filthy and sweaty, knowing full well that if I saw me walking beside the road, I would drive on. Just some unlucky hippie. Tough break.

And sure enough, people did drive on. I was passed by Winnebagos and pickup trucks and big black SUVs, and I just knew that the air conditioning was blowing full blast inside those monsters.

And then a tiny two-seat coupe packed to the ceiling with people, camping gear, and junk food pulled over and offered me a lift. It was a husband and wife, both of them economy sized, but they somehow found a place for my spare on the back of the pile in the back seat, the wife straddled the console, and I squeezed inside enough to close the door.

They introduced themselves and told me that they were on their way back from a VA hospital in Albuquerque to their home in West Texas and had camped along the way to save money. The husband had fought in Vietnam and come home with serious PTSD and a ruined back. Although my father, grandfather, and great-grandfather were in the service, I thought of myself then and now as a Christian pacifist, and my most recent engagement with conflict had been speaking at a peace rally before the Iraq War. I could also tell by their diction that they hadn't had much formal education, and although this certainly does not mark me as better or them as worse, I had a lot of education.

We were very, very different people.

The man and his wife were deeply conservative, deeply patriotic, and deeply kind. When we reached Roswell, they dropped me off at the giant Wal-Mart where I could get my tire fixed, and although I told them I could rent a car, they insisted on taking me back, a total of two hundred miles out of their way. The wife stayed at a truck stop in Roswell; the husband and I rocketed north as the sun began to set, and as we drove, he began to tell me about his life as a soldier. He had been in black ops in Vietnam, sometimes operating in places where Americans were not supposed to be, doing things American were not supposed to do. He and his wife had also pegged me as someone who wasn't much like them, and at one point he looked over at me and told me, gruffly, "Some of the things I had to do were not very nice."

I nodded, and told him that I knew it had been hard, and I thanked him for his service. When we finally reached my car, it was full dark, but he pulled in behind me so that I could see from his headlights to change the tire, and when my jack began to wobble, he braced his ruined back against my car and held it firm.

When all was fixed, we shook hands, he waved off any offer of payment, and he raised a hand in benediction as he drove off into the night.

I stood there, tears in my eyes, knowing full well that in this clash of cultures, in this world filled with danger and suspicion, I had been treated with love and respect, with grace I had not earned, that I had been rescued by Samaritans.

Jesus tells the Parable of the Good Samaritan in the tenth chapter of Luke, and it is one of the two most recognizable stories of Jesus (the other being the Parable of the Prodigal, also in Luke). When Jesus taught that we are called to love God and love our neighbor, a student of the law asked the logical question: "Who then is my neighbor?" and he told this story in response. In the story, a Jewish man is traveling down from Jerusalem to Jericho on a mountain road and is set upon by thieves, who beat him within an inch of his life and take all that he has. Two people from the religious establishment, Professional Religious People, we might call them, see the man lying bruised and bloody, and instead of stopping to help, they walk to the other side of the road and pass him by. But a man from Samaria, a region hated and vilified by Jews, saw the man lying there, and although the wounded Jew would probably not have done the same for him, came to his aid. The Samaritan bound up his wounds, put him on his donkey, and carried him to an inn, where he paid the innkeeper to take care of him.

"Who then," Jesus asked, "was a neighbor to the man in need?"

"The man who helped him," was the only possible response.[21]

"Go then, and do the same," Jesus said.

When Dr. King preached or spoke about this story—which he did for his parishioners, and also for sanitation workers in Memphis on the night before he was killed—he taught it as a parable for how we respond in dangerous times. Dr. and Mrs. King drove the road from Jerusalem to Jericho on a visit to the Holy Land, and he said it was a dangerous road, once known as the Bloody Pass, steep and treacherous, and with lots of places for a person or persons to lie in ambush of travelers. Perhaps, Dr. King said, the reason that the Professional Religious People passed by was not because they were in a hurry, or that touching *dangerous* what might be a dead body would make it impossible to perform their *unselfish* ceremonial religious functions. Perhaps, he said, they rushed past because they were afraid that if they stopped to help, they too might become victims: "I imagine the first question which the priest and the Levite asked was: 'If I stop to help this man, what will happen to me?' But by the very nature of his concern, the good Samaritan reversed the question: 'If I do not stop to help this man, what will happen to him?' The good Samaritan engaged in a dangerous altruism."[22] ("Altruism" is a good preaching word, but in Memphis, King used the phrase "dangerous unselfishness.")

When Officer Hanson intervenes in the standoff where Cameron is about to be shot, or picks up a black man hitchhiking on a dark night, he is displaying a dangerous unselfishness, even though the events lead to very different outcomes. When Officer Ryan, bigot and bully, crawls into a car—and then back into it as it burns—he is displaying some version of dangerous unselfishness (although at the end it is certainly leavened by guilt and responsibility). When Anthony turns down the lucrative offer for the slaves in his van and instead releases them, he is displaying a dangerous unselfishness. When Lara sees her father in the yard being threatened by a man with a gun, realizes she is now wearing his impenetrable cloak, and rushes to save him, she is practicing dangerous unselfishness. When Graham, who has been taking care of his addict mother, is accused by her of being the reason his brother Peter is dead, and hears her giving his brother credit for things that Graham actually did for her, his silence offers dangerous unselfishness. When Christine goes to meet Cameron at work to apologize for her vicious words after their traffic stop, even though he walks away, she is offering dangerous unselfishness. And when Cameron, at movie's end, takes her phone call, hears her request "Come home," and does, it is dangerous unselfishness.

Although it does not happen in every situation, person after person in *Crash* responds to physical and emotional danger with bravery, with grace, with dangerous unselfishness. Sometimes, of course, this grace is offered to people the characters know well, but sometimes it is offered to strangers, because of course, as Augustine said, the lesson from Jesus's story is that all people, even those we do not know, even those we hate, are our neighbors. It is our responsibility to try and respond to their hatred or bigotry (as the Samaritan does) with love and generosity, and this teaching is not simply a Christian teaching. Every wisdom tradition has a version of the Golden Rule, where we are asked to treat others as we hope to be treated. James Baldwin, in his letter to his nephew, tells him that in the end, it is irrelevant whether white people accept him: "The really terrible thing, old buddy, is that *you* must accept *them*. And I mean that very seriously. You must accept them and accept them with love."[23]

Who then is my neighbor? Everyone. But this teaching—and this dangerous unselfishness—becomes more difficult when we are reaching across identity gaps, and when the world seems dangerous (hence the terrible ethical decision of the professional ethicists in Jesus's parable), and this may be *Crash*'s great gift to us. Living in a post-9/11 world in which we are constantly confronted by fear, and a wired world in which we are informed about dangers and violence around the globe 24/7, it takes extra courage and extra mindfulness to be a good neighbor, to do the right thing.

Scott Bader-Saye has carved out a niche writing about how we do the right thing in this world in which we are confronted with threats, real and imagined. He cites the teachings of Aquinas, who asks us to think about whether our fears are appropriate or not, near at hand, or far off and extremely unlikely.[24] We have heard Professor Bader-Saye define courage as doing the right thing in the face of our fear and when we act for something larger than our own safety, and facing our fear is important because in the face of fear, our moral options seem to contract. "If I do this," we ask ourselves in fear, "what will happen to me?" rather than asking, properly, "If I do not do this, what will happen to them?" "In a culture of fear," as Bader-Saye has said, "then our lives will be oriented primarily around the spiritually-dubious value of self-preservation."[25]

Most in danger, Bader-Saye tells us, of being trampled by our post-9/11 fear and dread are the spiritual practices that define what it is to live well, with grace and unselfishness: hospitality, peacemaking, and generosity.[26] Hospitality is about our response to the stranger. Will we react to this encounter with fear, hostility, even violence? In the film, we see horrible offenses against hospitality, people immediately leaping to attack and vicious stereotypes, as when Ria insults the Asian American woman who crashed into her car at the beginning of the film. But we also see hospitality displayed by Daniel, who refuses to take offense at Jean's slanders of him, who responds to Farhad's insults with patience instead of losing his cool. We see hospitality when Graham cleans out the rancid food in his mother's refrigerator and goes to Whole Foods to refill it, even though she believes Peter did it. We see hospitality offered, even though it goes wrong, when Officer Hanson invites Peter into his car on a cold night.

Peacemaking is another hard practice in a time we feel threatened. It is easier to attack preemptively, to hold a weapon in hand rather than offer an open hand of greeting and reconciliation. "We are tempted," Bader-Saye writes, "to believe that if we make others afraid of us, we will not have to be afraid of them."[27] But Stanley Hauerwas places peacemaking at the center of his work, arguing in *The Peaceable Kingdom* that "peaceableness as the hallmark of Christian life helps illumine other issues, such as the nature of moral argument, the meaning and status of freedom, as well as how religious convictions can be claimed to be true or false."[28] If we practice peacemaking, we will cultivate other virtues as well. The most substantial scene of peacemaking in *Crash* has to be when Officer Hanson intervenes in Cameron's attempt to commit suicide at the hands of the police. He walks into a dangerously charged situation, hands up, weapon holstered. He could be shot by Cameron—or a stray shot from his police colleagues—but, as we have seen, he brokers a peace at the risk of his own life that makes many things possible. Cameron's words to Anthony help change him into a person ultimately willing to do more than get paid; Cameron himself remains alive to return home to Christine, and we trust that they will be able to forgive each other and move forward.

Finally, there is generosity, a reshaping of our priorities away from ourselves, our perceived needs, and our own perceived scarcity, and toward a generous concern for others. Many people have a worldview defined by scarcity thinking: There is not enough food, there are not enough jobs, we don't have enough resources, all of these tribal ways of thinking. If we give to others, will I have enough? Will my family have enough? Will my tribe, my caste, my class, my race have enough? *Crash* offers us examples of this scarcity thinking, of this fear. Jean wants to be locked up safe behind her walls at night. Graham initially responds to his relationship with Ria by withholding, because giving is vulnerability. "Why do you keep everybody at a certain distance?" she asks. "What, you start to feel something and panic?" Of course, we learn the reasons: because his mother is an addict, his father is not on the scene, and his brother is a twice-convicted felon. He was, as he tells her, raised badly. But he learns to do better, to offer generosity even though it makes him vulnerable. In *Crash*, Graham offers us a retelling of the Prodigal Son parable, where, for once, the older brother in the story proves generous to the younger.

I have said that *Crash* is not a feel-good movie, that it is not a racial reconciliation fantasy. Officer Ryan, chastened as he may be by what happened with Christine in the burning car, is still a bigot who uses his power as an agent of the state to humiliate black people. Officer Hanson, although he rose above his inaction on the traffic stop to demonstrate great bravery in saving Cameron's life, reacts with fear instead of courage when he shoots Peter. The movie's central song, "In the Deep," and the montage of characters as it plays, acknowledges that this is a hard world, and that sometimes we are in over our heads.

But those Good Samaritan moments—Anthony and the Chinamen, and Cameron and Anthony, and Officer Hanson and Cameron, and Maria, allowing Jean to embrace her because she must recognize her human brokenness—are the things that remain with us. We still live in a world of fear and hatred, a world where perhaps it feels safer not to offer hospitality, peace, generosity to a stranger. But we can also still demonstrate a dangerous unselfishness. And we should.

7

Get Out

Black Bodies Matter

Black Lives, White Power

For all of us who wanted to believe that the election of a black president might mean the end of racism in America (and I was one of those hopeful people, saying so to friends, opining on BBC Radio on numerous occasions that Donald Trump could not be elected on the strength of his appeals to racism), it's important to look at some snapshots from recent American racial history. "The past isn't dead," said William Faulkner; "It's not even past." And so it is with race in America, especially when it comes to the long, tortured American legacy of violence and coercion against black bodies that started with their kidnapping in Africa and shows no signs of ending.

On February 26, 2012, an armed amateur neighborhood watch captain in Sanford, Florida, George Zimmerman, shot and killed seventeen-year-old Trayvon Martin, whom he saw walking through his neighborhood, tracked, and accosted. Martin, an African American high schooler, was clothed in a dark hoodie, which became a symbol of violence against black men, and he was unarmed except for a bag of Skittles and an iced tea he'd gone out to buy. Although Zimmerman claimed he'd been attacked by Martin and shot him in self-defense, the case caused national outrage, with even President Barack Obama chiming in. The president, visibly moved, spoke in detail about why the case was so close to home for him and many other African Americans:

> You know, when Trayvon Martin was first shot I said that this could have been my son. Another way of saying that is Trayvon Martin could have been me thirty-five years ago. And when you think about

why, in the African American community at least, there's a lot of pain around what happened here, I think it's important to recognize that the African American community is looking at this issue through a set of experiences and a history that doesn't go away.

There are very few African American men in this country who haven't had the experience of being followed when they were shopping in a department store. That includes me. There are very few African American men who haven't had the experience of walking across the street and hearing the locks click on the doors of cars. That happened to me—at least before I was a senator. There are very few African Americans who haven't had the experience of getting on an elevator and a woman clutching her purse nervously and holding her breath until she had a chance to get off. That happens often.

And I don't want to exaggerate this, but those sets of experiences inform how the African American community interprets what happened one night in Florida. And it's inescapable for people to bring those experiences to bear. The African American community is also knowledgeable that there is a history of racial disparities in the application of our criminal laws—everything from the death penalty to enforcement of our drug laws. And that ends up having an impact in terms of how people interpret the case.[1]

Black families refer to the moment when they have to tell their sons that they may be threatened with police violence solely because they're black as "the talk." It is not a part of white experience. ("The talk" in my family was the talk about sex, and while it encompassed a lot of discomfort, the consequences were not presented as life threatening.) Ta-Nehisi Coates, in the letter to his son that is the National Book Award–winning *Between the World and Me*, writes that in his fifteenth year his son had already had to absorb the fact of white violence against black people, "that the police departments of your country have been endowed with the authority to destroy your body," and that even if that destruction is an overreach, a misunderstanding, a product of foolish law or policy, it doesn't matter: "The destroyers will rarely be held accountable."[2] In Trayvon Martin's case, although he was not shot by a police officer, this was certainly true: Zimmerman was acquitted of his death under Florida's "stand your ground" law, a statute that permits people to use deadly force if they feel that their lives are in danger. Zimmerman was larger than Martin, and he was armed, but he said he felt threatened by the slender black teenager. In the days and months that followed, many angrily asked if Martin would have been acquitted under the same statute had he killed Zimmerman. Clearly, his life was the one more in danger.

On August 9, 2014, Michael Brown, an unarmed black eighteen-year-old suspected of stealing a box of Swisher cigarillos, was killed in Ferguson, Missouri, by a white police officer who fired twelve shots at him. While the details of the case were again widely disputed, the community began to repeat the story that Brown raised his hands and asked the officer not to shoot. As President Obama pointed out in his response to Trayvon Martin's shooting, this common black experience of being mistrusted and assumed dangerous resonated throughout the country; in December 2014, after a grand jury decided not to indict Officer Darren Wilson for the shooting, members of the Rams football team of nearby St. Louis ran onto the field with their hands up, part of a national expression of outrage against violence against black people. As Nick Wright put it, " 'Hands Up, Don't Shoot' is not just about Mike Brown, or Ferguson, or police shooting unarmed black people. 'Hands Up, Don't Shoot' is about a fundamental question that gets to the core of what this country stands for. It's a question that's been open to debate since long before Darren Wilson shot and killed the unarmed Brown four months ago: Do black lives matter, and if so, how much?"[3] For Wright and thousands of protestors around the country, the answer continued to be "no," or if "yes," not much.

The shooting in Ferguson brought up a familiar defense, the very same defense cited by Zimmerman in the Trayvon Martin shooting: that black bodies represent physical danger. His friends and family described Michael Brown as a gentle giant: he was a large man, well over six feet tall, weighing almost 300 pounds. In his grand jury testimony, Officer Wilson spoke at length about the size and ferocity of Mr. Brown, and how, just before he shot him, Brown grunted and charged him, like an insane person. Like a beast.

The myth of the ferocious black man permeates society. It's the myth that informs the characterization of Gus in *The Birth of a Nation*; it's the myth that leads to Radio Raheem's death in *Do the Right Thing*; it's the myth that haunts Sandra Bullock's Jean when she sees two black men in the street in the opening moments of *Crash*; and it's the myth that, as President Obama said, makes real live white people speed up their steps when they encounter a black man in an unmediated encounter: the myth that black people possess powerful, potent, physical bodies that can and do overwhelm the less potent bodies of white people. While this seems like the stuff of tabloid headlines, even such sterling news organizations as the *New York Times* have fallen prey to the myth in years past. The blogger Undercover Black Man found that the *Times* (and many other newspapers) had regularly used the phrase "giant Negro" as a headline or in news stories from the late nineteenth century well into the 1940s, expressing the fear and fascination the supposedly superhuman physical prowess of black bodies inspired in white people: "GIANT NEGRO DISABLES 4 POLICEMEN IN FIGHT."[4] Even though Officer Wilson was himself a big man—a big man with a Sig Sauer P229 pistol that fired .40-caliber bullets, and a lot of them—he professed that he was afraid of (and simultaneously, perhaps, in awe of) the threat that Brown represented to him and to the community.

Michael Brown's death also prompted outrage and community responses to violence against black people. What began as spontaneous expressions of grief after the shooting escalated into formal protests and rioting, which continued for weeks in Ferguson. It jumpstarted the Black Lives Matter movement, which had begun on social media but now grew into marches and organizing all across America and even in foreign countries. The point of the movement, simply, was that black people were disproportionately losing their lives at the hands of law enforcement, often with no real justification. But outside of black communities, not all understood; Robert Jones notes that many white Americans were "baffled or frustrated" by the news coverage of the movement, and pushed back.[5] In response to Black Lives Matter, supporters of the police, politicians, pastors, and pundits asked, "Don't all lives matter?" Rick Warren, the tremendously influential pastor of the Willow Creek Church, introduced the theological hashtag #AllLivesMattertoGod. Daniel Victor pointed out that while all lives certainly matter, not all people are in equal peril: "Saying 'All Lives Matter' in response would suggest to them that all people are in equal danger, invalidating the specific concerns of black people."[6] Philosopher Judith Butler responded that it was simply a truly logical response to the history of black bodies and black life in this country:

> When and where did black lives ever really get free of coercive force? One reason the chant "Black Lives Matter" is so important is that it states the obvious but the obvious has not yet been historically realized. So it is a statement of outrage and a demand for equality, for the right to live free of constraint, but also a chant that links the history of slavery, of debt peonage, segregation, and a prison system geared toward the containment, neutralization and degradation of black lives, but also a police system that more and more easily and often can take away a black life in a flash all because some officer perceives a threat.[7]

One final horrifying snapshot, witnessed by millions: On July 6, 2016, Philandro Castile, a thirty-two-year-old African American school cafeteria worker, was pulled over in Falcon Heights, Minnesota, for questioning in a nearby robbery. His only connection with the robbery was being of the same race of the supposed culprit. His girl-friend and her four-year-old daughter were riding in the car with him. Castile told the officer who stopped him that he had a firearm—he was licensed to carry—and the officer cautioned him repeatedly not to reach for it. "I'm not pulling it out," Castile said, which was seconded by his girlfriend, Diamond Reynolds. Despite these affirmations, the officer fired seven shots at Castile, hitting him five times. Reynolds livestreamed what happened on Facebook: Castile dying from his wounds as Reynolds told the officer that he had not been reaching for a firearm, that he was simply getting his license and registration. Within 24 hours, the video had been viewed more than two million times, even though Facebook took it down temporarily because of its graphic content.[8] The video was also widely broadcast, reaching millions more in that way, and fueling more outrage about the continuing violations of black bodies. Castile did things right, everything black mothers and fathers tell their sons to do in "the talk." He told the police officer he had a gun and was not going to reach for it. But nonetheless, he bled out live on Facebook for the entire world to see.

Set aside for a moment, if you can, every lesser offense that people of color have endured and still endure, the personal microaggressions, the suspicions, the misunderstandings, the sexualization of black bodies. Set aside, even, the systemic inequities in education, incarceration, income, and institutional racism of every kind. At the end of the day, there is no greater offense against black bodies after slavery than this, that black people, particularly black men, are unsafe even (or especially?) in the hands of those who are supposed to preserve the peace in our society—that even a brilliant man like writer Vann Newkirk feels that he has to do everything exactly right to survive an encounter with the police. Simon Vosick-Levinson, reflecting on more than a decade of such killings in *Rolling Stone*, said, "Sadly, there's nothing new about this pattern of lethal racial profiling. For far too long, African-Americans in this country have had to worry about whether police will kill their loved ones on the slightest pretext without facing any meaningful punishment. Racist violence is a deep-rooted part of this country's history, and it's going to take substantial nationwide reform of the policing and court systems to change this awful reality."[9]

Outrage at the persistence of this reality fueled Black Lives Matter, making it a powerful force that, as Michael Lowery wrote in *The Guardian*, expanded outward from Ferguson, Missouri, in concentric circles: "What happened in Ferguson would give birth to a movement and set the nation on course for an ongoing public hearing on race that stretched far past the killing of unarmed residents—from daily policing to Confederate imagery to respectability politics to cultural appropriation."[10] Social media and the ubiquity of smartphones made it possible to chronicle, broadcast, and decry this awful reality. The now more-widespread awareness of the unfair treatment of people of color by institutions of justice invited people of good conscience to think about other ways in which racism was an endemic part of our culture. In 2016, some of the organizations affiliated with Black Lives Matter compiled a comprehensive antiracism platform; activist Janae Bonsu told Vann Newkirk, "It's never just been about, 'Oh, we're mad and we want you to stop killing black people.' It's about way more than that."[11] Black Lives Matter has morphed into a new and necessary civil rights movement, calling not just for changes in policing but opposing inequities affecting black people throughout the culture. As

Jill Lepore puts it, "Black Lives Matter [is] Black Power."[12] Some white people will always be frightened by Black Power and will try to reassert themselves—to hold on to privilege, power, and symbols of their dominance such as Confederate flags and war memorials. I was recently at Arlington National Cemetery and was stunned to find a Confederate Memorial, featuring a sculpture of a Confederate officer headed off to war with his devoted Mammy looking on, atop the sacred hill. The monument, funded by the United Daughters of the Confederacy, was dedicated by Woodrow Wilson in 1914, long after the conflict ended.

The incidents of violence against people of color we've explored so far in this chapter happened during the Obama presidency, under a president who offered thoughtful and moving statements about race, who shared the color of his skin with the violated. But on January 20, 2017, Donald J. Trump assumed the office of president of the United States after a hard and divisive campaign that, according to Lepore, "had stoked fears, incited hatreds, and sown doubts about American leadership in the world."[13] Many of those fears, hatreds, and doubts centered on race, immigration, and white privilege. President Trump has a long and complicated history with race: His first entry into a lifetime of celebrity and notoriety was when he and his father settled what Newkirk calls a "mountain of allegations" that in their real estate properties the Trumps discriminated against black and Puerto Rican potential tenants, a clear violation of the federal Fair Housing Act.[14] Later, the president was a powerful voice in the "birther" movement that denied that President Obama was actually an American by birth. When Trump descended from his penthouse apartment in Trump Tower to launch his candidacy, he marked the occasion by railing against immigrants from Mexico, whom he characterized as murderers and rapists. At campaign rallies, Trump, when faced by African American protesters, spoke nostalgically of the days when protesters could be beaten and jailed. Upon ascending to office, he encouraged law enforcement officers not to be too respectful of the rights of the accused. He issued executive orders banning people from Muslim-majority countries from entering the United States and spoke about places where brown people live as "shithole countries."

And then, in August 2017, when white supremacists marched in Charlottesville, Virginia, sparking conflict and violence that left one woman dead after a white supremacist rammed his car into a crowd of counterprotestors, the president crystallized his position on race. Trump did not categorically condemn the white supremacists and neo-Nazis who marched through the streets of Charlottesville chanting "Jews will not replace us," "White lives matter," and the Nazi slogan "Blood and soil." Instead, he said that there were "good people on both sides" of the protest. It seemed to many that at best he was turning a blind eye to racism, and at worst, he was offering tacit support to neo-Nazis. David Duke, former Grand Wizard of the Ku Klux Klan, spoke out in support of the president's stance (or non-stance). Writers for the *New York Times* argued that

> President Trump buoyed the white nationalist movement on Tuesday as no president has done in generations—equating activists protesting racism with the neo-Nazis and white supremacists who rampaged in Charlottesville, Va., over the weekend.
>
> Never has he gone as far in defending their actions as he did during a wild, street-corner shouting match of a news conference in the gilded lobby of Trump Tower, angrily asserting that so-called alt-left activists were just as responsible for the bloody confrontation as marchers brandishing swastikas, Confederate battle flags, anti-Semitic banners and "Trump/Pence" signs.[15]

The venerable *Atlantic* published a powerful piece by Ta-Nehisi Coates in which he called President Trump a white supremacist whose most significant pleasure in office is in rolling back all the achievements of the first black president. While previous presidents had surely benefited from their whiteness and many had used racism in an inexplicit way, Trump had consciously changed that equation: "It is often said that Trump has no real ideology, which is not true—his ideology is white supremacy, in all its truculent and sanctimonious power."[16] For decades before Trump's ascension, writers had observed that politicians had used dog-whistle phrases to encourage racists and white supremacists to believe that they shared their concerns. Trump's election seems to have led to a widespread belief that covert racism could now emerge into the open.[17]

Days after the 2016 presidential election, Baylor University, the fine Christian university where I have taught for thirty years, witnessed an event that had no precedent in all my time there. On November 9, 2016, a white male student shoved a black female student off a Baylor sidewalk, knocking her to the ground, saying "no niggers allowed on the sidewalk." He told another, outraged student that he was just making America great again, Trump's campaign slogan. To Baylor's credit, in addition to the rapid formal condemnation of this vile action, hundreds of Baylor students and faculty—and the university's president—mobilized via social media to walk the assaulted student to her classes and to demonstrate our collective outrage, but the racism displayed in this incident was hardly unique to our campus. Shortly after the election, a friend with a black daughter at Texas State University posted that her daughter's apartment door had been defaced with racial epithets. These anecdotes from my own experience are merely part of a larger pattern. The *Washington Post* reported that hate offenses rose beginning the day after the election, and the NAACP has chronicled a continued and dramatic rise in public hate incidents since Trump became president.[18] Their report postulated a direct correlation between these hate crimes and Trump's own actions (or inactions): "The NAACP believes there is a direct relationship between the rise in hate crimes exemplified by the continual #LivingWhileBlack incidents and other reported crimes and President Donald J. Trump's xenophobic rhetoric and racist policies."[19] And #DrivingWhileBlack, #ShoppingWhileBlack, #SwimmingWhileBlack, and simply #LivingWhileBlack moments continue to multiply as of this writing in 2019; rarely does a day go by without one or more of these racist incidents popping up in my newsfeed.

Many commentators had written—had earnestly hoped—that with the election of Barack Obama, America was entering a new postracial phase. How could America be racist, they wondered, if we had elected and celebrated the election of a black commander in chief? But with the election of Donald Trump and a seeming green light to racism, writers, directors, and filmgoers had a new reality to live into. In his National Book Award–winning history of racism, *Stamped from the Beginning*, Ibram X. Kendi argues that the hopeful progressive narrative of inexorable racial progress is false. It is, he says, an "easy-to-predict, two-sided Hollywood battle of obvious good versus obvious evil, with good triumphing in the end."[20] Instead, Kendi argues, racism and antiracism in this country are always involved in an elaborate three-sided dance, in which racist segregationist and assimilationist arguments are aligned in opposition to antiracist ideas, and for every seeming step forward against racism, a backlash causes a step backwards. The election of Barack Obama made some Americans feel that the battle against racism had been won; the election of Donald Trump, who affirmed or ignored white supremacists, made it clear that the battle continues.

Many white people do not understand the Black Lives Matter movement, or find it in itself prejudiced. Those struggling economically in a society where the rich grow richer and the middle class shrinks continue to worry about their own survival. There is nothing new about this white backlash, the fear that if people of color achieve more parity, whites will suffer as a consequence. We spoke about scarcity in the last chapter, the fear that there is not enough for me and mine. Martin Luther King, Jr. also spoke of this often. In 1964 he wrote about it for the *Saturday Evening Post*. When black people asked for equality, he said, some whites saw it as "a demand for privileges rather than as a desperate quest for existence."[21] We have come a long, long way; there is still a long, long way to go.

Hollywood stepped in to this ongoing racial struggle of Black Lives Matter and Charlottesville, as culture always does. The #HollywoodSoWhite movement reflected Hollywood's desire to do better, as did the production of critical darlings like *Moonlight* and blockbusters like *Black Panther*, both made by black filmmakers and celebrating all- or almost-all-black casts. But at the same time, the number of black screenwriters, directors, and producers continued to be tiny, and many films and TV shows still focused solely on the experiences of white viewers. However, in 2017 and 2018, Jordan Peele's *Get Out* confronted all the problems facing Hollywood (and America), appropriated long-standing genres, and rewrote American history in a painful, compelling, and liberating film about black bodies and white supremacy that vividly illustrates the final phase of our conversation together about racism, film, American culture, and human flourishing. The film is about a white woman, Rose (Allison Williams), bringing her black boyfriend Chris (Daniel Kaluuya) home to meet her family. It is a story familiar to us from *Guess Who's Coming to Dinner*, but in its twists and turns, and its movement from romantic comedy to horror, it offers a pointed commentary on how racism and violence against black bodies still continues.

In 2018, Peele participated in an interview with the screenwriter and producer James V. Hart (for which Hart asked me to formulate some questions about race, narrative, and genre). Peele spoke of how the historical moment, all these recent snapshots, joined the images of the past to shape the story he ultimately wrote:

> Trump was basically elected between when I shot the movie and when it came out. . . . The climate surrounding race was becoming more out in the open, and this discussion of Black Lives Matter was happening in a way we hadn't seen, and more specifically, there was the tension of black people being murdered by the police. Because the Obama era was surrounded by this post-racial lie, as I like to call it, all of a sudden I was showing this movie and testing it in a world that was race weary . . . Because the state of the world had evolved and these conversations were happening, that's when I made the decision to give us a happy ending.[22]

Get Out was both an acknowledgment of the difficulty of the moment and a hope that something better and more just might be possible. It offered audiences not just a recognition of the ways that race continues to shape all of our realities, but an opportunity for white audiences to recognize their own complicity in racism and take action to change it. After viewing *Get Out* at the National Cathedral in February 2018, my Baylor student Maddie Ebrey, who is white, told me that stories such as this one can "serve as a call to action for those individuals who should feel entitled to use their means to enact change." *Get Out* is indeed a powerful call to action, a visceral experience of racism, and one of the most important films ever made about race in America.

Don't Go in There: Genre and Film
Tradition in *Get Out*

Get Out, although set in upstate New York, was filmed in Alabama, largely around the small and picturesque town of Fairhope. I have spoken and preached in Fairhope and have twice signed books at its independent bookstore, Page and Palette. On my first visit I marveled at the downtown, which looks like Disneyland, or Switzerland, as though elves come out in the middle of the night to redo the flower arrangements—which, I discovered, is not far from the truth. Fairhope is, without casting aspersions on the town or on my friends who live there, notable for several things. Its lovely resort hotel, a Marriott, has a singular backstory. *Southern Living* reports that "what makes this resort so special—and so beloved by generations of Southerners—is its history. Built in 1847, it served as a Confederate hospital during the Civil War, and the hotel's military past is still honored every day with a ceremonial cannon firing at 4:00 pm."[23] The town itself was founded as a utopian community. And Fairhope is, again without casting aspersions, white. Staggeringly, blindingly white. People of color stand out. Actor Daniel Kaluuya (Chris) would go running there during the shooting of *Get Out*. Lil Rel Howery, who plays Chris's best friend Rod, said, "Daniel used to run at night, which I thought was crazy. When I first got there, I was coming from dinner and I saw Daniel in this hoodie and shorts . . . I was like, 'Man, what are you doing?' 'I'm just running.' 'At night? Around here?'" Yet, as Peele remarked, the people were kind and welcoming, and he grew to love Alabama.[24] All in all, Fairhope could not be a more perfect setting for a film about the things black people fear and that white people are afraid to face about themselves—but must.

   Peele came up with the idea of a film about a black man going home with his white girlfriend some years before the film was made. One of the movies that helped him make sense of the story, as he told Jim Hart, was *Guess Who's Coming to Dinner*. The concept, he thought all along, was "about being black in a white space," and "at some point, I realized, it's *Guess Who's Coming to Dinner.*" There's a universal quality, Peele said, to the fear of meeting your potential in-laws for the first time, a problem that would make this film about being black in a white space also accessible for a white audience.[25]

But there are also obvious differences from this source material. As the theologian Kelly Brown Douglas says, while it was inspiring for black viewers like her to see Sydney Poitier on the screen, *Guess Who's Coming to Dinner* was made for white audiences, not for people who looked like her. As Richard Lawson noted in *Vanity Fair*, unlike its ancestor, *Get Out* does not exist to make white audiences feel better about themselves. Not only is it a movie intended first for black audiences, he argues that *Get Out* is "a nasty, and necessary, perversion of racism panaceas like *Guess Who's Coming to Dinner*, which reassure white audiences about how they'd surely behave if such an anomaly—a black person in our home??—were to happen in their lives."[26] It is not, he says, a film seeking to soothe racial tensions. Yet, he says, it is the film that we need right now.

Not that there aren't plenty of similarities to the earlier film beyond simply the plot of a young white woman bringing her black beau home to meet the parents. Chris Washington is a paragon, if not quite the Black Wonder Doctor played by Poitier about whom James Baldwin protested. He's a respected professional photographer whose images of black urban life are exhibited in galleries, an artist who—the film both tells and shows us—has an amazing eye. But he's also a real human being with fears and foibles who doesn't overlook the many irritations placed in his path.

In *Guess Who's Coming to Dinner*, Spencer Tracy, a liberal icon, plays Matt Drayton, a San Francisco newspaper publisher who is also a liberal icon. *Get Out* develops similar expectations and character archetypes. Bradley Whitford, who plays Dean, the father in *Get Out*, is a contemporary liberal icon, famous for his Emmy-winning depiction of Deputy White House Chief of Staff Josh Lyman in the television series *West Wing*. Few other actors could have had the same impact in the role. According to Whitford, "Dean was a delicious opportunity for self-parody. I mean, I say lines like 'I would have voted for Obama for a third time.' In my defense, I say them to white people as often as I say them to African-Americans. I didn't realize how much of a laugh line that was."[27] When Dean proves to be something different from what we expect—as when Spencer Tracy's Matt holds out against his daughter's marriage—audiences can't help but be disappointed, and perhaps, to see themselves in Dean's betrayal of their values.

Ultimately, the differences between *Guess Who's Coming to Dinner* and *Get Out* can be ascribed to genre. *Guess Who's Coming to Dinner* is a hybrid of romantic comedy and social problem film. *Get Out* takes the same storyline and explores it through different and perhaps more problematic genres. Many critics called it a horror film; others called it social satire; Peele himself preferred to think of it as a social thriller, since "horror" carries a set of not-so-positive associations and keeps some people away; remember the hundred-year-old woman in Houston who was upset about being asked to watch a horror film? I myself put off seeing *Get Out* because I am not drawn to the horror genre as I was when I was seventeen. But horror (like comedy) can also be deadly serious. In the *New York Times*, Jason Zinoman wrote that *Get Out* is both a horror film and a "trenchant indictment of liberal white orthodoxy," and that it is misguided to think of horror as a juvenile genre, unconcerned with political and social issues.[28]

After we watched *Get Out* in February 2018 in the nave of the National Cathedral, Korva Coleman asked me to start the conversation with the subject of genre. I suggested that

> There are a couple of classic films that are very closely related to this one: *Night of the Living Dead*, which is fifty years old this year, *The Stepford Wives*, *Invasion of the Body Snatchers* . . . are really powerful horror films that are chock full of social commentary. You know, they're tremendously political films. And this is a film that takes a genre that can be used to make very serious points, but it turns a lot of stuff around. . . . Instead of the black character being the first one out, which is a typical horror film trope, Jordan Peele talks about this: usually the white virgin is the last one in the film. And he said very consciously, "No, Chris is the white virgin in this film. I'm turning everything around and making it possible, you know, for him to stick around until the end." And that's one of a lot of really interesting reversals, in terms of the genre in this film.[29]

Peele has said that, in addition to *Guess Who's Coming to Dinner*, films that influenced his conception of *Get Out* were precisely these horror films with a social message and meaning: *Night of the Living Dead, Invasion of the Body Snatchers*, and *The Stepford Wives*. In all of those films, it becomes apparent to characters that business as usual is no longer possible, that something strange and different is at work that threatens their lives and maybe even their souls. Film critic Owen Gleiberman suggested that *Rosemary's Baby* and other films by Roman Polanski might also be essential ingredients in Peele's recipe, a "cinema of plausibly unsettling paranoia."[30] Peele was indeed a huge fan of *Rosemary's Baby*—he grew up in Manhattan a few blocks from the Dakota, the huge apartment building that was the setting of that film. If *Get Out* is in one sense a film about white people closely watching a black person who gradually becomes aware of their malign interest, this evocation of Polanski's cinema of paranoia as influential also makes a great deal of sense.

Critics and filmgoers sometimes tend to trivialize the horror genre and associate it with a teenage audience, but the horror genre can carry significant social criticism under the guise of entertainment. In the 2018 preface to the second edition of his book *Monsters in America*, Scott Poole wrote that

> Monster tales ultimately do not let you hide. . . . There are empathetic monsters, subversive monsters, monsters that we contemplate in order to ponder our own mortality. . . . There are also monsters born from the systems of exploitation, corruption, and oppression. You will not like all you learn here about American history. But I am telling you that this book reveals . . . an American horror story, *the* American horror story.[31]

There are all kinds of monsters, and they stand in for all sorts of fears. Frankenstein's monster, is, according to Alberto Manguel, "a reflection of that which we do not want to or do not dare remember."[32] Accepting the award for Best Director at the 2018 Golden Globes, Guillermo del Toro lauded monsters as "patron saints of our blissful imperfections."[33] Horror films can be serious explorations of societal horrors, and *Get Out* is a serious entertainment based on what critic Aisha Harris calls "all of the real-life anxieties of Existing While Black."[34]

Peele observed, "Black audiences are obsessed with horror films but consistently frustrated with them. Part of the reason goes back to the Eddie Murphy routine about how a black family would be much different than a white family in a horror movie. There is a heightened awareness that black Americans have developed in looking out for racism and the real horrors that we've been subjected to for years."[35] In *Between the World and Me*, Ta-Nehisi Coates repeatedly points out that the black experience in American consists of a constant and conscious awareness about the things that can go badly and violently wrong at any moment. Rod, the TSA agent in *Get Out*, represents the black audience's experience of reaction and judgment. Don't go in that house, black audiences say, because they know that around every corner and in every dark corridor, there is the potential for violence and death for black bodies.

Get Out takes on century-old realities that should be thought of as horrific—black people in servitude to white people, black people as sexual objects for white desire, black people imprisoned by white people—subject matter that sparks from *Guess Who's Coming to Dinner* but goes far beyond it. Korva Coleman and I talked about this at the National Cathedral in 2018:

GREG GARRETT: We were talking last night about the idea of the Faithful Retainers in *Guess Who's Coming to Dinner*—it's a term that comes from James Baldwin, who, as some of you heard last night, talked about having gone to see *Birth of a Nation* and *Guess Who's Coming to Dinner* on the exact same day and discovering that there were scenes in both of those films that were almost identical to each other, in which we had these sort of stereotypical characters portrayed. And so here we have the Faithful Retainers again. They look very much like the ones in *Birth of a Nation* from 1915. But it is clear that what their loyalty means is something very creepy, I mean supernaturally odd. And that's actually what it's been all along. And just as we saw the character of Tilly last night sort of giving so much loyalty to her white family that that's all that she has to give, we realize there is something really crazy about this dynamic. And what Jordan Peele has done with it is to say, "Okay, this is not just off in a cultural or political way. I'm going to take this and make something science-fiction-supernatural, to at least give you an explanation for this kind of supernatural loyalty, which should not have any basis in fact."

KORVA COLEMAN: There is something, I think it was Ryan Coughlin who said this, that basically the African American experience is one of science fiction. Aliens come to your land, they abduct you, they take your language, they take your culture, they take everything about you, plant you down in an alien landscape, and you must survive or die. Science fiction, but expressed in horror, but expressed as the African American experience.[36]

But the film also takes—and overturns—horror tropes in racially aware ways. The film opens with Dre (Lakeith Stanfield), a black man walking through a white suburb at night. As Aisha Harris points out, this is a scene instantly recognizable to fans of horror films, which specialize in importing death and terror into our supposedly safe spaces. When a lone figure walks a deserted street at night in a horror movie, we suspect the monster is watching—or approaching. This image is complicated when we overlay society's fear of a black man on white streets; too often in actual neighborhoods and on actual streets white people have perceived him as the monster. Here, we quickly see that Dre is not the menace, but the menaced. "You know how they like to do motherfuckers out here," he mutters. The reference is to scenes of menace in neighborhood settings as in *Halloween*, but also an echo of contemporary society, as Harris notes: "[N]ot unlike the black teen whose name became a rallying cry for the Black Lives Matter movement, he can't avoid trouble."[37] Trayvon Martin didn't intend to become a victim; he was just going to the convenience store. And Dre did not intend to become the next victim of the Armitage family; he was just trying to find the right house on the right street.

Get Out also moves quickly to another staple of horror: the haunted house. Chris enters the isolated Gothic house of the Armitage family. This typically spells doom for a black character. It does not mean the end for him, although he will be pressed to his limits to survive, as it is indeed a haunted house. We are shown this during the house tour that takes place shortly after Chris and Rose arrive. A picture of Dean's father Roman, who lost a race to Jesse Owens and "almost got over it," is a first sign. Roman's resentment and envy of Owens's prowess seems to have led directly to the Coagula Project; his brain now resides in Walter's body (Marcus Henderson), and he exults in the feeling of running, of using that black body for his own enjoyment. Dean tells Chris that the basement is closed off because of "black mold," which becomes morbidly funny after we have seen the entire film and realize what has happened to black people down there. And then Dean says that they still keep a little piece of his mother in the kitchen—as the camera shows us Georgina (Betty Gabriel), in whose body his mother's brain now resides.

Like any good haunted house, the Armitage house is isolated. Peele's screenplay presents it this way:

EXT. BACKYARD - LATE AFTERNOON
The yard is huge and the woods beyond it ominous. The wind RUSHES through the trees. Dean leads Chris out through the yard towards a gazebo.
DEAN: Smell that . . . ? Space! I love it. I'm tellin' you, the nearest house is practically on the other side of the lake. It's total privacy out here.[38]

The house and its grounds grow more and more ominous. Later that night, Chris goes downstairs and then outside to smoke a cigarette. We experience the first shock cuts as he is startled by Georgina appearing out of nowhere and Walter sprinting toward him in the night. Isolation is an essential horror trope, as in *Psycho* (1960), *The Texas Chainsaw Massacre* (1974), *The Shining* (1980), *Friday the 13th* (1980), and *Cabin in the Woods* (2011). The fact that a cast of characters is brought into this remote estate from the outside world is also genre specific. This is the world of *Rosemary's Baby* and *The Stepford Wives*—a world in which our main characters are encouraged to think (or hope) that the world remains normal while all is actually falling to pieces around them.

In *Get Out*, Peele populates the Armitage house party with microaggressions, some of them benign—a character who tells Chris he knows Tiger Woods, and another who asks how he is enjoying the African American experience—and others more offensive, like the woman who asks Rose if sex with a black man is better and fondles

Chris's bicep—and others simply ominous, as when all the guests at the party fall silent and gaze at the ceiling when Chris walks upstairs, or the silent scene in which Dean, standing in front of a portrait of Chris, auctions off Chris's body to his party guests.

The movie also presents a truly hair-raising image of captivity and powerlessness, as horror films often do. Nothing is more terrifying than that feeling; perhaps like me, you have had that nightmare that someone or something is in your house and you are paralyzed, unable to move? The Sunken Place, where Chris is put when he is hypnotized by Missy Armitage (Catherine Keener), is a place of awareness; Chris can see what is happening in the world around him but can't move a muscle to change it. He is trapped, unable to escape, and he faces the threat that this will be his fate for the rest of the life: He will see the world but forever lose any agency in it. In the *New York Times Magazine*, Wesley Morris described the Sunken Place as "the movie's most potent metaphor" and recounted how Peele came to associate it with the mass incarceration of African American men: "The first moment in the writing process where I sat there and cried ... was realizing that while I was having fun writing this mischievous popcorn film, there were real black people who were being abducted and put into dark holes, and the worst part of it is we don't think about them."[39]

In her bestselling *The New Jim Crow: Mass Incarceration in the Age of Colorblindness*, Michelle Alexander writes that the fictional Sunken Place is a reality for far too many African Americans, locked out of the mainstream society and its economy. Alexander speaks of mass incarceration as "a system that locks people not only behind actual bars in actual prisons, but also behind virtual bars and virtual walls—walls that are invisible to the naked eye but function nearly as effectively as Jim Crow laws once did at locking people of color into a permanent second-class citizenship." The position of African Americans in America today is, she says, as a permanent undercaste, "permanently barred by law and custom from mainstream society." One could not find a more accurate—or chilling—statement of the relevance of the Sunken Place.[40]

Since the release of the film, the Sunken Place has entered the more general discourse, coming to represent not just incarceration and control but concepts like disenfranchisement and racial self-estrangement (an idea that Morris puts forward as an explanation for the behavior of people of color who may seem to be under the control of white people: Clarence Thomas, Ben Carson, O. J. Simpson, "Kanye West and any black person with something nice to say about President Trump").[41] The Sunken Place represents a great number of things we fear—and that we see in everyday life where race is concerned. The close-ups on the black characters who have lost their bodies and now reside only in the Sunken Place are among the most horrific of the film. Georgina's teary, smiling, head-shaking response to Chris's statement that he gets nervous when too many white people are around—the chilling "No, no, no"—became a widely shared meme, and Dre, momentarily brought to the surface by the flash from Chris's camera, screams at him to get out before he too loses himself forever.

Get Out represents things we fear, whether black or white. Peele has talked about how the movie represents everything he is scared by. He told the *New York Times* that "to me, it was the missing piece of the conversation. I'd never seen my fears as an African-American man onscreen in this way."[42] Morris agreed, saying that *Get Out* is "a movie made by a person having the same bad dream I and lots of other black people have had." Movies about the things we fear fit solidly into the horror genre. But the film also works in a second genre, as social satire, exploring the things black people fear and white people should be ashamed of with a deft comic touch that should surprise no one, seeing that Peele came to fame as a standup comic in the sketch comedy show *Key & Peele* with Keegan-Michael Key.[43] Zadie Smith writes that what the film explores with a deft touch is "a compendium of black fears about white folk. White women who date black men. Waspy families. Waspy garden parties. Ukeleles. Crazy younger brothers. Crazy younger brothers who play ukuleles. Sexual psychopaths, hunting, guns, cannibalism, mind control, well-meaning conversations about Obama."[44]

The movie is genuinely horrifying but often genuinely funny as well; it puts its fingers on serious issues but also identifies genuine behaviors recognizable to both black and white audiences. Owen Gleiberman says that *Get Out* is not only a "slashing satire of white people" that permits white audiences to understand, perhaps for the first time, their faux pas and what racism feels like to people of color but also "a slashing satire of black identity and anxiety."[45] Satire holds things up to ridicule in the hope of teaching something. It is Jonathan Swift in *Gulliver's Travels* holding his culture up to the light and showing his readers what is stupid about it. It is Jon Stewart or Trevor Noah on *The Daily Show*, rolling their eyes at the day's news. Communications scholar Jennifer Keohane writes that "satire has an uncanny ability to speak truth to power. And that in a world where many Americans get their news from satirical shows, the host of *The Daily Show* matters a great deal."[46] Satire can help us come to grips with details of our lives we hadn't realized were ridiculous and help us see the news of the day through a filter that enables us to both laugh at it and somehow appropriate it.

Horror is a hot medium; it inserts you in a story. Satire is cold; it invites you to sit back and laugh at something. By combining them, *Get Out* offers audiences an inside/out experience. At times we are Chris, trapped in the Sunken Place. At other times we are standing back at some remove and recognizing the absurdity of white superiority and the violence against black lives. Even though Peele made *Get Out* for a black audience, white people can enter into it and learn from it. My student Maddie Ebrey said that before she saw *Get Out* in the National Cathedral and listened to the panel conversation following it, she had never really understood all the aggressions, micro and macro, that white people impose on people of color. The possibility of evoking such empathy was a part of Peele's intent for the film. Morris notes that, because of our identification with Chris, "White audiences are pushed into an uncomfortable new experience. 'One of the reasons this movie clicked with more than just a black audience,' Peele said, 'is because you get to be black while you're watching it.' "[47] Producer Jason Blum says that *Get Out* is a movie about racism in "liberal, elite America . . . The truth is, there's a lot of racism that exists in that thinking, and inside me, that I wasn't aware of. There are things that I would have done two years ago that I would not do now as a result of making the movie. It's impossible for me not to imagine that many, many people have had the same experience."[48]

It's difficult for a white viewer to experience the movie and be unmoved and unchanged. I told the audience in the National Cathedral that this film had been a transformative experience for me, a moment of huge grace and understanding:

> One of the great cinematic and theological things that comes together in this film is that Jordan Peele has made such an amazing film, and he's used so many cinematic devices to make any kind of audience identify with the main characters in it that he has actually offered white audiences this incredible gift of grace, to have that sort of moment that Spencer Tracy had in [*Guess Who's Coming to Dinner*] last night where he says, "Well, I'll be a son of a bitch." If you can watch this film and not have in your very bones a sense of, "Oh my God, I've been watching this happen from the sidelines, and this is what it feels like." Because Jordan Peele asks all of us to inhabit Chris. And I can understand that it's incredibly powerful for a black audience to see that, but for me as a middle-class white man, to have that grace extended where I can see through the eyes of Chris and see what this feels like, even, you know, the tiniest bit of it. I mean, every time I watch this movie, I have an "I'll be a son of a bitch" moment where I am woke, maybe, for a little bit.[49]

It is this power of story that, in the face of all the horrors, offers us hope that we might be able to move past where we've been, all the offenses against black bodies, all the misunderstanding of white minds. *Get Out* offers to open a conversation between black people and newly empathetic people outside the black experience that might lead in the direction of greater awareness, greater compassion, and greater justice.

The Power of Hope: Black Bodies Reclaimed

My work with the Very Rev. Dr. Douglas has been an instrument of grace and understanding for me during the writing of this book. I am too white to claim to be "woke," but our collaboration and friendship has helped me to become more awake. She has taught me much about the African American experience, not simply how she watches a film differently than I do as a middle-class white man, but how she lives life differently, and how the people she loves live life differently as well. In her book *Stand Your Ground: Black Bodies and the Justice of God*, she speaks of how very personal the Trayvon Martin shooting was for her, how it was "another young black male killed for no other reason than the fact of his blackness." And, just as Barack Obama understood that Trayvon Martin could have been his son, as the mother of a black man, she understood all too well that "[p]arents of black male children know that the world poses a much greater danger to our sons than they do to the world."[50]

It seems sometimes, in fact, that black bodies are simply here to be overpowered, to be imprisoned, to be lynched, to be murdered. In the films we've discussed, consider the following: Gus's body is dumped on a front porch in *The Birth of a Nation*; Radio Raheem's body is flung into the back of a police car at the end of *Do the Right Thing*; Peter's body is tossed out of a car in the Hollywood Hills after Officer Hansen shoots him in *Crash*; Chris in *Get Out* is strapped to a chair in a basement as he awaits his own extinction.

One of the most potent tropes in horror films is the convention that a black character in a horror film (as in many genres) will be the first to die. One of the most important changes—and one of the most affirmative—that Peele rings on the horror genre is simply changing that convention. Normally the white virgin survives to scream another day. As Morris puts it, "'Final Girl' is a horror trope. 'Final Brother' is not." Peele reverses not only that tired trope—he says that in *Get Out*, "Daniel [Kaluuya becomes] the final girl"—but also the well-founded expectation that an encounter between a person of color and law enforcement must mean incarceration or a violent death.[51] By rewriting the ending of the film after Trump's election, Peele felt he was offering the necessary hope his community required and acknowledging the possibility of black power. Some lament the loss of the original ending, in which Chris is taken into custody and imprisoned, but having watched this movie multiple times with an audience, I can tell you that the moment at the film's climax when we see the flashing lights as the police car pulls up, a collective groan goes up from the crowd. They get that Chris's guilt or innocence is irrelevant. As Bradley Whitford put it, "The ending he ended up with does a brilliant thing, because when Chris is strangling Rose in the driveway, you see the red police lights, and then you see the door open and it says 'Airport' and it's a huge laugh and everybody has that same laugh and release. You understand from Chris's POV that if the cops come, he's a dead man. That is absolutely brilliant, non-lecturing storytelling."[52]

It is also necessary storytelling. In a time of despair and renewed oppression, this ending offers the possibility of change, the power of hope. Marcus Henderson, who played Walter in the film, says

> I remember when they gave the verdict that Darren Wilson wouldn't be indicted [in the Ferguson shooting], and you felt defeated. Like, "Man! Can't we catch a break?" What the original ending said was, "No, you can't catch a break," because that's our reality. But the new ending gave us a break, and I think that's why we enjoyed it so much because we want it so badly. The similarities of the narrative are so parallel to what actually happened in Ferguson. When I have conversations with people about it, we talk about the importance of watching that black body get away to tell his story. Because you know who didn't get to tell their own story? Trayvon Martin. Mike Brown. Philandro Castile.[53]

Peele told Hart that a happy ending seemed essential given the present moment, given the reemergence of open racism as a tangible force in American society: "I remember specifically feeling that when I showed the original ending . . . It's meant to be a gut blow, but it's also a downer . . . Because the state of the world had evolved, that's when I made the decision to give us a happy ending, which I don't know if I would have in the Obama era . . . when everyone seemed certain that race wasn't a thing anymore."[54] *Get Out* producer Sean McKittrick similarly recalled how, when they showed the original ending to test audiences, it seemed to suck all the air out of the room: "The country was different. We weren't in the Obama era, we were in this new world where all the racism crept out from under the rocks again. It was always an ending that we debated back and forth, so we decided to go back and shoot the pieces for the other ending where Chris wins."[55] (If in fact, we can consider it a "win"; Chris will live with his memories, his heartbreak, and his trauma forever. But survival against the odds is always a potent narrative.)

The Very Rev. Dr. Douglas wrote that "[a]fter Trayvon's killer was acquitted, one of my church members, with tears in her eyes, despaired, 'There is no hope; our black children will never be safe.' I said to her, 'As long as there is a God, there is hope.'"[56] Hope is one of the greatest human needs, and happy endings are important, not just as reflections on contemporary culture, but as theological statements. J. R. R. Tolkien, in his essay "On Fairy Stories," talks about the concept of the "eucatastrophe," a word he coined to describe how in great stories the world ends—but for a character who survives that cataclysm, transformation becomes possible, and perhaps for the larger world as well.

In Tolkien's *The Lord of the Rings*, the old world passes, yet characters live through the disaster, and the new world offers an opportunity for change and growth, a concept described by the word "metanoia." *Metanoia* is typically translated in the Christian Testament as "repentance," as though what we are called to do is refrain from doing things in the old way. But the true meaning of *metanoia* is "turn," a 180-degree turn away from the person we have been and into the person we might become.

Get Out offers us—as members of the audience—the possibility of metanoia. By overturning so many horror tropes—the black man as the first to die, the survival of the white woman, the ineffectual comic best friend—and by offering us the satirical gift of recognition, *Get Out* tells us that a new world is possible. Possible? No: necessary. The way things have always been leads us only to more people of color sunk in the Sunken Place, more white people controlling black bodies. There must be a new way, in which slavery, incarceration, and control are no longer the story in which we live. Owen Gleiberman writes that "part of the film's catharsis is that its very existence proves that we're strong enough, as racially diverse moviegoers, to unite and giggle in fearful suspense at a vision that hits this luridly close to home. We may not—yet—be one nation under a groove, but we're one nation under a megaplex roof. And we're more than ready for a horror movie that uses the elixir of organic storytelling to bring us together by laying bare the ways that we remain scandalously apart."[57] Narrative can help us, can offer hope, can lead us into conversation.

African American theology also offers us hope and the possibility of conversation. When Trayvon Martin's killer was acquitted, his father, Tracy Martin, said, "My heart is broken, but my faith is unshattered." The Very Rev. Dr. Douglas concluded from his statement that "[t]he father's faith claim points to the story of the God who liberated the Israelites from a land where their bodies were being devalued and destroyed . . . The faith of a father points to an Exodus God who is with a people through a wilderness journey to forge a new life."[58]

The Exodus story is seminal for both Jews and Christians. It is recounted in the Hebrew Testament books of Exodus, Numbers, Deuteronomy, and Joshua. The Exodus story tells how the descendants of Joseph escaped slavery in Egypt and found the place where they belonged. In Exodus, we are told that a new pharaoh arose who did not remember Joseph and his contributions to Egypt, and so the Children of Israel, Joseph's descendants, were forced into bondage. "After a long time," Exodus tells us, "the king of Egypt died. The Israelites groaned under their slavery and cried out. Out of the slavery their cry for help rose up to God. God heard their groaning, and God remembered his covenant with Abraham, Isaac, and Jacob. God looked upon the Israelites, and God took notice of them."[59] God raised up a leader, Moses, to confront the pharaoh and demand the release of the Israelites so that they could travel to a land that God would give them. God worked ten wonders to force the Egyptian ruler to release the Israelites; God turned water to blood, brought forth plagues of frogs and flies, and sent the Angel of Death to slay the first-born animals and children of Egypt.

When the pharaoh had let them depart, God told Moses, "I will harden Pharaoh's heart, and he will pursue them, so that I will gain glory for myself over Pharaoh and all his army; and the Egyptians shall know that I am the Lord."[60] Then God parted the waters of the Red Sea so that the Israelites could cross on dry land—and sent the waters cascading down on their enemies to destroy them. Afterwards, the Israelites wandered for a long time in the wilderness because they lost faith in the Lord, but ultimately they were shown the land of Canaan, a land of milk and honey, and in the Book of Joshua they took possession of that land God had granted them.

The Exodus story—how the Israelites were taken from a reality of slavery and oppression in Egypt to a new life in the Promised Land—has for hundreds of years been one of the central narratives of black American Christianity. Slaves clung to this biblical story of liberation as a pillar of hope. Dr. King drew from the Exodus narrative of liberation in sermons, speeches, and essays, perhaps most notably at the conclusion of his "I Have a Dream" speech, delivered on the Washington Mall in 1963: "Free at last, free at last, thank God Almighty, we are free at last!" And liberation is at the heart of much black theology, as evidenced by the words of James H. Cone in his seminal *God of the Oppressed*: "If asked the theological question, 'Who Is God?' one black person might say: 'I don't know much about him. All I know is that I was weak and God gave me strength. I was lost and God found me. I was crying and Jesus wiped away the tears from my eyes.'" What characterizes the identity of God—as reflected in this story of the Exodus—is "the verbal assent to the power of God to grant identity and liberation."[61] God is a God who is with the suffering; God is a God who liberates from the Sunken Place.

That liberation is not just for black bodies and lives; it is also for the white people who directly or indirectly have participated in a system that dominates and destroys black bodies. Saint Anthony the Great said that our salvation is with our brother (and sister). Truer words were never spoken. Dr. King often said that prejudice and oppression imprisoned the white race as well as the black; Baldwin told his beloved nephew James that he must accept white people, and accept them with love, for they had no other hope, trapped as they were in a history that for the most part they did not understand: "We cannot be free until they are free."[62] Our salvation, in other words, is with our neighbor.

While writing this book, I was privileged to meet the Rev. Robert W. Lee IV (a distant nephew of General Robert E. Lee), who lost his church after speaking out against Charlottesville, after speaking in favor of taking down statues of Confederate war heroes like his ancestor, after speaking out for Black Lives Matter. The Rev. Lee has thought deeply about how God is working in conversations and transformations in the South, where he lives, and around the country as we face racism and seek liberation. Toward the end of his memoir, Lee wrote about liberation, remembering how his professor Stanley

Hauerwas had said that "[t]he same God who brought the Israelites out of Egypt is the God who brought Jesus out of the tomb." This God of liberation and life, Lee wrote, is "a God who is deeply concerned and invested with the liberation of the South and its history."[63] Liberation for white America cannot come until all are liberated. Until all of us are free, Dr. King said, none of us is free. And all of us are not free yet, as the snapshots from recent history—and ongoing violence and oppression—prove.

African Americans are not unique in their oppression; many people have been enslaved in the history of the world, many have been treated as inferior, many have been marginalized. But in this story of the Exodus, in this story of a God who identifies with the suffering and set aside, in this story of liberation and new life, we come to the place where we all hope to arrive: the place of hope. If God exists, as the Very Rev. Dr. Douglas says, there is always hope, and the end of *Get Out* offers that hope for audiences still sunk in a racist society. A black man can emerge from bondage, another black man can be his rescuer, and he can survive even a story intended to take away every part of him that matters.

Our society can perhaps get out of the Sunken Place where we find ourselves and enter into a story of liberation, but it will require recognition and conversation and true repentance along the way. We will not know exactly what the future will look like until we arrive there. In our conclusion, we'll consider how our conversations about these films might serve as part of a larger societal conversation about race, prejudice, reconciliation, and healing—and of individual conversations that lead to real change.

8

Conclusion

Remembrance, Contrition, and Hope

A great nation does not hide its history. It faces its flaws
and corrects them.
George W. Bush, dedicating the Museum of African
American History and Culture

In September 2018, I was in Washington, DC, for a planning meeting
for the "Long, Long Way" film festival. On a football game day,
I walked across the campus of Georgetown University. I had been
coming to Georgetown for over thirty years, and the university looked
much as I remembered it. But my reaction this time was shaped by
ongoing news reports about the university's response to the recognition that in 1838 it had been rescued from financial ruin by the sale
of 272 slaves. I walked past the well-kept graves of Jesuits—some of
whom may have been involved in that slave sale, others who may have
benefited directly during their lifetimes from slave labor. Healy Hall,
a great, gray, grim Hogwarts of a building, commanded the eye at the
campus entrance on O Street, as did the statue of Father Healy in front
of the building. At first it seemed that not much had changed.

But then I saw a banner touting Georgetown's diversity, and as
I looked around at the students, gathering at tables and on sidewalks
before the game, I discovered a rainbow of colors. Whatever happened
here 180 years ago, something had shifted—has shifted, even over the
last thirty years. Where once white people were privileged and powerful, now I saw amazing diversity.

I passed Healy Hall and turned down the hill on Library Walk,
where I saw signs for the two buildings I was seeking: Isaac

Hawkins Hall, named after the first slave on that 1838 sale manifest, and Anne Marie Becraft Hall, named for a pioneer African
American Catholic educator. These buildings had previously been
named for past presidents of Georgetown, the very presidents who
had overseen the sale of the college's slaves to buyers in Louisiana.
Now they were memorials to a past that could not be changed but
could be remembered, regretted, and repented. That naming and
claiming of a hard story could become the basis for honest conversation and, maybe someday, for reconciliation. In the words of
Joe Ferrara, vice president and chief of staff to Georgetown's president, it was "acknowledging our history and making sure we never
forget it. This has to be a part of the fabric of how we understand
the university."[1]

A Working Group on Slavery, Memory, and Reconciliation was established at Georgetown in 2015 to explore "how best to acknowledge
and recognize this history." After a period of soul-searching involving
participants from President John J. DeGioia on down, on April 18,
2017, the university rededicated the newly named buildings, offering a
"Liturgy of Remembrance, Contrition, and Hope."[2] Presiding over the
liturgy, the Rev. Matthew Carnes acknowledged Georgetown's history
of racism and asked forgiveness for it:

> For the participation of our predecessors in the national tragedy of
> slavery, for the failure of moral imagination and conviction to call
> into question the perpetuated evil, and for the privilege and benefit
> accrued from their complicity, we pray:
>> Forgive us, O Lord.
> For the treatment of the 272 men, women, and children who were
> considered as property to be sold, whose lives were valued as little
> more than monetary worth, and whose labors were proffered not by
> choice but by force we pray:
>> Forgive us, O Lord.
> For the many women, men, and children, those known, those
> whose names are yet to be discovered, and those forgotten,
> that came here without choice and toiled here without consent,
> we pray:
>> Forgive us, O Lord.

From the desire to hide from our histories, to flee from the failures of the past, and the impulse to avoid shining the bright light of truth in the dark shadows of yesterday, we pray:

Deliver us, O Lord.[3]

James Baldwin, who has been a guide on our journey together, wrote, "To accept one's past—one's history—is not the same thing as drowning in it; it is learning how to use it."[4] We have drawn attention to past and present depictions of race and prejudice in American film, mourning the harmful and celebrating the helpful, and we have entered into conversation with critics, theologians, and filmgoers across the decades. I hope we have arrived at a place from which we can accept that past, acknowledge it, and regret it. How do we move forward from this point?

During that trip to Washington, DC, I also met with the Very Rev. Randolph Hollerith, dean of Washington National Cathedral. The previous September, I had heard Dean Hollerith preach on the Cathedral's decision to remove stained-glass windows honoring Robert E. Lee and Stonewall Jackson, which had been donated by the Daughters of the Confederacy. In that sermon, Dean Hollerith described a similar process of recognition, prayer, and conversation leading to action:

I know some of you are relieved that this decision has been made and others are quite sad, disappointed, even angry that these two windows have been removed from the sacred fabric of the Cathedral. What I can tell you is that this was not an easy decision, a quick decision, or one that anyone took lightly. Rather, after almost two years of conversation and programming around these windows and the larger issues of race, racism and the legacy of slavery, the Bishop and I, along with the Chapter, came to the decision that these windows were an obstacle to our mission to be a house of prayer for all people; they were an obstacle to the work of building the Beloved Community, and we needed to let them go. In short, as the body of Christ we came to the decision that the people we serve are more important than the fabric we protect.[5]

The experiences of Georgetown University and of Washington National Cathedral, and the larger national conversation about memorials to Confederate heroes and the honored dead, offer us the possibility that we can do more than just think and talk; it allows us to hope that we can act for a society in which justice and freedom are more accessible. As New Orleans mayor Mitch Landrieu said on the occasion of removing the last Confederate memorial in his city, "To literally put the Confederacy on a pedestal in our most prominent places of honor is an inaccurate recitation of our full past. It is an affront to our present, and it is a bad prescription for our future. History cannot be changed. It cannot be moved like a statue."[6] But in these real-world attempts at reconciliation, we see the process carried to logical lengths that might help us move into a brighter future.

In all of these cases, people and institutions with power and history on their side opted to revisit and revise their stories, and people in a position of privilege expressed regret for past expressions of racism and a desire to move in the direction of healing. It strikes me that this is exactly the situation of America and its cultural history. During the past three years, as I've shown American films about race and prejudice around the country and spoken with experts and audience members, I've found a similar process at work, a process I've tried to replicate in this book. These powerful stories about racism past and present have given viewers new insights into the personal and institutional bases of prejudice and have often led them to confront racism in their own experiences. They have offered people the chance to talk about race with less defensiveness, to begin the truly difficult conversations that must be ongoing if our nation—if our world—is ever to have a chance of being whole.

Theologian Kelly Brown Douglas and I have often talked about the necessity of beginning these conversations. For both of us, there is a faith component involved. "These conversations are not optional," she has often said. "They are the Gospel." She also says, "These conversations aren't always easy, but they are necessary for getting to a better place . . . Building more authentic institutions starts with learning how to talk, and listen, authentically about who we have been, who we are, and who we dream to become."[7]

I know that these conversations are often difficult, just as the subject matter of the films is difficult: Stories about racism and prejudice show us human beings at their worst, shatter us with scenes of human suffering, and, if we are white, confront us with realities that may not be apparent to us in our daily lives. I was so strongly affected by *12 Years a Slave* that I could not rise from my seat when the lights came up in the theater, and I was far from the only audience member so afflicted. But I remember, with affection, that hundred-year-old woman from Houston who watched her first horror film ever with me, and who committed to see *Get Out* again because she wanted to understand her racist society better.

Why have I given the last three years of my life to these conversations and to this writing? Why as a middle-aged and middle-class white male did I feel compelled to speak, write, and preach on race? I hope by this point in the book, that is no longer a question. But I still encounter resistance from some white people, sometimes even after screenings and conversations about these films. The other night, after a conversation about *Casablanca*, a white Episcopalian man asked why we had to take on the guilt of our forefathers and protested that these conversations made him feel bad. I assured him that I understood—but that, nonetheless, we were called to have them. Kevin O'Brien, a Jesuit theologian who was part of the Georgetown Working Committee, told me that it is important to be pulled to the truth, no matter how painful it may be, to avoid being defensive, and to be really engaging history so as to push it out into the light of day: "What we were naming—well, the truth really does set us free."[8]

Brené Brown would agree that it is important to name that hard truth, even when it makes us cringe. She says, "To opt out of conversations that are difficult, or that we won't do perfectly because they're uncomfortable, is the definition of privilege. It boils down to a very simple question on those big fault lines of racism, sexism, homophobia, class: Are you choosing your own human comfort over making a decision that is in line with our faith?"[9] These conversations are not optional. "What is the conversation you don't want to have?" Dr. Catherine Meeks asked. "Go and have it."[10]

One epiphany does not a just society make. While the truth can begin to set us free, it is not definitive. Georgetown's Joe Ferrara recognizes that the working report of the committee did not end the university's work of reconciliation, or of reparation. (On April 12, 2019, in a nonbinding referendum, Georgetown students voted to create a fund to provide reparations to the descendants of the slaves.)[11] This ongoing process, Ferrara says, "is very much a permanent part of our work. We didn't wake up one day and declare victory."[12] Similarly, Randolph Hollerith told me that removing the Lee and Jackson windows (and ultimately exhibiting them with historical and cultural context supplied) does not complete the National Cathedral's work: "It's going to take time. The historical memories of the Cathedral's past racism will last awhile. But we're working to change all that." The Cathedral reinstituted the position of Canon Missioner. The Rev. Canon Leonard L. Hamlin, Sr., formerly minister of Macedonia Baptist Church in Arlington, Virginia, took office in April 2018 and now heads the Cathedral's efforts on racial reconciliation. The Cathedral seeks to be more racially balanced in worship, consciously offering preachers and readers who reflect the makeup of the larger community. Dean Hollerith also cited the "Becoming Beloved Community" initiative of the national Episcopal Church as a set of guiding principles for the ongoing work of reconciliation.[13]

For us, naming and claiming, expressing contrition, and even engaging in conversation about race, violence, justice, policing, and privilege are not the end; rather, they are only the beginning of an ongoing process of learning to live together and recognizing our biases and prejudices. Catherine Meeks has said that she no longer even uses the word "reconciliation" in her work toward racial healing. "Everyone is anxious to jump straight to reconciliation," she told me. People seem to think it is a sprint—I confess that I am certainly ready for a just society—when actually, Dr. Meeks suggests, it is a marathon.[14]

But that long, long way cannot begin without the first steps, which is where we will conclude. America's history swells with stories of racism and prejudice, narratives, images, and stereotypes we are called to mark, name as offensive, and seek to replace with something more true, more just. And our personal reflection, our own awareness is an important step, but, as Baldwin wrote, in this country we have to live, to heal, and to find new stories together: "The price of the liberation of the white people is the liberation of the blacks—the total liberation, in the cities, in the towns, before the law, and in the mind . . . In short, we, the black and the white, deeply need each other here if we are really to become a nation—if we are really, that is, to achieve our destiny, our maturity, as men and women."[15] In other words, contra *The Birth of a Nation*, which depicted America as one Aryan nation, now and forever united in opposition to anyone who isn't part of the white mainstream, we have to continue to have the conversations about race and division that might be sparked by that film and *Guess Who's Coming to Dinner* and *Do the Right Thing* and *Get Out*.

At the Liturgy of Remembrance, Contrition, and Hope, Jeremy Alexander, one of the descendants of the Georgetown slaves, followed the Intercessions for Contrition by offering Intercessions for Hope, ending with this:

> May a commitment to those pushed aside and forgotten be renewed, may a sense of personal accountability for their struggles abide, and may the light of love radiate out and heal the abiding wounds of our nation, we pray:
> Give us hope, O Lord.[16]

We have come a long, long way; there is still a long, long way left to go. But we can choose to journey in hope instead of despair, to journey together instead of in segregated groups of people who look like us and love like us and spend like us. We can recognize stories that divide us. And we can watch and celebrate stories that remind us that we all want to be loved and valued and seen, that we are so much more alike than we are different.

That is the end of our work together.

And the beginning.

Acknowledgments

All of my books have been collaborative acts, but none more so than this one. During the three years I have been thinking about the book, I have also been continually engaged in reading, film viewing, and conversations that taught me things I hadn't known when I first proposed this project. For the screenings and conversations that first launched this idea, I am grateful to the Rev. David Andrews and the Church of Saints Andrew and Matthew in Wilmington, Delaware. Other screenings or presentations on race and reconciliation that shaped the writing of this book took place at the American Cathedral in Paris; Westmoreland Congregational United Church of Christ in Bethesda, Maryland; the Hines Center and Christ Church Cathedral in Houston, Texas; Wilshire Baptist Church in Dallas, Texas; the Episcopal Diocese of the Central Gulf Coast in Fairhope, Alabama; and the full-blown film festivals that have grown from this work at Trinity Wall Street, New York City, and the Long, Long Way Film Festival at Washington National Cathedral.

At both festivals I was privileged to work with the Very Rev. Kelly Brown Douglas, and one of the great treasures of these past few years has been our friendship and ongoing collaboration. At Trinity Wall Street, it was also a joy to work with Bob Scott, Ruth Frey, Angelica Roman-Jimenez, and all of Trinity's great staff in Formation, Education, Justice, Programming, and Publicity. At the National Cathedral, I am grateful for the support of Dean Randy Hollerith and the excellent work of Program Director Michelle Dibblee, who, with Dean Douglas and me, created and continues to administer the Long, Long Way Film Festival. I also owe a huge debt to my onstage conversation partners, including, in New York City, Dean Douglas, Melissa Harris-Perry, Catherine Meeks, Michael Gillespie, Stanley Talbert, Lisa Thompson, and Daveed Diggs; in Washington, DC, Korva Coleman,

Vann Newkirk, Lenika Cruz, Yolanda Pierce, and Dean Douglas; and in Houston, Sean Palmer and Alexander Johnson.

Baylor University has offered funding on multiple levels for my research, writing, and continued exploration of these important topics. The University supported this work through a major internal grant, the Dr. Benjamin F. Brown IV Fund for Interdisciplinary and Collaborative Scholarship, which offered me the chance to travel widely and build up a library of books on race and reconciliation. The Baylor College of Arts & Sciences (along with the National Cathedral and the Austin Film Festival) sponsors the Long, Long Way Film Festival, and the College and Baylor's Department of English together have paid for me and for Baylor undergraduates to attend it each year. The Department also offered me the expert help of research assistants Daniel Smith and Mackenzie Balken during the research phase of this book. My gratitude to Dean Lee Nordt and my department chair, Kevin Gardner, cannot be measured. Thank you, gentlemen. There would be no book without your generous support, and I am so proud of Baylor's involvement in this ongoing work of racial reconciliation.

I've been privileged to work with the great editor Cynthia Read at Oxford University Press on three books now and have benefited from a team of great public relations professionals in the United Kingdom and in the United States. Each book has been a pleasure to talk about, and I look forward to the conversations that will emerge from this work.

At the American Cathedral in Paris, this work has been supported and encouraged by Dean Lucinda Laird, Zach Ullery, Tony Holmes, Dennis Mana-Ay, Bill Tompson, Gabriella Meloni, and Nicholas Criss. My work at the American Cathedral as Theologian in Residence offered opportunities to initiate conversations through programming on race, to screen *Moonlight* in the Cathedral nave, and to do research and write at the American Library in Paris, where I am a grateful member. I worked on this book over three summers and assorted visits in Paris, and again, without the Cathedral's advocacy, this book could not exist. It is dedicated to the American Cathedral in recognition of its essential work on the frontlines of faith and culture, and of my ongoing appreciation.

Allen Fisher and Jenna de Graffenried helped me navigate the riches of the Lyndon Baines Johnson Presidential Library in Austin, Texas. Joseph Ferrara took time from his busy schedule to talk about the ongoing racial reconciliation work at Georgetown University, in particular their response to the slave sales of the nineteenth century. I also had a valuable conversation on the aims of the Georgetown Working Group with Kevin O'Brien, who is now president of Santa Clara University in Santa Clara, California. Thanks also to Vann Newkirk and Lenika Cruz, both of *The Atlantic*, for meeting and talking with me about race, films, and this project outside of the public programs on which we appeared together.

The Austin Film Festival, in addition to cosponsoring the important public programs that shaped this work, offered me the chance to speak with many writers and filmmakers; the AFF team members have devoted themselves to diversity and to the telling of everyone's stories. I am grateful to director Barbara Morgan and conference director Colin Hyer, as well as to the entire AFF team, and am so thankful for our continued work together.

Terry Nathan (of blessed memory), and his daughter Alison Nathan Huxel, offered me space and time for much of the writing of this book in 2018 and 2019. Their homes in the Texas Hill Country have become treasured places where I've written well. Thanks to both of them and to Alison's husband Jeff for their generosity and friendship over the years.

St. George's Episcopal Church, Austin, offered me an office after I concluded my term as writer in residence at the Seminary of the Southwest, also in Austin. I am grateful for the Rev. Kevin Schubert and the vestry of St. George's for the space and time to read and write there, and to Scott Bader-Saye and the Very Rev. Cynthia Kittredge for my eleven good years of fellowship and writing at Seminary of the Southwest.

I owe much to friends who have talked with me about these topics, too many to remember, let alone name, but including Rowan Williams and his family, Greg and Marti Rickel, Martyn Percy, Tim Ditchfield and his family, Ken Malcolm, Kevin Schubert, Hulitt Gloer, Danielle Tumminio Hansen, Richard Russell, Tom Hanks, Deanna Toten Beard, Tim Tutt, and many, many others. I am especially grateful for writers, producers, and directors who have talked with me about our shared passion for movies, including James V. Hart, Peter Hedges, Mark Protosevich, and Scott Myers. I am rich in friendships.

As I am in family. Without the forbearance of my daughters, Lily and Sophie; the encouragement of my son, Chandler; and the sustaining love of my wife, Jeanie, you would be holding only empty pages. My greatest thanks are to them.

Notes

Chapter 1

1. James Baldwin, *The Devil Finds Work* (1976; New York: Vintage, 2011), 35.
2. Oliver Jones, "Some of the Best 'BlacKkKlansman' Scenes Serve No Plot Purpose—And Save the Film," *The Observer*, August 8, 2018, http://observer.com/2018/08/review-spike-lees-blackkklansman-might-be-his-most-ambitious-movie/.
3. With thanks to the good people of Wilshire Baptist Church, Dallas, Texas, and to Senior Pastor George Mason, who helped me formulate this contrasting description in conversations and worship over a weekend in August 2018.
4. David Brooks, "How Cool Works in America Today," *New York Times*, July 25, 2017, https://www.nytimes.com/2017/07/25/opinion/how-cool-works-in-america-today.html.
5. "A Long, Long Way," Washington National Cathedral, February 17, 2018.
6. Kimberly Kindy et al., "Fatal Shootings by Police Are Up in the First Six Months of 2016, *Post* Analysis Finds," *Washington Post*, July 7, 2016, https://www.washingtonpost.com/national/fatal-shootings-by-police-surpass-2015s-rate/2016/07/07/81b708f2-3d42-11e6-84e8-1580c7db5275_story.html.
7. "On Views of Race and Inequality, Blacks and Whites Are Worlds Apart," pewsocialtrends.org, June 27, 2016, http://www.pewsocialtrends.org/2016/06/27/on-views-of-race-and-inequality-blacks-and-whites-are-worlds-apart/.
8. Michael Eric Dyson, *The Black Presidency: Barack Obama and the Politics of Race in America* (Boston: Houghton Mifflin Harcourt, 2016), ii.
9. Nicky Woolf, "Idris Elba and Tina Fey Invited to More Diverse Academy After #OscarsSoWhite," *The Guardian*, June 30, 2016, http://www.theguardian.stfi.re/film/2016/jun/29/oscars-motion-picture-academy-diversity?CMP=oth_b-aplnews_d-3&sf=exwpjax&utm_content=buffer87d8b&utm_medium=social&utm_source=twitter.com&utm_campaign=buffer#ab.

10. "Most Americans Say Trump's Election Has Led to Worse Race Relations in the U.S.," Pew Research Center, December 19, 2017, http://www.people-press.org/2017/12/19/most-americans-say-trumps-election-has-led-to-worse-race-relations-in-the-u-s/.

11. Martin Luther King, Jr., "Transcript of Dr. Martin Luther King Jr.'s Speech at SMU on March 17, 1966," smu.edu, January 10, 2014, https://www.smu.edu/News/NewsSources/MLKatSMU/mlk-at-smu-transcript-17march1966.

12. One important caveat I should insert is that a disproportionate number of Hollywood film moguls and filmmakers in Hollywood's first half-century were Jewish. These were certainly people who knew more than a little about being an oppressed minority. But they were also trying to create mass entertainment for a mainstream white culture, and their films usually demonstrate that fact, whatever sympathy or subversion might sneak into their narratives. See Neil Gabler's *An Empire of Their Own: How the Jews Invented Hollywood* (New York: Crown, 1988).

13. James Baldwin, "The Fire Next Time," in *The Fire Next Time* (1963; New York: Vintage, 1993), 25–26.

14. Ta-Nehisi Coates, *Between the World and Me* (New York: Spiegel & Grau, 2015), 43.

15. Emma G. Fitzsimmons, "As Second Avenue Subway Opens, a Train Delay Ends in (Happy) Tears," *New York Times*, January 1, 2017, http://www.nytimes.com/2017/01/01/nyregion/as-second-avenue-subway-opens-a-train-delay-ends-in-happy-tears.html?_r=0.

16. Hurr Murtaza, email, July 12, 2018.

17. Scott Feinberg, "LA Film Critics Association Awards: Big Nights for 'Moonlight,' Other Indie Darlings," *Hollywood Reporter*, January 14, 2017, http://www.hollywoodreporter.com/race/la-film-critics-association-awards-big-night-moonlight-indie-darlings-964423.

18. "A Long, Long Way: Race and Film 1968–2018," Washington National Cathedral, Washington, DC, February 16, 2018.

19. Julia Joffe, "We Can't Make Our Elections About Being Against Trump," *The Atlantic*, April 2018, 29.

20. Kelly Brown Douglas, "A Long, Long Way," February 16, 2018.

21. Donald Bogle, *Toms, Coons, Mulattoes, Mammies, and Bucks: An Interpretive History of Blacks in American Films*, 5th ed. (New York: Bloomsbury, 2016), 1.

22. "An Offer He Couldn't Refuse: Al Pacino Reveals Marlon Brando Kept Him in *The Godfather* when Francis Ford Coppola Wanted to Sack Him," *Daily*

Mail, December 7, 2010, http://www.dailymail.co.uk/tvshowbiz/article-1336468/Al-Pacino-reveals-Marlon-Brando-kept-The-Godfather-Francis-Ford-Coppola-wanted-sack-him.html#ixzz4K3NgWLI4.

23. Pamela S. Deane, "Good Times," *Museum of Broadcast Communications: Encyclopedia of Television*, http://www.museum.tv/eotv/goodtimes.htm.

24. Toni Morrison, "Comment," *The New Yorker*, October 5, 1998, http://www.newyorker.com/magazine/1998/10/05/comment-6543.

25. Nia-Malika Henderson, "Race and Racism in the 2016 Campaign," CNN, August 31, 2016, http://www.cnn.com/2016/08/31/politics/2016-election-donald-trump-hillary-clinton-race/index.html.

26. David Leonheardt and Ian Prasad Philbrick, "Donald Trump's Racism: The Definitive List," *New York Times*, January 15, 2018, https://www.nytimes.com/interactive/2018/01/15/opinion/leonhardt-trump-racist.html..

27. Mark Binelli, "Hamilton Mania," *Rolling Stone*, June 16, 2016, 38.

28. Lin-Manuel Miranda, as told to Frank DiGiacomo, "'Hamilton's' Lin-Manuel Miranda on Finding Originality, Racial Politics (and Why Trump Should See His Show)," *Hollywood Reporter*, August 12, 2015, http://www.hollywoodreporter.com/features/hamiltons-lin-manuel-miranda-finding-814657; Christopher Mele and Patrick Healy, "Hamilton' Had Some Unscripted Lines for Pence. Trump Wasn't Happy," *New York Times*, November 19, 2017, https://www.nytimes.com/2016/11/19/us/mike-pence-hamilton.html..

29. Baldwin, *Devil Finds Work*, 47.

30. Library of Congress, https://www.loc.gov/programs/national-film-preservation-board/film-registry/complete-national-film-registry-listing/.

31. "On Views of Race and Inequality, Blacks and Whites Are Worlds Apart," Pew Research Center, June 27, 2016, http://www.pewsocialtrends.org/2016/06/27/on-views-of-race-and-inequality-blacks-and-whites-are-worlds-apart/.

32. Hadley Freeman, "'Don't Play Identity Politics! The Primal Scream of the Straight White Male," *The Guardian*, December 2, 2016, https://www.theguardian.com/commentisfree/2016/dec/02/identity-politics-donald-trump-white-men.

33. "Hope," *Black-ish*, NBC, February 24, 2016.

34. Vernon E. Jordan, Jr., "The Power of Movies to Change Our Hearts," *New York Times*, February 18, 2017, https://www.nytimes.com/2017/02/18/opinion/sunday/the-power-of-movies-to-change-our-hearts.html.

35. Manohla Dargis, A. O. Scott, and Stephen Holden, "The Best Movies of 2016," *New York Times*, December 7, 2016, https://www.nytimes.com/2016/12/07/movies/the-best-movies-of-2016.html.

36. Jordan, "Power of Movies."

37. "Scene and Unseen: Facing Race Through Film," St. Paul's Chapel, New York City, February 9, 2019.

38. Jonathan Capehart, "'It's Like He Took a Knee to Putin': Mitch Landrieu on Helsinki, Race, Democrats' Identity Crisis," *New York Times*, July 24, 2018, https://www.washingtonpost.com/blogs/post-partisan/wp/2018/07/24/its-like-he-took-a-knee-to-putin-mitch-landrieu-on-helsinki-race-democrats-identity-crisis/?utm_term=.2c173bcd3866.

Chapter 2

1. Joe Heim, "Recounting a Day of Rage, Hate, Violence and Death," *Washington Post*, August 14, 2017, https://www.washingtonpost.com/graphics/2017/local/charlottesville-timeline/?utm_term=.a2c57d624745.

2. James Baldwin, *The Devil Finds Work* (1976; New York: Vintage, 2011), 46.

3. John Milton Cooper, Jr., *Woodrow Wilson: A Biography* (New York: Knopf, 2009), 272.

4. Mark Benbow, "Wilson the Man," in *A Companion to Woodrow Wilson*, ed. Ross A. Kennedy (Malden, MA: Wiley-Blackwell, 2013), 30.

5. Gary Gerstle, "Race and Nation in the Thought and Politics of Woodrow Wilson," in *Reconsidering Woodrow Wilson: Progressivism, Internationalism, War, and Peace*, ed. John Milton Cooper, Jr. (Washington, DC: Woodrow Wilson Center Press and Baltimore: Johns Hopkins University Press, 2008), 121; Cooper, *Woodrow Wilson*, 272–73.

6. Paul McEwan, *The Birth of a Nation* (London: Palgrave, 2015), 10.

7. Xan Brooks, "*The Birth of a Nation*: A Gripping Masterpiece . . . and a Stain on History," *The Guardian*, July 29, 2013, https://www.theguardian.com/film/filmblog/2013/jul/29/birth-of-a-nation-dw-griffith-masterpiece.

8. Abraham Lincoln, November 19, 1863, http://rmc.library.cornell.edu/gettysburg/good_cause/transcript.htm.

9. Langston Hughes, "Let America Be America Again," Poets.Org, https://www.poets.org/poetsorg/poem/let-america-be-america-again.

10. "'Birth of a Nation' History in Motion," *Dallas Morning News*, October 5, 1915.

11. Mimi White, "*The Birth of a Nation*: History as Pretext," in *The Birth of a Nation: D. W. Griffith, Director*, ed. Robert Lang (New Brunswick, NJ: Rutgers University Press, 1994), 218.

12. Donald Bogle, *Toms, Coons, Mulattoes, Mammies, and Bucks: An Interpretive History of Blacks in American Films*, 5th ed. (New York: Bloomsbury, 2016), 11.

13. Ibid.

14. Ibid.

15. Albin Krebs, "Lillian Gish, 99, a Movie Star Since Movies Began, Is Dead," *New York Times*, March 1, 1993, https://www.nytimes.com/1993/03/01/movies/lillian-gish-99-a-movie-star-since-movies-began-is-dead.html.

16. bell hooks, *Black Looks: Race and Representation* (New York: Routledge, 1992), 7.

17. James Baldwin, *The Fire Next Time* (1962; New York: Vintage, 1993), 4.

18. Jere Downs, "Pancake Flap: 'Aunt Jemima' Heirs Seek Dough," *USA Today*, October 7, 2014, https://eu.usatoday.com/story/money/business/2014/10/06/aunt-jemima-lawsuit/16799923/.

19. "Aunt Jemima Frozen Breakfast," Pinnacle Foods, http://pinnaclefoods.com/brands/aunt-jemima.

20. Downs, "Pancake Flap."

21. "The Mammy Caricature," Jim Crow Museum of Racist Memorabilia, https://ferris.edu/jimcrow/mammies/.

22. Melissa V. Harris-Perry, *Sister Citizens: Shame, Stereotypes, and Black Women in America* (New Haven, CT: Yale University Press, 2011), 80.

23. Ibid., 83.

24. Joshua Zeitz, "Fact-Checking 'Lincoln': Lincoln's Mostly Realistic; His Advisers Aren't," *The Atlantic*, November 12, 2012, https://www.theatlantic.com/entertainment/archive/2012/11/fact-checking-lincoln-lincolns-mostly-realistic-his-advisers-arent/265073/.

25. Baldwin, *Devil Finds Work*, 50.

26. Ibram X. Kendi, *Stamped from the Beginning: The Definitive History of Racist Ideas in America* (New York: Nation, 2016), 42.

27. Bogle, *Toms, Coons*, 11.

28. The Jezebel stereotype is not limited to black or biracial women. Bette Davis starred in the 1938 historical epic *Jezebel*, and in this film we see a white woman who is sexual, volatile, conniving, and amoral. The film's portrayal of the stereotype is only spoiled when Davis's Julie Marsden makes a predictable third-act conversion to compassion and selflessness.

29. Bogle, *Toms, Coons*, 4–5.

30. Joneath Spicer, "European Perceptions of Blackness as Reflected in the Visual Arts," in *Revealing the African Presence in Renaissance Europe*, ed. Joneath Spicer (Baltimore: Walters Museum of Art, 2013), 36–37; Kendi, *Stamped from the Beginning*, 28–29.

31. Amy Louise Wood, *Lynching and Spectacle: Witnessing Racial Violence in America, 1890–1940* (Chapel Hill: University of North Carolina Press, 2009), 179–80. I am also grateful to *Waco Tribune Herald* film critic Carl Hoover for information on the reception of *Birth of a Nation* in Waco.

32. Jamiles Lartey and Sam Morris, "How White Americans Used Lynchings to Terrorize and Control Black People," *The Guardian*, April 26, 2018, https://www.theguardian.com/us-news/2018/apr/26/lynchings-memorial-us-south-montgomery-alabama.

33. Bogle, *Toms, Coons*, 7.

34. Baldwin, *Fire Next Time*, 10.

35. Universal Declaration of Human Rights, http://www.un.org/en/universal-declaration-human-rights/.

36. As, for example, in Walter Brueggemann, *Old Testament Theology: An Introduction* (Nashville: Abingdon Press, 2008), 143–50.

37. Exodus 1:11–14 (NRSV).

38. Exodus 3:7–8 (NRSV).

39. Barry L. Schwartz, "For You Were Strangers in the Land of Egypt," *Jewish Publication Society*, February 10, 2017, https://jps.org/for-you-were-strangers-in-the-land-of-egypt/.

40. Oliver Sacks, "Mishpatim (5768)—Loving the Stranger," *Office of Rabbi Sacks*, http://rabbisacks.org/covenant-conversation-5768-mishpatim-loving-the-stranger/.

41. N. T. Wright, *Paul and the Faithfulness of God* (Minneapolis: Fortress, 2013), 9.

42. Galatians 3:28 (NRSV).

43. Marlena Graves, "'It's Not a Matter of Obeying the Bible': 8 Questions for Walter Brueggemann," *OnFaith*, https://www.onfaith.co/onfaith/2015/01/09/walter-brueggemann-church-gospel-bible/35739.

Chapter 3

1. John Silk, "Racist and Anti-Racist Ideology in Films of the American South," in *Race and Racism: Essays in Social Geography*, ed. Peter Jackson (London: Allen and Unwin, 1987), 271.

2. Sean Axmaker, "Hollywood Goes to War—The Documentaries of 'Five Came Back' on Netflix," Stream on Demand, April 1, 2017, https://streamondemandathome.com/war-documentary-midway-san-pietro-streaming-vod/.

3. James Baldwin, *I Am Not Your Negro*, ed. Raoul Peck (New York: Vintage, 2017), 20.

4. Donald Bogle, *Toms, Coons, Mulattoes, Mammies, and Bucks: An Interpretive History of Blacks in American Films*, 5th ed. (New York: Bloomsbury, 2016), 137–38.

5. James Baldwin, *The Devil Finds Work* (1976; New York: Vantage, 2011), 20.

6. "Race and Hollywood: Black Images on Film," Turner Movie Classics, 2007.

7. Bim Adewumni, "Why Are There So Few Oscar-Winning Roles for Black Actresses?" *The Guardian*, February 27, 2012, https://www.theguardian.com/film/shortcuts/2012/feb/27/few-black-actresses-win-oscars.

8. Noah Isenberg, *We'll Always Have Casablanca: The Life, Legend, and Afterlife of Hollywood's Most Beloved Movie* (New York: Norton, 2017), 74.

9. John Dollard, *Caste and Class in a Southern Town* (New Haven, CT: Yale University Press, 1937), 302.

10. Isabel Wilkerson, *The Warmth of Other Suns: The Epic Story of America's Great Migration* (New York: Random House, 2010), 15.

11. Robert A. Gibson, "The Negro Holocaust: Lynching and Race Riots in the United States, 1880–1950," Yale-New Haven Teacher's Institute, http://teachersinstitute.yale.edu/curriculum/units/1979/2/79.02.04.x.htmlhttp://teachersinstitute.yale.edu/curriculum/units/1979/2/79.02.04.x.html.

12. Justin McCarthy, "Gallup Vault: 72% Support for Anti-Lynching Bill in 1937," Gallup.com, May 11, 2018, https://news.gallup.com/vault/234371/gallup-vault-support-anti-lynching-bill-1937.aspx.

13. Susan Stamberg, "Denied a Stage, She Sang for a Nation," *National Public Radio*, April 9, 2014, https://www.npr.org/2014/04/09/298760473/denied-a-stage-she-sang-for-a-nation?t=1544617149795.

14. Ibid.

15. Robert L. Harris, Jr. and Rosalyn Terborg-Penn, "Interpreting African American History Since 1939," in *The Columbia Guide to African American History Since 1939* (New York: Columbia University Press, 2006), 7.

16. Louis Menand, "The Hammer and the Nail," *The New Yorker*, July 20, 1992, https://www.newyorker.com/magazine/1992/07/20/the-hammer-and-the-nail.

17. Irving Howe, "Black Boys and Native Sons," *Dissent* (Autumn 1973), http://www.writing.upenn.edu/~afilreis/50s/howe-blackboys.html.

18. Michael Laris, "Tuskegee Airman Charles McGee Celebrates His 99th Birthday in the Co-pilot's Seat," *Washington Post*, December 8, 2018, https://www.washingtonpost.com/history/2018/12/08/tuskegee-

airman-charles-mcgee-celebrated-his-th-birthday-co-pilots-seat/?utm_
term=.76a4a746b12a.

19. "Executive Order 8802: Prohibition of Discrimination in the Defense
Industry (1941)," *Our Documents*, https://www.ourdocuments.gov/
doc.php?flash=true&doc=72; William J. Collins, "Race, Roosevelt, and
Wartime Production: Fair Employment in World War II Labor Markets,"
American Economic Review 91, no. 1 (March 2001): 272.

20. Richard Corliss, "Analysis of the Film," *Casablanca: The Complete Script
and Legend Behind the Film*, ed. Howard Koch (Woodstock, NY: Overlook
Press, 1973), 188.

21. Dan Burley, "Wilson's Role in *Casablanca* Tops for Hollywood," *New York
Amsterdam News*, February 6, 1943; cited in Isenberg, *We'll Always Have
Casablanca*, 76.

22. "Casablanca," *Variety*, December 1, 1942, https://variety.com/1942/film/
reviews/casablanca-2-1200413952/.

23. Bosley Crowther, "'Casablanca,' with Humphrey Bogart and Ingrid
Bergman, at Hollywood—'White Cargo' and 'Ravaged Earth' Open,"
New York Times, November 27, 1942, https://www.nytimes.com/1942/11/
27/archives/casablanca-with-humphrey-bogart-and-ingrid-bergman-at-
hollywood.html.

24. Corliss, "Analysis of the Film," 189.

25. Isenberg, *We'll Always Have Casablanca*, 77.

26. Noah Isenberg, personal email, December 18, 2018.

27. Isenberg, *We'll Always Have Casablanca*, 74.

28. Isenberg, personal email, December 18, 2018.

29. Brian T. Edwards, *Morocco Bound: Disorienting America's Maghreb, from
Casablanca to the Marrakech Express* (Durham, NC: Duke University
Press, 2005), 71.

30. Edward W. Said, *Power, Politics, and Culture: Interviews with Edward
W. Said*, ed. Gauri Viswanathan (New York: Pantheon, 2001), 31.

31. Edwards, *Morocco Bound*, 67.

32. David Robson, "You Must Remember This," *Jewish Chronicle*, November
23, 2017, https://www.thejc.com/culture/film/casablanca-1.448636.

33. Ibid.

34. David Mikics, "Here's Looking at You, Kid," *Tablet*, February 14, 2017,
https://www.tabletmag.com/jewish-arts-and-culture/224670/casablanca-
isenberg.

35. Isenberg, *We'll Always Have Casablanca*, 27.

36. Tambay Obensom, "'Green Book': The Feel-Good Oscar Contender
Has a 'Magical Negro' Problem—Opinion," *IndieWire*, November 23,

2018, https://www.indiewire.com/2018/11/green-book-mahershala-ali-magical-negro-1202022226/.

37. Eric Deggans, "Latest TV Trend? The Black Best Friend," *Washington Post*, October 28, 2011, https://www.washingtonpost.com/lifestyle/style/latest-tv-trend-the-black-best-friend/2011/10/25/gIQAwYw4OM_story.html?utm_term=.e144593d2473.

38. Genesis 2:18.

39. 1 Samuel 18:1 (NRSV); Ruth 1:16 (NRSV).

40. John 11:33 (NRSV).

41. Moses Maimonides, *The Guide of the Perplexed*, trans. Shlomo Pines (Chicago: University of Chicago Press, 1963), 601–602.

42. Peter Brown, *Augustine: A Biography* (Berkeley: University of California Press, 2000), passim.

43. Augustine, *Letter 130*, 2.4.

44. Donald X. Burt, *Friendship & Society: An Introduction to Augustine's Practical Philosophy* (Grand Rapids, MI: Eerdmans, 1999), 56–57.

45. *City of God* XIX.3.

46. "About Ellis Island," The Statue of Liberty/Ellis Island Foundation, https://www.libertyellisfoundation.org/about-the-ellis-island.

47. Emma Lazarus, "The New Colossus," Poetry Foundation, https://www.poetryfoundation.org/poems/46550/the-new-colossus.

48. Vincent J. Cannato, *American Passage: The History of Ellis Island* (New York: HarperCollins, 2009), 12.

49. Charles Kimball, *When Religion Becomes Evil* (New York: HarperSanFrancisco, 2002), 39.

50. Augustine, *Sermon 299D*, 1.

51. Jürgen Moltmann, *History and the Triune God: Contributions to Trinitarian Theology* (New York: Crossroad, 1992), xii/xiii, 64.

52. *The Sayings of the Desert Fathers*, ed. Benedicta Ward, rev. ed. (Kalamazoo, MI: Cistercian, 1984), 3.

53. *The Rule of Augustine*, 1.1, 4.2.

54. Pope Benedict XVI, *Caritas in Veritate*, June 29, 2009, http://www.vatican.va/holy_father/benedict_xvi/encyclicals/documents/hf_ben-xvi_enc_20090629_caritas-in-veritate_en.html.

55. Frank Griswold, *Going Home: An Invitation to Jubilee* (Cambridge, MA: Cowley, 2000), 67.

56. Barbara Brown Taylor, *The Seeds of Heaven: Sermons on the Gospel of Matthew* (Louisville, KY: Westminster John Knox, 2004), 89.

57. Desmond Tutu, *God Has a Dream: A Vision of Hope for Our Time* (New York: Image, 2004), 27.

58. Desmond Tutu, "Who We Are: Human Uniqueness and the African Spirit of Ubuntu," Templeton Foundation, April 3, 2013, https://www.youtube.com/watch?v=0wZtfqZ271w.

59. Samuel T. Lloyd, III, "Practicing the Hope of the World," *Cathedral Voice*, September 2008, 1.

60. Koch, *Casablanca*, 143.

61. Joseph Campbell, *The Hero with a Thousand Faces* (1949; Princeton, NJ: Princeton University Press, 1972), 16.

62. Ibid., 38.

63. Joseph Campbell with Bill Moyers, *The Power of Myth* (New York: Anchor, 1988), 82.

Chapter 4

1. *Loving v. Virginia*, 388 U.S. 1 (1967), Justia, https://supreme.justia.com/cases/federal/us/388/1/.

2. Mark Harris, *Pictures at a Revolution: Five Movies and the Birth of the New Hollywood* (New York: Penguin, 2008), 57.

3. Margaret Talbot, "Wedding Bells," *The New Yorker*, May 21, 2012, https://www.newyorker.com/magazine/2012/05/21/wedding-bells.

4. Tom Dreisbach, "Behind the Motorcycles in 'Easy Rider,' a Long-Obscured Story," *NPR*, October 11, 2014, https://www.npr.org/2014/10/11/354875096/behind-the-motorcycles-in-easy-rider-a-long-obscured-story.

5. James Baldwin, *The Devil Finds Work* (1976; New York: Vintage, 2011), 71.

6. Rick Lyman, "Stanley Kramer, Filmmaker with Social Bent, Dies at 87," *New York Times*, February 21, 2001, https://www.nytimes.com/2001/02/21/movies/stanley-kramer-filmmaker-with-social-bent-dies-at-87.html.

7. Benedict Nightingale, "Whatever Happened to Drawing Room Comedy?" *New York Times*, April 28, 1985, https://www.nytimes.com/1985/04/28/theater/whatever-happened-to-drawing-room-comedy.html.

8. A recent memoir and documentary casts some doubts on Hepburn and Tracy's sexual relationship (these claims are disputed), but their long-time companionship is never in question. See Anne Thompson, "'Scotty and the Secret History of Hollywood' Exposes Star Myths, from Tracy & Hepburn to Cary Grant," *IndieWire*, August 2, 2018, https://www.indiewire.com/2018/08/gay-expose-scotty-and-the-secret-history-of-hollywood-hollywood-myths-matt-tyrnauer-1201989716/.

9. Ruthe Stein, "Looking Back at 'Guess Who's Coming to Dinner,'" *SF Gate*, February 28, 2008, https://www.sfgate.com/entertainment/article/Looking-back-at-Guess-Who-s-Coming-to-Dinner-3293149.php.

10. David A. Hollinger, "After Cloven Tongues of Fire: Ecumenical Protestantism and the Modern American Encounter with Diversity," *Journal of American History* (June 2011): 23.

11. Martin Luther King, Jr., "The Other America," Stanford University, April 14, 1967, https://auroraforum.stanford.edu/files/transcripts/Aurora_Forum_Transcript_Martin_Luther_King_The_Other_America_Speech_at_Stanford_04.15.07.pdf.

12. "A Tragedy," *Washington Post*, April 6, 1967, A20.

13. These materials are drawn from archives at the Lyndon Baines Johnson Presidential Library, Austin, Texas, including letters and other correspondence in the White House Central Files (WHCF) Subject File, and the WHCF Name File. I am grateful to archival librarian (and one of my favorite former students) Jenna de Graffenried and the LBJ Presidential Library for assistance and access to these essential records, including correspondence between Dr. King and his family and President Johnson.

14. Baldwin, *Devil Finds Work*, 75.

15. Ibid., 74.

16. "A Long, Long Way: Race and Film 1968–2018," Washington National Cathedral, Washington, DC, February 16, 2018.

17. Keli Goff, "Can 'Belle' End Hollywood's Obsession with the White Savior?" *Daily Beast*, May 4, 2014, https://www.thedailybeast.com/can-belle-end-hollywoods-obsession-with-the-white-savior.

18. Wesley Morris, "Why Do the Oscars Keep Falling for Racial Reconciliation Fantasies?" *New York Times*, January 23, 2019, https://www.nytimes.com/2019/01/23/arts/green-book-interracial-friendship.html.

19. *My Next Guest Needs No Introduction*, HBO, February 9, 2018.

20. "Guess Who's Coming to Dinner," Roger Ebert.com, original review January 25, 1968, https://www.rogerebert.com/reviews/guess-whos-coming-to-dinner-1968.

21. "A Long, Long Way: Race and Film 1968–2018."

22. Samantha Cooney, "Bishop Michael Curry Delivered a Powerful Royal Wedding Sermon. Read the Full Transcript," *Time*, May 19, 2018, http://time.com/5283953/royal-wedding-sermon-transcript/.

23. Michael Curry, "An Invitation from Presiding Bishop Michael B. Curry to Practice the Way of Love," episcopalchurch.org, https://www.episcopalchurch.org/way-of-love/invitation.

24. Julian of Norwich, *Showings*, trans. Edmund Colledge and James Walsh (Mahwah, NJ: Paulist Press, 1977), 342.

25. Augustine, *Sermons on the First Epistle of John* (Io. ep. tr.) VII.8, https://www.ecatholic2000.com/fathers/untitled-680.shtml.

26. Thomas Aquinas, *Summa* II-II, 23.7.

27. C. S. Lewis, *The Four Loves* (1960; New York: HarperOne, 2017), 47.

28. Ibid., 61.

29. Ibid., 89.

30. Ibid., 138.

31. Ibid., 155.

32. John 15:12–13 (NRSV).

33. I John 3:14–18 (NRSV).

34. Martin Luther King, Jr., *Strength to Love* (1963; Philadelphia: Fortress, 1981), 52.

35. Ibid.

36. Scott Bader-Saye, *Formed by Love: Church's Teaching for a Changing World* (New York: Church, 2017), v–vi.

Chapter 5

1. Roger Ebert, "Great Movies: *Do the Right Thing*," Roger Ebert.com, May 27, 2001, https://www.rogerebert.com/reviews/great-movie-do-the-right-thing-1989.

2. Jason Bailey, "When Spike Lee Became Scary," *The Atlantic*, August 22, 2012, https://www.theatlantic.com/entertainment/archive/2012/08/when-spike-lee-became-scary/261434/.

3. Roger Ebert, "Do the Right Thing," Roger Ebert.com, June 30, 1989, https://www.rogerebert.com/reviews/do-the-right-thing-1989.

4. Vann Newkirk II, personal conversation, Washington, DC, January 30, 2019.

5. Matt Haber, "The Little-Known Story Behind 'Do the Right Thing,'" Atavist.com, https://mentalfloss.atavist.com/the-little-known-story-behind-do-the-right-thing.

6. Spike Lee and Lisa Jones, *Do the Right Thing: A Spike Lee Joint* (New York: Simon & Schuster, 1989), 50.

7. Joe Klein, *New York Magazine*, June 26, 1989. Quoted in Christopher Rosen, "The 'Do The Right Thing' Reviews Spike Lee Called 'Uncut, Unfiltered Racism,'" *HuffPost*, June 30, 2014, https://www.huffingtonpost.com/2014/06/30/do-the-right-thing-anniversary_n_5543293.html.

8. David Denby, *New York Magazine*, June 26, 1989. Quoted in Christopher Rosen, "The 'Do The Right Thing' Reviews Spike Lee Called 'Uncut, Unfiltered Racism,'" *HuffPost*, June 30, 2014, https://www.huffingtonpost.com/2014/06/30/do-the-right-thing-anniversary_n_5543293.html.

9. Jack Kroll, *Newsweek*, July 3, 1989. Quoted in Christopher Rosen, "The 'Do The Right Thing' Reviews Spike Lee Called 'Uncut, Unfiltered Racism,'" *HuffPost*, June 30, 2014, https://www.huffingtonpost.com/2014/06/30/do-the-right-thing-anniversary_n_5543293.html.

10. Mike Fleming, Jr., "No Cannes Do: Why Spike Lee Nixed 'Do The Right Thing' Silver Anniversary for Black Fest Fete," Deadline.com, May 13, 2014, https://deadline.com/2014/05/no-cannes-do-why-spike-lee-nixed-do-the-right-thing-silver-anni-for-black-fest-fete-729355/.

11. Bailey, "When Spike Lee Became Scary."

12. Ebert, "Do the Right Thing."

13. Ed Guerrero, *Do the Right Thing* (London: Palgrave, 2001), 18–19.

14. Wesley Morris, "Why Do the Oscars Keep Falling for Racial Reconciliation Fantasies?" *New York Times*, January 23, 2019, https://www.nytimes.com/2019/01/23/arts/green-book-interracial-friendship.html.

15. Haber, "The Little-Known Story."

16. Guerrero, *Do the Right Thing*, 27.

17. "A Long, Long Way: Race and Film 1989–2019," Washington National Cathedral, February 1, 2019.

18. Guerrero, *Do the Right Thing*, 21.

19. Jill Lepore, *These Truths: A History of the United States* (New York: W. W. Norton, 2018), 648.

20. Brooke Minters and Blake Hounshell, "'I Don't Have the Answer': Spike Lee on Race in Trump's America," *Politico*, February 7, 2019, https://www.politico.com/magazine/story/2019/02/07/spike-lee-interview-race-america-blackkklansman-2019-224822.

21. Bailey, "When Spike Lee Became Scary."

22. Guerrero, *Do the Right Thing*, 23.

23. Ibid., 32.

24. Ebert, "Do the Right Thing."

25. Minters and Hounshell, "'I Don't Have the Answer.'"

26. Rowan Williams and Greg Garrett, *In Conversation: Rowan Williams and Greg Garrett* (New York: Church Publishing, 2019), 55.

27. "Scene and Unseen: Facing Race Through Film," St. Paul's Chapel, New York City, February 8, 2019.

28. Guerrero, *Do the Right Thing*, 54.

29. Ibid., 54–56.

30. "A Long, Long Way."

31. Ebert, "Do the Right Thing."

32. Guerrero, *Do the Right Thing*, 86.

33. "A Long, Long Way."

34. Williams and Garrett, *In Conversation*, 55.

35. Stanley Hauerwas, *The Peaceable Kingdom: A Primer in Christian Ethics* (Notre Dame: University of Notre Dame Press, 1983), 26

36. Scott Bader-Saye, *Formed by Love: Church's Teaching for a Changing World* (New York: Church, 2017), 11.

37. "Sunday Morning with . . ." BBC Radio Scotland, January 31, 2016.

38. Guerrero, *Do the Right Thing*, 83.

39. Romans 7:19 (NRSV).

40. "Scene and Unseen: Facing Race Through Film."

41. Ibid.

42. Ibid.

43. Ibid.

44. H. Richard Niebuhr, *The Responsible Self* (San Francisco: HarperSanFrancisco, 1963), 60, 140.

45. Scott Bader-Saye, *Following Jesus in a Culture of Fear* (Grand Rapids, MI: Brazos, 2007), 27.

46. "Scene and Unseen: Facing Race Through Film."

47. James Baldwin, *The Last Interview and Other Conversations* (Brooklyn: Melville House, 2014), 9.

48. Bader-Saye, *Following Jesus*, 67.

49. Richard Harries, *The Re-Enchantment of Morality: Wisdom for a Troubled World* (London: SPCK, 2008), 29.

Chapter 6

1. Brookes Barnes, "In 'Green Book' Victory, Oscar Critics See an Old Hollywood Tale," *New York Times*, February 25, 2019.

2. Lisa Schwarzbaum, "*Crash*: Movie," *Entertainment Weekly*, May 16, 2005, https://ew.com/article/2005/05/16/crash-2/.

3. Ella Taylor, "Space Race," *LA Weekly*, May 5, 2005, https://www.laweekly.com/film/space-race-2139874.

4. Peter Travers, "Crash," *Rolling Stone*, https://www.rollingstone.com/movies/movie-reviews/crash-90132/.

5. Roger Ebert, "In Defense of the Year's 'Worst Movie,'" Roger Ebert.com, January 8, 2006, https://www.rogerebert.com/rogers-journal/in-defense-of-the-years-worst-movie.

6. Ibid.

7. Roger Ebert, "Crash," Roger Ebert.com, May 5, 2005, https://www. rogerebert.com/reviews/crash-2005.

8. Taylor, "Space Race."

9. Jim Wallis, *God's Politics: Why the Right Gets It Wrong and Left Doesn't Get It* (New York: HarperSanFrancisco, 2005), 308.

10. Steve Davis, "Crash," *Austin Chronicle*, May 6, 2005.

11. Ebert, "Crash."

12. Matt Fagerholm, "Paul Haggis on 'Third Person,' 'Crash,' Scientology and Truth," Roger Ebert.com, June 16, 2014, https://www.rogerebert. com/interviews/paul-haggis-on-third-person-crash-scientology-and-truth.

13. Martin Luther King, Jr., "Letter from a Birmingham Jail," *I Have a Dream* (New York: HarperSanFrancisco, 1992), 92.

14. David Denby, "Angry People," *The New Yorker*, May 2, 2005, http://www. pages.drexel.edu/~ina22/+355/$355-Readings-9.html.

15. Desson Thompson, "'Crash': Meet It Head-On," *Washington Post*, May 6, 2005, http://www.washingtonpost.com/wp-dyn/content/article/2005/05/06/AR2005062901190.html.

16. Stephen Hunter, "'Crash': The Collision of Human Contradictions," *Washington Post*, May 6, 2005, http://www.washingtonpost.com/wp-dyn/content/article/2005/05/06/AR2005062901114.html.

17. Rachel Martin, "'Women's Work' Delves into Gender Roles at Home and Relationships with Domestic Help," National Public Radio, April 15, 2019, https://www.npr.org/2019/04/15/712741576/womens-work-delves-into-gender-roles-at-home-and-relationships-with-domestic-hel.

18. Fagerholm, "Paul Haggis."

19. Thompson, "'Crash.'"

20. Hunter, "'Crash.'"

21. This is my rendering of the story, which is told in Luke 10:25–37.

22. Martin Luther King, Jr., *Strength to Love* (1963; Philadelphia: Fortress, 1981), 34.

23. James Baldwin, *The Fire Next Time* (1962; New York: Vintage, 1993), 8.

24. Aquinas teaches about fear in the *Summa Theologica* I–II, Q. 42.

25. Scott Bader-Saye, *Following Jesus in a Culture of Fear* (Grand Rapids, MI: Brazos, 2007), 27.

26. Ibid., 102.

27. Ibid., 119.

28. Stanley Hauerwas, *The Peaceable Kingdom: A Primer in Christian Ethics* (Notre Dame: University of Notre Dame Press, 1983), xvii.

Chapter 7

1. Barack Obama, "Remarks by the President on Trayvon Martin," The White House, July 19, 2013, https://obamawhitehouse.archives.gov/the-press-office/2013/07/19/remarks-president-trayvon-martin.

2. Ta-Nehisi Coates, *Between the World and Me* (New York: Spiegel and Grau, 2015), 9.

3. Nick Wright, "'Hands Up, Don't Shoot' Is Bigger Than Ferguson and Bigger Than the Rams," *Vice Sports*, December 2, 2014, https://sports.vice.com/en_us/article/jpz933/hands-up-dont-shoot-is-bigger-than-ferguson-and-bigger-than-the-rams.

4. "Attack of the GIANT NEGROES!!" *Undercover Black Man*, July 10, 2007, http://undercoverblackman.blogspot.com/2007/07/attack-of-giant-negroes.html.

5. Robert P. Jones, *The End of White America* (New York: Simon & Schuster, 2016), 100–101.

6. Daniel Victor, "Why 'All Lives Matter' Is Such a Perilous Phrase," *New York Times*, July 15, 2016, https://www.nytimes.com/2016/07/16/us/all-lives-matter-black-lives-matter.html.

7. George Yancy and Judith Butler, "What's Wrong with 'All Lives Matter'?" *New York Times*, January 12, 2015, https://opinionator.blogs.nytimes.com/2015/01/12/whats-wrong-with-all-lives-matter/.

8. Andrea Peterson, "Why the Philandro Castile Police-Shooting Video Disappeared from Facebook—Then Came Back," *Washington Post*, July 6, 2016, https://www.washingtonpost.com/news/the-switch/wp/2016/07/07/why-facebook-took-down-the-philando-castile-shooting-video-then-put-it-back-up/.

9. Simon Vosick-Levinson, "Black Lives Matter: 11 Racist Police Killings with No Justice Served," *Rolling Stone*, December 4, 2014, https://www.rollingstone.com/politics/politics-news/black-lives-matter-11-racist-police-killings-with-no-justice-served-40001/.

10. Wesley Lowery, "Black Lives Matter: Birth of a Movement," *The Guardian*, January 17, 2017, https://www.theguardian.com/us-news/2017/jan/17/black-lives-matter-birth-of-a-movement.

11. Vann R. Newkirk II, "The Permanence of Black Lives Matter," *The Atlantic*, August 3, 2016, https://www.theatlantic.com/politics/archive/2016/08/movement-black-lives-platform/494309/.

12. Jill Lepore, *These Truths: A History of the United States* (New York: Norton, 2018), 767.

13. Ibid., 782.
14. Vann R. Newkirk II, "Five Decades of White Backlash," *The Atlantic*, January 15, 2018, https://www.theatlantic.com/politics/archive/2018/01/trump-massive-resistance-history-mlk/550544/.
15. Glenn Thrush and Maggie Haberman, "Trump Gives White Supremacists an Unequivocal Boost," *New York Times*, August 15, 2017, https://www.nytimes.com/2017/08/15/us/politics/trump-charlottesville-white-nationalists.html?mcubz=0.
16. Ta-Nehisi Coates, "The First White President," *The Atlantic*, October 2017, https://www.theatlantic.com/magazine/archive/2017/10/the-first-white-president-ta-nehisi-coates/537909/.
17. Alex Hearn, "Top Five Racist Republican Dog-Whistles," *NewStatesmanAmerica*, July 12, 2012, https://www.newstatesman.com/world/2012/07/top-five-racist-republican-dog-whistles.
18. "Hate Crimes Rose the Day After Trump Was Elected, FBI Data Show," *Washington Post*, March 23, 2018, https://www.washingtonpost.com/news/post-nation/wp/2018/03/23/hate-crimes-rose-the-day-after-trump-was-elected-fbi-data-show/.
19. "NAACP Sees Continued Rise in Hate Crimes, Legacy of Trump's Racism," NAACP.org, June 28, 2019, https://www.naacp.org/latest/naacp-sees-continued-rise-hate-crimes-legacy-trumps-racism/.
20. Ibram X. Kendi, *Stamped from the Beginning: The Definitive History of Racist Ideas in America* (New York: Nation, 2016), 4.
21. Dr. Martin Luther King, Jr., "Negroes Are *Not* Moving Too Fast," *Saturday Evening Post*, November 7, 1964, http://www.saturdayeveningpost.com/wp-content/uploads/satevepost/19641107-martin-luther-king.pdf.
22. "Jordan Peele: 'Get Out,' Austin Film Festival," *HartChart*, November 2, 2018, https://www.youtube.com/watch?v=MsdS3RZ9Gdc&feature=youtube.
23. Sid Evans, "7 Reasons You'll Fall in Love with Fairhope, Alabama," *Southern Living*, https://www.southernliving.com/travel/what-to-do-fairhope-alabama.
24. Jada Yuan and Hunter Harris, "The First Great Movie of the Trump Administration," *New York Magazine*, February 19, 2018, https://www.vulture.com/2018/02/making-get-out-jordan-peele.html.
25. "Jordan Peele: "Get Out,' Austin Film Festival."
26. Richard Lawson, "*Get Out* Is Thrilling, Terrifying, and Timely," *Vanity Fair*, February 23, 2017, https://www.vanityfair.com/hollywood/2017/02/get-out-jordan-peele-review.

27. Yuan and Harris, "First Great Movie."

28. Jason Zinoman, "Why Are We Ashamed to Call 'Get Out' and 'The Shape of Water' Horror Films?," *New York Times*, January 18, 2018, https://www.nytimes.com/2018/01/18/movies/get-out-the-shape-of-water-horror-oscars.html.

29. "A Long, Long Way," Washington National Cathedral, February 17, 2018.

30. Owen Gleiberman, "The Audacity of 'Get Out': A Racial Horror Film That Dares to Be a Real Movie," *Variety*, February 26, 2017, https://variety.com/2017/film/columns/get-out-jordan-peele-1201996782/.

31. Scott Poole, *Monsters in America: Our Historical Obsession with the Hideous and the Haunting* (Waco, TX: Baylor University Press, 2018), xiii.

32. Alberto Manguel, *Fabulous Monsters: Dracula, Alice, Superman, and Other Literary Friends* (New Haven, CT: Yale University Press, 2019), 158.

33. Zinoman, "Why Are We Ashamed."

34. Aisha Harris, "Get Out," *Slate*, February 23, 2017, https://slate.com/culture/2017/02/get-out-jordan-peeles-horror-movie-reviewed.html.

35. Yuan and Harris, "First Great Movie."

36. "A Long, Long Way."

37. Harris, "Get Out."

38. Jordan Peele, *Get Out*, http://www.universalpicturesawards.com/site-content/uploads/2017/09/GET-OUT.pdf.

39. Wesley Morris, "Jordan Peele's X-Ray Vision," *New York Times Magazine*, December 20, 2017, https://www.nytimes.com/2017/12/20/magazine/jordan-peeles-x-ray-vision.html.

40. Michelle Alexander, *The New Jim Crow: Mass Incarceration in the Age of Colorblindness*, rev. ed. (New York: New Press, 2012), 12–13.

41. Morris, "Jordan Peele's X-Ray Vision."

42. Cara Buckley, "'I'd Never Seen My Fears as an African-American Man Onscreen,'" *New York Times*, December 26, 2017, https://www.nytimes.com/2017/12/06/movies/jordan-peele-get-out-african-american-biracial.html.

43. Morris, "Jordan Peele's X-Ray Vision."

44. Zadie Smith, "Getting In and Out: Who Owns Black Pain?" *The Atlantic*, July 2017, https://harpers.org/archive/2017/07/getting-in-and-out./

45. Gleiberman, "The Audacity."

46. Jennifer Keohane, "Serious Satire: Trevor Noah and the Daily Show," *Rhetorically Speaking*, April 9, 2015, http://rhetoric.commarts.wisc.edu/?p=286.

47. Morris, "Jordan Peele's X-Ray Vision."

48. Ibid.

49. "A Long, Long Way."
50. Kelly Brown Douglas, *Stand Your Ground: Black Bodies and the Justice of God* (Maryknoll, NY: Orbis, 2015), xi.
51. Morris, "Jordan Peele's X-Ray Vision."
52. Yuan and Harris, "First Great Movie."
53. Ibid.
54. "Jordan Peele: 'Get Out,' Austin Film Festival."
55. Yuan and Harris, "First Great Movie."
56. Douglas, *Stand Your Ground*, 134.
57. Gleiberman, "The Audacity."
58. Douglas, *Stand Your Ground*, 137.
59. Exodus 2:23–25 (NRSV).
60. Exodus 14:4 (NRSV).
61. James H. Cone, *God of the Oppressed*, rev. ed. (Maryknoll, NY: Orbis, 1997), 21.
62. James Baldwin, *The Fire Next Time* (1962; New York: Vintage 1993), 8, 10.
63. Robert W. Lee IV, *A Sin by Any Other Name: Reckoning with Racism and the Heritage of the South* (New York: Convergent, 2019), 155.

Chapter 8

1. Joseph Ferrara, telephone conversation, August 27, 2018.
2. "Liturgy of Remembrance, Contrition, and Hope" and "Dedication of Isaac Hawkins Hall and Anne Marie Becraft Hall," Georgetown University, Washington, DC, 2017, 5.
3. "Liturgy of Remembrance, Contrition and Hope," Georgetown University, April 18, 2017, https://www.youtube.com/watch?v=tO4Xsz36kTU.
4. James Baldwin, *The Fire Next Time* (1963; New York: Vintage, 1993), 81.
5. Randolph Hollerith, Washington National Cathedral, September 10, 2017.
6. "Full Speech: Mitch Landrieu Addresses Removal of Confederate Statues," May 31, 2017, https://www.youtube.com/watch?v=csMbjG0-6Ak.
7. Kevin Eckstrom, "Beloved, Let Us Love One Another," *Cathedral Age*, Winter 2018, 14.
8. Kevin O'Brien, telephone conversation, September 4, 2018.
9. Brené Brown, Washington National Cathedral, January 21, 2018.
10. Catherine Meeks, "Scene and Unseen: Facing Race Through Film," St. Paul's Chapel, New York City, February 9, 2019.
11. Martin Pengelly, "Georgetown Students Vote to Pay Reparations for Slaves Sold by University," *The Guardian*, April 15, 2019, https://

www.theguardian.com/world/2019/apr/15/georgetown-students-reparations-vote-slaves-sold-by-university.

12. Ferrara, phone conversation.
13. Hollerith, September 10, 2018.
14. Catherine Meeks, Atlanta, Georgia, October 19, 2018.
15. Baldwin, *Fire Next Time*, 97.
16. "Liturgy of Remembrance, Contrition and Hope."

About the Author

Greg Garrett is the author of two dozen works of fiction, nonfiction, and memoir. He is perhaps best known as a writer and thinker exploring the intersections of theology, literature and culture, race, and politics; BBC Radio calls him one of America's essential voices on religion and culture. His previous books for Oxford University Press have been *Entertaining Judgment: The Afterlife in Popular Imagination* (2015) and *Living with the Living Dead: The Wisdom of the Zombie Apocalypse* (2017). Dr. Garrett has discussed his work with FOX News, National Public Radio, BBC Radio, DublinTalk Radio, *Playboy*, *Christianity Today*, *Church News*, the *Los Angeles Times*, *The Spectator*, and many other publications and media sources. He is Professor of English at Baylor University in Texas and Theologian in Residence at the American Cathedral in Paris, and lives with his wife, Jeanie, and their family in Austin, Texas.

Index

white supremacy ideology in American culture reflected in, <u>106f</u>, 27–32, 48–49, 50, 70–71, 101–2

white womanhood depicted in, 17–18, 33–36, 43–44

Wilson and, <u>108f</u>, 26–27, 31, 79–80

Black-ish (television show), <u>19</u>

BlacKkKlansman (2018), <u>111f</u>, 1, 6, 44, 119–20

Black Lives Matter movement, 15, 173–74, 175–76, 179

Black Panther (2018), 6, 9, 16–17, 179–80

Blaxploitation films, 14

The Blind Side (2009), 89, 90

Blum, Jason, 190

Bogart, Humphrey, <u>107f</u>, 12, 51, 74

Bogle, Donald
on *The Birth of a Nation*, 32–33, 41
on *Gone With the Wind*, 52
stereotypical representations of African Americans in film identified by, 11, 37–38, 42, 44–45
sympathetic representations of African Americans in film identified by, 52

Bonnie and Clyde (1967), 80

Bonsu, Janae, 175–76

Booker, Cory, 10

Borg, Marcus, 37

Boyz in the Hood (1991), 14

Braham, Harry, 29–30

Brawley, Tawana, 120–21

Breil, Joseph Carl, 32

Brexit referendum (2016), 4

Broderick, Matthew, 89–90

Brokeback Mountain (2005), 147, 148–49

Brooks, David, 3

Brooks, Xan, 27–28

Brown, Barry Alexander, 127

Brown, Brené, 202

Brown, Michael, 172–74, 193

Brown, Peter, 70

Brown v. Board of Education, 54

Brueggemann, Walter, 46, 48

Bullock, Sandra, 89, 149–50, 152, 153, 159, 172–73

Bumpers, Eleanor, 120–21

Burley, Dan, 57–58

Burt, Donald, 70–71

Bush, George W., 198

Butler, Judith, 173–74

Cabin in the Woods (2011), 187

Campbell, Joseph, 76–77

Cannato, Vincent J., 71

Capra, Frank, 51

Caritas in Veritate (Benedict XVI), 73

Carnes, Matthew, 199

Casablanca (1942)
Arab and Berber characters' absence from, 64–65
"As Time Goes By" and, 57, 60–61, 63
Everybody Comes to Rick's and, 57–58, 63
Jewish characters' absence from, 65
Jews' involvement in the production of, 65–66
"La Marseillaise" scene in, 63, 75
Motion Picture Production Code and, 76
opening titles of, 58–59
Paris flashback scene in, <u>107f</u>, 62–63
Rick's comment about not selling human beings in, 12, 51, 60
Sam character in, <u>107f</u>, 12, 52, 53, 56–57, 70–71, 72–73, 74, 75–76, 77, 80, 94–95
"Shine" in, 57–59

Castile, Philando, 174, 193

Central Park Five incident (1989), 120–21

Chang, Justin, 146

Charlottesville "Unite the Right" rally (2017)
counterprotests at, 25, 176–77
killing of counterprotestor at, 176–77
Trump and, 15, 176–77
white supremacy ideology and, 25, 37, 48–49, 176–77, 196–97

Cheadle, Don, 15–16, 150, 152

Chekhov, Anton, 130–31

Cheyenne Autumn (1964), 12

Christine, Virginia, 87

Civil Rights Movement of the 1960s, 83–86

The Clansman (Dixon), 17–18, 26–28, 40, 41, 43–44

Clifton, Elmer, 28–29